For Reading Out Loud!

A GUIDE TO SHARING BOOKS WITH CHILDREN

Revised and expanded edition

Margaret Mary Kimmel & Elizabeth Segel

Drawings by Michael Hays

Foreword by Fred M. Rogers

A Dell Trade Paperback

A DELL TRADE PAPERBACK

Published by
Dell Publishing
a division of
Bantam Doubleday Dell Publishing Group, Inc.
666 Fifth Avenue
New York, New York 10103

Grateful acknowledgment is made for permission to reprint the following material:

Excerpt from *Recipe for a Magic Childhood* by Mary Ellen Chase. Copyright 1951 The Curtis Publishing Company. Reprinted by permission of Macmillan Publishing Co., Inc.

Excerpt from *American Dreams: Lost and Found* by Studs Terkel. Copyright © 1980 by Studs Terkel. Reprinted by permission of Pantheon Books, a division of Random House, Inc.

Excerpt from *Word Music and Word Magic: Children's Literature Methods* by James A. Smith and Dorothy M. Park. Copyright © 1977 by Allyn and Bacon, Inc., Boston. Reprinted with permission.

"Demonstrations, Engagement and Sensitivity: The Choice Between People and Programs" from *Language Arts,* September 1981. Reprinted with the permission of the National Council of Teachers of English.

Third stanza from "Charlotte's Web" reprinted from *Woman Before an Aquarium* by Patricia Hampl by permission of the University of Pittsburgh Press. © 1978 by Patricia Hampl.

Text copyright © 1983, 1988, 1991 by Margaret Kimmel and Elizabeth Segel
Illustrations copyright © 1988 by Michael Hays
Foreword copyright © 1988 by Fred M. Rogers

The trademark Dell® is registered in the U.S. Patent and Trademark Office.

ISBN: 0-440-50400-7

Reprinted by arrangement with Delacorte Press, New York, New York

Printed in the United States of America

Published simultaneously in Canada

August 1991

10 9 8 7 6 5 4 3 2

BVG

To our families . . .
those who once read to us
and those who have listened

Contents

Foreword

When someone says to me, "One of my favorite things to do is to curl up with a good book and spend the evening reading," I always wonder, Who read to you when you were a child? Who curled up with you and helped you to feel good about yourself before you ever knew how to read the words in all those books? Who gave you the feeling (and what a gift it is!) that books are good and reading is good and an evening can be a favorite thing in the company of yourself and a book?

One of my childhood "heroes" was "Aunt" Sarah McComb, the librarian in my hometown. Everyone my age called her Aunt Sarah even though the only way we were related to her was through our love of books—which she helped grow in us. First of all, she herself delighted in books. You could tell by the way she held them and looked at them and turned their pages and smiled when she offered them to us . . . or put them back up on the shelves. She respected words and authors and thoughts and when she read to us, it seemed we all were "someplace else."

"Aunt Sarah" wore an ancient scarab ring. It was a mysterious-looking ring, and I often wondered what it would be like to have something from so far away that was made so long ago: before our hometown ever had one house in it—long before there were even any printed books. (Aunt Sarah obviously helped us to wonder about such things!) Anyway, through the years I have often thought of Sarah McComb when I read to myself or to others. I told her so before she died. I told her that I hoped my television "neighbors" would know that I loved books, and I told her I knew for sure that she had helped me love them. She said, "I think they'll know. Children usually know the truth about us."

Aunt Sarah died in her late eighties. Shortly afterwards, a box came to me from the people to whom she had willed her "estate." In it was the scarab ring. "I want Freddy Rogers to have this," she had told them. You can imagine what that ring means to me! What it signifies means even more: a lifetime love of books and reading . . . and knowing how to help people feel good about themselves. Maggie Kimmel and Elizabeth Segel have provided us with a valuable tool to help us pass on an invaluable gift.

Fred M. Rogers

Preface to the 1988 Edition

Writing this expanded and revised version of *For Reading Out Loud!* has been more work than we dreamed, as the piles of books mounted, the search for elusive volumes dragged on, and endless decisions were wrestled with. But the joys were substantial too: the pleasures of working with each other, the discovery and rediscovery of all those extraordinary children's books, and the knowledge that through our labors, the delights of those books would reach more children and parents, teachers and librarians, across the country.

Soon after we wrote the first edition of this book, we knew we wanted to compile an expanded and updated version. The day the manuscript was in the mail was the day we began to find newly published books, funny and beautiful and touching books that we were eager to share with other lovers of reading aloud. Since the book was published, we've been asked to give many talks about reading to children, and at each one people asked good questions and shared their successes and difficulties in reading aloud. Some of our new titles are books they recommended to us. Many of their questions are answered for everyone in the new chapter "Queries and Quandaries."

Then, too, the climate was changing. The importance of reading to children was gaining wide acceptance by the general public and the educational establishment. But none of us can rest on our laurels, for significant challenges remain before we can say that all children benefit from what reading aloud has to offer, challenges we discuss in the new Chapter I.

Another change concerned preschool children. In 1982 it seemed that many parents were reading to their toddlers and preschoolers, but very few continued read-aloud sessions after the children learned to read. And little reading aloud was going on in the schools. So we focused our book on the neglected activity of reading to school-age children. Since then we've learned that many parents *don't* read to their little ones. They weren't read to as children and they don't know where or how to begin. We found that most are willing to try, however, given a little encouragement and guidance with book selection.

Also, we've been alarmed by the reported increase in parents who mistakenly think that doing right by their babies means buying workbooks and kits and games—all to teach their children to read before they go to school. Combine these observations with the requests of many new parents that we include material on reading to younger children, and we readily decided to add a completely new and extensive chapter, "Off to a Good Start: Books in the Early Years," and a new list of 125 books recommended for reading to children from infancy through kindergarten. As with our first list, we restricted ourselves to one entry per author, so as to present a wide variety, but readers are encouraged to seek out other books by those authors and artists whose work they particularly enjoy.

As for our original list of 140 recommended books for reading to school-age children, we've dropped a few, most of them out of print, and added with full annotations more than 50 titles, for a new total of 175. We also added to a number of the original annotations brief comments on new books by that author which are good choices for reading aloud. We've updated the bibliography, too, of course, selecting from the greatly increased writing on this subject those books and articles we have found most useful.

Again we are grateful to our close professional colleagues and friends, Amy Kellman and Marilyn Hollinshead, for their suggestions and cheerful assistance in supplying us with books, and to Joan Friedberg for wise advice and warm encouragement. Thanks also to the many librarians, teachers, parents, and children we've talked or corresponded with about reading aloud. Their generous sharing has enriched this revision. We thank, too,

Jill Locke for help under the pressure of deadlines and Marcy Livingston for her hours at the word processor. Finally, we appreciate deeply the patience and moral support of our families and friends.

We hope this new edition will lead many more children and grown-ups to discover the joys of reading aloud and will provide new and welcome possibilities for those who already know that there's no substitute FOR READING OUT LOUD!

Preface to the 1991 Edition

As we complete this update, we are struck with what riches for ear, eye, mind, and spirit lie waiting in children's books for those who can take advantage of them. We urge those reading this to do what they can to see that *all* young children have access to good books. Our involvement with Beginning with Books—Elizabeth is founder and codirector and Maggie is first chair of its advisory board—has confirmed for us that the best children's books are loved by children and parents of all economic strata. We think of little Chelsea, sobbing because the copy of *Goodnight Moon* she had received from Beginning with Books was damaged in a quarrel with her sister. Her mother, whose public assistance check was often stretched to the limit, reported Chelsea saying between sobs: "Mama, when you get your check, after you get your shoes you need, will you buy me another *Goodnight Moon?*"

We've seen that with a little encouragement, many parents struggling to surmount all the problems associated with poverty will devote themselves to a daily read-aloud time once they understand how it can benefit their children. "I read to them until my throat is hoarse and my back is breaking," one mother told us after participating in a Read-Aloud Parent Club. She described how she sits on the steps outside her housing project apartment when it becomes too unbearably hot inside and reads to her two daughters and the neighbor children, too.

We remember a father who missed his bus and arrived for a Read-Aloud Parent Club meeting after everyone else had gone home. "I wanted to come anyway to be sure I knew what time to be here next week," he said. Elizabeth replied that we were glad he hadn't gotten discouraged. "Oh, I can't get discouraged, ma'am. I have to get him started out right," he replied, nodding at his four-year-old.

We think of other families, in other circumstances, equally amazed at the power of sharing stories. A young lawyer father we met told about the excitement he and his son shared when they read their first "chapter" book, an excitement that caused him to tape two bedtime episodes when he had to be away on business.

We are heartened by inspirational teachers, like the one who reads aloud stories of the great heroes of the past to her sixth-graders. Then she tells them: "Their names have lasted a thousand years. I wonder whose name from today will last that long. Will it be yours?"

We think of the teacher's aide in a high school class of kids with many problems, both in reading and in life. After she attended a workshop we gave, the aide won these discouraged students to books by reading to them every day. Skeptical at first, they soon were mesmerized, and their gratitude was evident when her husband died. They bought and touchingly inscribed a copy of the first book she had read to them—and gave it to the school library in her husband's name.

Finally, we think of all the librarians we meet around the country, from Minneapolis to Morgantown, from Ellen's Hill to the Mon Valley, many of whom are underpaid and overworked, who nonetheless are there each and every day, helping all those who read to children. Many of them direct programs that reach out to mothers and babies in hospitals, in day-care centers, or homeless shelters—to busy parents, hurried teachers, and even to older kids to find just the book that will delight their listeners. We're proud to be working with all these lovers of books and children to spread far and wide the joys of reading aloud.

NOTE

For this paperback edition, we have removed some out-of-print titles and added about thirty books that have appeared since the second edition went to press. The number of books described in full annotations is now well over three hundred; the number of recommended titles totals more than four hundred.

We are on the dock.
My mother reads
Charlotte's Web *and stops*
when I cry.
"Darling! Don't cry!"
"Keep reading, keep reading," I sob.
The voice starts up again
dry as hazelnuts,
slow voice that doesn't try to get away,
voice that does what I want,
softly bringing the story I love,
voice with more ocean than the ocean that laps near us,
voice, woman who cries for the death of a spider too.
Mother! We are on the dock,
rising and falling with fiction.

—*from "Charlotte's Web"*
by Patricia Hampl

Reprinted from *Woman Before an Aquarium* by Patricia Hampl by permission of the University of Pittsburgh Press. © 1978 by Patricia Hampl.

I/Why Bother?

THE CASE FOR READING ALOUD

"I remember little from my childhood, but the soft voice reading to me still lingers inside my mind."

How vividly most people remember the experience of being read to as children! They can tell you exactly whether it was mother or dad who read at bedtime. They know it was Aunt Lou who specialized in Kipling, and Mrs. Rossi in third grade who read *Charlotte's Web* the last thing every afternoon.

A loved adult's voice conjuring up a colorful story-world . . . the memory evokes such warm and contented feelings as recollections of infant nursing might hold, if we could remember back that far. Indeed, the two experiences have common elements: the physical and emotional closeness of adult and child, the adult's attentiveness to the child, and the aim of satisfying a hunger. Clearly, both activities are nurturing ones.

A middle-aged woman recalls "a sweet, familiar voice" reading at bedtime. "I remember little from my childhood," she says, "but the soft voice reading to me still lingers inside my mind."

Augusta Baker, now retired from her long service as Coordinator of Children's Services for the New York Public Library, confesses that she, too, has few memories from her primary school years. "I don't remember the teachers who poured the information in my head, who taught the basic skills . . . [though] they were important. My vivid memory is that of a teacher—probably fourth grade—who read a chapter every week of *Beautiful Joe,* a story which was the 'Perils of Pauline' of the canine world." She feels she owes her love of books and reading in large part to that teacher.

A colleague's face brightens when the subject of children's books comes up in party conversation. "You know," he confides, "when I was a boy, I went to a camp where, along with the usual games and sports, the owner read to us every day after lunch. Boys lay sprawled about everywhere while from the dining-hall steps this small white-haired lady read another installment of *Tom Sawyer* or whatever the current novel happened to be." The small white-haired lady was Laura Richards, best known as an accomplished writer of humorous verse for children; the poets Ogden Nash and David McCord were among the sprawling boys who benefited from the Camp Merryweather tradition of reading aloud.

As another, younger poet, Karla Kuskin, says: "Those were the days when a channel was simply a deep waterway, sesame was only a seed and people read aloud for entertainment" (*The New York Times Book Review,* November 15, 1981, p. 57). Such entertainment wasn't just for children, either; whole families often gathered in the evening and someone read from a classic novel or the latest magazine serial while the others worked—sewed or hooked a rug, mended tools or shelled nuts.

Nor were communal reading sessions limited to the home and family. Studs Terkel, for his book *American Dreams* (Pantheon Books, 1980), interviewed ninety-four-year-old Dora Rosenzweig, who immigrated to Chicago as a child from a Jewish ghetto in Russia. At twelve, having completed sixth grade, she took a job as a cigar maker, where she worked in a room of thirty to forty people. She recalls: "They elected me a reader. I used to roll fifty cigars an hour. That was my piecework limit. So if I read for an hour, they would donate the fifty cigars I missed. If I read for two hours, they'd give me a hundred . . . I would choose the books. Whoever heard of a twelve-year-old girl reading Flaubert's *Salammbô*? Whatever struck me, I'd read to the others. Tolstoi, anything" (Terkel, p. 108).

But by the 1970s, reading aloud in the home was largely limited to middle-class parents reading to preschool children, and read-aloud sessions in schools were few and far between. Furthermore, little attention was paid to that loss. Some no doubt viewed it as just a case of having replaced one pleasant pastime with others— gathering around the television set for *Monday Night Football,* for instance. After all, if children of the 1970s were born too late for group reading sessions, Dora Rosenzweig was born too early to have known the satisfaction of racking up a high score on a space-combat video game. Maybe it balanced out.

But no. We can now see that the loss was a real loss, not just a change, and that the shared pleasure of reading aloud was not the only casualty. Many children were growing up with negative attitudes toward books and reading in any form. The media called it "a literacy crisis." The schools were trying new methods of teaching reading and were testing children more often, but nothing seemed to cure the problem. Publishers brought out attractive books geared to poor readers; teachers reported that these students were so turned off by books that the new formats didn't entice them at all. Worried parents invested in expensive teach-your-child-to-read kits and high-powered electronic learning games, only to see their children growing up reading nothing on their own but an occasional comic book.

Meanwhile, research data was slowly accumulating that suggested how we might resolve this crisis. Several studies of children from widely varied backgrounds who learned to read easily and remained good readers throughout their school years revealed that they had something in common. They all had been read to regularly from early childhood and had as models adults or older children who read for pleasure. Other studies showed that simple reading aloud on a daily basis improved children's independent reading skills and motivation. *In fact, reading aloud to children from literature that is meaningful to them has come to be widely acknowledged among experts to be the most effective, as well as the simplest and least expensive, way to foster in children a lifelong love of books and reading.*

The literacy crisis in the United States has not abated in the years since the first edition of this book was published, though public awareness of the problem has increased. A much needed national initiative to combat adult illiteracy has been launched, but the need far outstrips the resources to deal with it. These efforts must be supplemented with increased attention to *preventing* illiteracy. As Eleanor Holmes Norton has said: "Remedies for deep-rooted problems—from teen-age pregnancy to functional illiteracy—are bound to fail when we leave the water running while we struggle to check the overflow" (*The New York Times Magazine*, June 2, 1985). Add to the numbers of children who grow up unable to read those who simply don't read, and we see a critical national problem. A survey by the Book Industry Study Group in 1978 reported that 75 percent of Americans under twenty-one were book readers; when they repeated the survey in 1984, that figure had dropped to 63 percent (*The New York Times*, April 12, 1984), an abrupt and distressing decline.

Rays of hope exist within this gloomy picture, however. A significant revival of interest in reading aloud to children over the last few years suggests that more of the children now growing up will term themselves book readers at age twenty-one. The many parents and professionals who have promoted the joys and benefits of reading aloud can be proud that much more reading aloud is going on today than was the case ten years ago. We have witnessed a genuine "Read-aloud Revival," and it has been exhilarating to be a part of it. Besides the availability of books like this one, advice on reading aloud has been incorporated into a great many books on parenting; articles on reading to children appear regularly in popular magazines and daily newspapers; and at least one excellent television program has been broadcast on the subject, no doubt reaching many parents who don't read books and articles.

Dramatic recognition of these efforts appeared in the 1985 report of the Commission on Reading. This group of nationally recognized experts on reading surveyed research in all disciplines that had relevance to the reading process, in order to base educational policy on the best information available. The report is clear and emphatic on the subject of reading to children. It states: "The single most important activity for building the knowledge required for eventual success in reading is reading aloud to children" (p. 23). And the experts noted that "Children . . . whose parents simply read to them . . . performed as well on beginning reading tasks as those whose parents had . . . training and workbooks" (p. 24). Their recommendations were repeated in a report published for the general public by the U.S. Department of

Education, *What Works: Research About Teaching and Learning* (1986), which bluntly affirms: "The best way for parents to help their children become better readers is to read to them—even when they are very young" (p. 9).

In the flush of this strong consensus, it would be human to feel that the struggle for acceptance of this practice is over and to relegate the issue to a back burner. This would be a mistake, however. For one thing, there are still many children, particularly those from disadvantaged homes, who are growing up without hearing stories regularly. We need to develop and support programs that will encourage all literate parents to undertake this pleasurable and beneficial, but traditionally middle-class, activity. And we need to see that children whose parents cannot or will not read to them at home are read to elsewhere.

Another cause for concern is that in spite of the unequivocal endorsement of reading aloud in home and school by such respected bodies as the Commission on Reading and the U.S. Department of Education, and in spite of many fervent supporters of reading aloud in schools, a great many educators who are in a position to implement this activity on a large scale fail to do so. Whether this is due to their having an entrenched interest in other approaches to promoting reading, or whether, as has been suggested to us by one school administrator, "they can't believe that anything this simple and inexpensive will work," the fact is that we need to go on pressing for daily reading aloud in the classroom.

Finally, though at present much attention is being focused on the costs of illiteracy and the value of reading aloud, media concern in our society tends to be fickle. Today's "issue of the day" becomes ho-hum news tomorrow. The trouble with revivals has always been that they come to town, they generate excitement and spiritual renewal, and then they depart, leaving the converted to slip back to their old ways. We need to make sure that the Read-aloud Revival becomes institutionalized: that listening to stories becomes as much a fixture of the school day as lunchtime, and that parents share books with their babies as readily as they change diapers. We know now that reading aloud will never be outdated as long as children need to learn how to read, and as long as young and old delight in hearing stories and in sharing them together.

II/Off to a Good Start:

BOOKS IN THE EARLY YEARS

"The single most important way to help children become good readers is to read to them—even when they are infants."

Infancy is the time to develop in children a love of words and stories that will become an appetite for books. In fact, it's never too early to begin. When we say "begin," however, we don't mean trying to interest a newborn baby in a book. Besides the fact that it's very difficult to turn the pages of a book while supporting a tiny infant properly, that baby has other, more pressing, needs. Very young babies need to see the human face, to which they respond with great interest. Introduce your new baby to words and to the rhythm and intonation of language, but don't try to get the baby to focus on a book. Let her watch your face instead.

Above all, *talk* to your baby. The earlier you do this, the sooner the baby will begin to understand words—which will happen long before she can speak, by the way. Buy or borrow that beautiful collection of nursery rhymes now, but use it first to brush up your own memory of these delightful bits of verse that have been treasured by generations of parents and children. Say the ones you like best to your baby when changing a diaper or enjoying a peaceful moment in a rocking chair. "Hickory, Dickory, Dock" can distract a fussy infant; "This Little Pig Went to Market" may elicit your baby's first real chuckle. Try singing "Hush, Little Baby" or "The Three Little Kittens" to soothe a wakeful baby to sleepiness. Talk to your baby about the world around him. You'll be helping him sort out the confusing swirl of objects and activities. There will be time enough to look at books together when he is comfortable sitting up—around five or six months. No need to rush things. As Elizabeth's mother used to tell her when she couldn't wait for her baby sister to crawl, to walk, and to talk: "Don't wish her life away. Babies grow up quickly enough as it is."

Valerie Willsher, a children's librarian, has described her attempt to interest her ten-week-old daughter in books as "fraught with frustration and irritation for both of us." She tried again when the baby was six months old, with results that were much more enjoyable for both mother and child ("Books for the Under-Twos," *Signal* 38 [1982], 105).

Each child is different, of course. Dorothy Butler tells in *Cushla and Her Books* (Horn Book, 1980) how her granddaughter Cushla became fascinated by vivid picture book illustrations as early as four months. Cushla had multiple disabilities including poor vision and apparently could not see well enough to focus on anything that was not very close to her eyes. Picture books were a godsend to her parents, who had the difficult task of amusing a child whose grave problems included being unable to sleep except in brief snatches.

Whenever you decide is the right time to introduce books to *your* baby, remember that this is supposed to be fun! If either one of you is not enjoying the experience, put the book away and go on talking and singing to your baby. But be sure to try again soon. Infants often take giant steps in development in just a few short weeks. You don't want to waste these months and years when your child's mind is at its most receptive. (Experts say 40 percent of his or her intelligence is developed by age five.) In these years, your child will benefit remarkably from hearing, looking at, and handling lots and lots of books. If your child is cared for by another person while you work, check to be sure that they see book-sharing sessions as an important everyday activity. Care-givers should include book purchases in planning budgets; parents should insist on it.

Some parents who weren't themselves read to as children have the mistaken impression that introducing a child to books is the school's job. Their children start kindergarten at a serious disadvantage, compared to their classmates who grew up with books. Educators say they may lag as much as two and one-half years in reading readiness behind children whose parents or care-givers read to them. It's very hard for a teacher with twenty-five or thirty children to make up for that deficiency, and such children often experience failure in learning to read. Sadly, they tend to fall farther and farther behind as they struggle through school. We need to get out the word to all parents that, as Diane Ravitch, professor at Teachers' College, Columbia University, puts it: "The single most important way to help children become good readers is to read to them—even when they are infants."

EARLY BOOK-SHARING

For your baby's first session with a book, choose a book that has clear pictures of familiar objects. A cup, a spoon, another baby, a cat, an apple—you may be surprised at how quickly the representation of these items on a page seizes the interest of an infant. Take the baby on your lap and open the book.

Now, very likely the baby will make a lightning-quick grab for the book. He wants to explore this interesting thing, and for a baby, that means touching and tasting. If the book is a "board book," one made of stiff, thick pages, go ahead and let the baby feel and taste the book and find out how the pages work. Then try again. This time (or right away if the pages are paper), give the baby a toy to keep his hands occupied, or hold the book just out of his reach. Point to a picture.

At first, you will probably do most of the asking. "What's this?" you'll ask, pointing to a picture of a shoe, a dog, or something else that your baby knows from daily life. If the baby doesn't try to say the word, give the answer yourself: "Shoe. See the shoe? . . . Can Matthew say 'shoe'?" Then it's a good idea to add a phrase that relates that pictured object to the child's experience: "Where's Matthew's shoe?" (It's better to say "Matthew's shoe" when talking to baby Matthew than "your shoe," since "your" and other pronouns refer to different people when used in different sentences, a very confusing situation for someone just learning the language.) If your baby points to his shoe or tries to say "shoe," be sure to praise him. He wants to please you, so this will be all he needs to try another word . . . and another.

Soon the baby will be asking *you* for words: "Whazzat? Whazzat?" one little girl we know used to say. Her cousin's way of asking was just to point and say "Uh? Uh?" in a way that was both a demand and a question. And so the two of you alternate asking and answering, and *voilà*! your baby discovers that conversation consists of turn-taking. Yes, it is conversation that you're having over that book, and that suggests one of the great advantages of bringing books into your daily routine. The young child's world is a small one and the subjects of conversation limited. From the beginning, books can extend that world for both of you.

You, as the adult, can help the child master language by trying to figure out what he is trying to say and then expanding his sentences. Below is a fragment of a book-sharing session between a not-quite-two-year-old and his aunt. They are looking at the book *500 Words to Grow On* (Random House), which is full of appealing groupings of the kind of familiar objects mentioned above. After they have looked together at a page of "Things That Go" and one of animals, the aunt has turned to a page of common household objects. The toddler immediately points to the picture of a flashlight.

TODDLER: Bubba.
AUNT: Bubba? Um . . . that's a flashlight.
TODDLER (emphatically): Bubba.
AUNT: (musing) Bubba. Hmm . . . Baby? Brother? [Neither of these is accepted by the toddler.] Bubba. Oh, I know. Bubba . . . Grandpa. [Big grin and nodding of head by toddler]. Grandpa has a flashlight, doesn't he?
TODDLER (with immense satisfaction): Uh-huh. On, off. On, off.

It took a bit of effort before the aunt remembered that "Bubba" was the closest this child could come to saying "Grandpa" and that Grandpa had let the little boy play with his flashlight. But her effort was well repaid by the delight of the child, who was able successfully to steer this book-conversation to a subject that interested him. This little one was learning that he had something worth saying and was gaining confidence that his efforts to speak would be rewarded.

These early book-sharing sessions should be short—perhaps only five minutes. Take your cue from the baby. An attack of the wiggles means it's time to shift to a knee-trotting game or other physical activity. In home or day-care center, reading a story can follow playtime, but be sure to find time every day to get out the books. Studies show that the benefits of introducing children to books early are most striking when book sharing is a daily activity.

Soon you can vary these sessions of identifying words and pictures with the actual reading of a story. At a surprisingly young age, about fifteen months, a child can appreciate a simple story, and there are many picture story books geared to a toddler's interests and attention span. Big sister's attempts to make Max talk in *Max's First Word* by Rosemary Wells are certainly something a toddler can relate to, as is the necessity of going to bed in a darkening room, which is depicted with genius in Margaret Wise Brown's *Goodnight Moon*. The latter is probably the best baby book ever published, with its objects to locate—mittens and kittens, red balloon and tiny mouse, its rhythmic prose, and the repetition that enables even tiny children to chime in as the bunny says good night to all the objects in his room. This book proved the favorite of four picture books distributed to one thousand disadvantaged families in Pittsburgh recently. "It makes bedtime so much easier," several parents reported. They were discovering that books read together as a part of the bedtime ritual, or at some other regular time of day, can provide a calming influence and a wonderful sense of security for a child.

Storybooks, like nursery rhymes, also feed a child's love of words—the love that's so evident when the child plays with nonsense syllables at the stage the linguists call "babbling," or later when play monologues are sprinkled with words that sound good. "This is my cacciatore window!" one child crowed as he peered down through the bars of a climbing frame.

Be sure to "read with expression," as they used to tell us in elementary school. Be on the lookout for stories that allow you to vary your voice and ham it up a bit. The littlest listeners love to hear Papa Bear's throaty rumble, Mama Bear's gentle tones, and Baby Bear's comical squeak. The voices and the "trip-traps" of three Billy Goats Gruff should be different, too, and be sure to make the troll's voice rough and gruff (not *too* scary if you're reading to very little children, of course).

The best picture books often use unusual words and rhythmic refrains. We remember being enchanted by certain phrases from the picture books of our childhood: the "Scr-r-ritch, scratch, scratch, scritch" of Mr. McGregor's hoe in *The Tale of Peter Rabbit;* "One misty, moisty morning" from Mother Goose; and Wanda Gág's "Cats here, cats there, cats and kittens everywhere" from *Millions of Cats.*

Add to these entrancing sounds the wealth of illustrations in today's picture books, and you have a formula guaranteed to delight both child and adult. While you read the story, the child will be scrutinizing the accompanying picture. Because it can be lingered over and come back to, unlike television images, a book illustration is especially well suited to further your child's powers of visual discrimination. And at the same time, he or she will be developing a responsiveness to textures, shapes, colors, and visual patterns, the beginning of an appreciation of art.

Be sure to leave some books—indestructible or inexpensive ones—within your toddler's reach, though you will want to shelve library books and particularly elegant volumes where she can't get at them when you're not with her. It's important that a child be able to initiate story time by bringing a book to an adult when she wants to be read to. Some parents even put books in a tod-dler's crib after she falls asleep. One mother reported that her twenty-one-month-old child can sit for half an hour looking at books first thing in the morning. "He seems to be careful as he turns pages and most of the time he never misuses them. When he does, he gets upset and shows me." Of course, there may be a torn page sometimes, but how much this child would be missing if his mother kept books out of his hands to protect them. Books do no one any good when they are sitting on the shelf.

When you read a new picture book to one or more toddlers or preschoolers, you may be frustrated because a child interrupts constantly to ask questions about the words or the illustrations. Be patient and answer the questions unless there are so many, you

feel you'll never reach the end of the story. This happens some-times with a very literal child. In that case, after answering a number of questions, say, "Let's see what the story says. Maybe it will answer some of your questions." Questions, though, are nor-mal when you introduce an unfamiliar book; it's even good to pause occasionally to allow children a chance to ask about some-thing that puzzles them. One reason children like to hear the same book over and over again is that during the first readings they are getting things sorted out; later readings enable them to "get lost in the story"—which is the ideal way to experience a story.

BOOKS TO BUY, BOOKS TO BORROW

You will want to buy some books for your baby, or suggest them when grandparents or friends inquire what gift they might buy the child: a volume of nursery rhymes, a word book, a collection of nursery tales, and a few special picture books are all that's needed if funds are short. Paperback editions are fine and less expensive. One's *own* books are special and arouse a special intensity of attachment in the small child.

No matter how many children's books you have at home, however, be sure to borrow others from the public library. Only by taking advantage of the library's resources can you satisfy the hunger for books you will stimulate by reading regularly to your child. In the children's section you can find old favorites and this season's newest hit. And the child who is familiar with the library will feel comfortable there when, years later, he needs to use the library to complete school assignments.

Day-care centers and preschools, too, should both buy books and borrow books from the public library. We know that budgets are tight for these agencies and the temptations to "let the library do it" is strong. Yet the children should have some books that are always available. The ideal is a good basic collection owned by the school, plus a rotating supply of library books on a regular basis. Request from your public library long-term loans on books, and choose a variety to supplement the permanent collection. Take advantage, too, of the library as a destination for group outings. You can probably arrange to have the librarian tell a story or two to the children. A library visit is an important social occasion for children, and their enthusiasm about the visit may make a library patron out of an initially reluctant parent.

An important ingredient in making reading fun for children is letting them frequently select the books they will be hearing. In a home reading session with a preschooler, this means letting the child decide what book to read next. If you have more than one child, of course, they can take turns choosing, as they must learn to do in so many activities. You should occasionally assert your right to choose too. Otherwise you might end up reading nothing but *Mike Mulligan and His Steam Shovel,* and your child would never discover *Where the Wild Things Are,* which she might enjoy just as intensely.

When visiting the library with your own child, establish that you will pick some books and the child will pick some. If selection is left entirely up to a three-year-old, you may find that you go home with the five biggest books in the children's room, or five red ones—selection principles not likely to produce books your child will enjoy hearing. If your child wants to take out from the library the same book over and over, consider buying that book. A children's librarian told us once about a little boy who came in with his mother and requested *Harry the Dirty Dog.* When she reported that the book was out, he burst into tears: "But I *need* it," he explained through his tears. I hope that mother went to the nearest bookstore to buy *Harry the Dirty Dog* for her son—or to order it if the store didn't have it in stock.

At bookstores, children invariably gravitate to the "pop-up" books and to those that are merchandised as spin-offs from television shows and mass-marketed toys. By pop-up books we mean any books in which the illustrations have parts that move, revealing something new when they are manipulated. They appeal to the child's natural fascination with seeing something disappear and come back again and to his desire to be active, in book reading as in all else. By all means buy him a few pop-up books if you can afford them, but make sure that the story and illustrations are well done. Because of the innate popularity of these books, publishers can save money by using inferior art and watered down, prosy versions of favorite stories. The best, however, are engineering feats that invite and intrigue.

As for the books that are TV and toy spin-offs, the great majority are insipid, with the exception of those that come out of the *Sesame Street* and *Mister Rogers* shows. It doesn't hurt to read stories that your child will like because (she or he) owns a Cabbage Patch Kid doll or a superhero figure, but many are either frenetic or so sticky-sweet that they should be marketed with fluoride. In any case, they are no substitute for books that have to be good enough to stand on their own.

Be sure to try out a variety of illustrating styles on your little one: the bright, bold clarity of Galdone's *The Little Red Hen*, the simplified, textured shapes of Lionni's collages in *Frederick*, and the warmth of Symeon Shimin's charcoal drawings that illustrate Ann Scott's *Sam*. Many people underestimate little children in assuming they like only bright primary colors. The numerous books with black-and-white drawings that have remained popular with children for decades show that to be untrue.

Vary the kind of text, too. You'll find family favorites that are stories in verse and others in prose. Stories about animals are popular with young listeners, and so are stories about families just like yours. Old folktales will alternate as favorites with books about the contemporary scene. Whether you are buying or borrowing books for young children, our list for younger children is designed to introduce you and your children to the riches that are available in that most appealing of twentieth-century art forms, the picture book.

HEARING STORIES AND LEARNING TO READ

Stories give shape to the chaotic world the child experiences. Psychiatrists tell us that when children are familiar with the way stories begin and develop and end, they can fit their own experiences into the form of a story and thus make sense of them. Their chances of surviving traumatic experiences without damage to the psyche are thus improved. This familiarity with story (some experts call it having "story awareness" or a "story schema") also enables children to predict what will happen next as they hear new stories—and that's a big help when they begin to learn to read.

Every parent or care-giver who reads to little children knows that they often want the same story over and over *and over* again. Pretty soon the child knows the story so well, she will roar with dismay if you change a single word. (And heaven help you, if, in your weariness you skip a page so as to hasten bedtime by a minute or two.) This familiarity, however inconvenient at times, benefits the child enormously and is probably a key step toward independent reading. A child, using the pictures as clues, will often pretend to "read" the story—to you or to her stuffed animals —before she can read any actual words at all. Older siblings have been known to jeer at such a performance: "You can't read! You just memorized that story." But the child is making a good start on reading and should be praised and encouraged. We know a two-year-old who "reads" to her toys the books her baby-sitter and parents have read to her. Half of her words are in a jargon that is incomprehensible to adults, but they can recognize enough words to know that she is indeed remembering the story and retelling it in her own way.

Later, such a child will begin to notice that a longer time between page turnings corresponds to more of the black squiggles on the page. If someone begins to point out some of the easier letters and to indicate their sounds, the child begins to understand what print is, and to pay attention to it, as well as to the pictures, while sitting beside a reading adult. This is the time to bring out again those word books with printed labels under pictures. The child will now try to guess the words—not just from the picture but from the letters underneath. That child is on the way becoming a real reader. The philosopher Jean-Paul Sartre describes in his autobiography, *Words,* how he learned to read:

> I would climb on my cot with Hector Malot's *No Family,* which I knew by heart, and, half reciting, half deciphering, I went through every page of it one after another. When the last was turned, I knew how to read.
> I was wild with joy. . . .

For some children this kind of breakthrough happens at four, but for most, not until six or seven. By reading often to your child, you can assure that it will happen when the child is developmentally ready. Don't rush it by pressuring the child, or you will rob that moment of the delight Sartre experienced.

As you can see, we are not recommending that you teach your child to read. The sets of books and materials that are marketed for that purpose are terribly dreary. (One set devotes a whole boring book to teaching the word for "cup.") As the Report of the Commission on Reading says, informal instruction by parents (such as looking at books, pointing out letters on signs, or spelling out a child's name with magnetic letters) "seems to work as well or better than formal, systematic approaches." The report cites a study showing that children whose parents simply read to them regularly performed as well on beginning reading tasks as those whose parents had special training and used workbooks to teach sounds and letters (p. 24).

Just by reading to your children, you will prepare them to understand what is expected of them at school. They will know how a book works, what print is, but most of all, they will know how much pleasure can be found between the covers of a book. "The single most important activity for building the knowledge required for eventual success in reading is reading aloud to children," state the distinguished authors of *Becoming a Nation of Readers* (p. 23). No ifs, ands, or buts about it.

Make sure that this activity gets top priority in your family life. All you need is a child, a book, and what will turn out to be the happiest fifteen minutes of your day.

III/Don't Stop Now!

THE BENEFITS OF READING TO SCHOOL-AGE CHILDREN

"Contrary to some parents' and teachers' fears, listening to stories doesn't make 'lazy readers.'"

Many adults understand the importance of reading aloud to a young child who can't yet read. But too often these same adults no more think of reading aloud to the child who has learned to read than they would continue to run alongside the child's first bicycle, steadying the vehicle, after the child had learned to ride alone.

This is a sad mistake. Remember the little girl on the dock, listening to her mother read *Charlotte's Web*, as they weep together over the death of a spider? Our message is the same one she addressed to the treasured reading voice: "Keep reading." READING ALOUD SHOULD CONTINUE ALL THROUGH THE SCHOOL YEARS, for many reasons.

- *To stop the read-aloud sessions of the preschool years ends a rich shared experience.* A mother and father we know were concerned because their son's first-grade year was nearly over and he showed no signs of being able to read. They expressed their concern to his teacher and asked if she thought he needed special help to overcome a problem or disability. She stared at them in surprise: "Why, Jason reads quite well—and has been for several months now." It turned out that Jason had been keeping his new skill a secret, worrying that if his parents knew he could read to himself, they might stop reading him a bedtime story. Needless to say, Jason's parents reassured him that he could enjoy reading to himself *and* have his nightly story, too.

    In many families now grown up, books read aloud together in childhood have become a treasured part of family history. "Remember when you read us *Five Children and It*, and we kids spent our entire week at the beach digging for a sand-fairy?" "I'll never forget when Mom was reading *Cheaper by the Dozen* in the car and Dad got laughing so hard that he had to pull over and stop."

In school, too, the shared experience that reading aloud provides creates a genuine bond in a group of diverse children that is unlikely to occur in any other way. As one teacher said after reading *Bridge to Terabithia* to her class: "By the end of that story, we had been through so much together."

And this kind of communal experience is becoming rarer. In automobile assembly plants these days, many workers are plugged into their individual "walkaround" tape players. No doubt these help dispel the tedium of the job, but such gadgets cut off one worker from another; each is operating in his or her own world rather than sharing, as the cigar workers did, one fictional world.

- *Being read to promotes, rather than retards, children's desire to read independently.* Contrary to some parents' and teachers' fears, listening to stories doesn't make "lazy readers." Rather, what the children hear seems to whet their appetites to read that book or others like it for themselves. One school librarian told us that when she asks children to name their favorite book, they almost always name the book she or their teacher has most recently read to them.

We all know that film and television adaptations increase interest in a book. When *The Secret Garden* was telecast on *Once Upon a Classic,* copies of the book were scarce as hen's teeth in the libraries. (We know one little girl whose popularity shot up considerably as her classmates competed to borrow the copy she owned.) Reading a story aloud is another form of book promotion and is just as effective with the children it reaches as a *Star Wars* movie or an *Afterschool Special* on television. And it has the decided advantage that the individual parent or professional—not Madison Avenue or Hollywood—can choose what book to promote to a particular child or group of children.

One reason that reading a book or story works so effectively to motivate independent reading is that learning to read is difficult and often frustrating. Going on to read more and more challenging books means repeatedly risking failure. Hearing a first-rate story read aloud makes the rewards of sticking to it clear and tangible.

• *Being read to fosters improvement of children's independent reading skills.* Studies of first- and second-graders and fourth-through sixth-graders have demonstrated that children who are read aloud to on a regular basis over a period of several months show significant gains in reading comprehension, decoding skills, and vocabulary. The gains were greatest for disadvantaged students but not limited to them—all the children benefited significantly compared to the control groups, who were read to only occasionally or not at all.

Besides making children more eager to tackle the difficult tasks involved in learning to read, hearing stories read gets children used to the written language they will meet in books, which is different from spoken language.

• *All through their school years, young people can enjoy listening to books that would be too difficult for them to read on their own.* How exciting it is for the first-grader, who is struggling to read brief and perhaps insipid primer stories, to share the delights and dangers of a whole prairie year when the teacher reads a daily chapter from one of Laura Ingalls Wilder's books. Similarly, seventh-graders might find *The Wizard of Earthsea* beyond their ability or ambition for independent reading yet become totally absorbed in listening to an adult read it aloud.

Listening experiences like these are especially valuable for the student whose home language is not English and for children whose chief exposure to English comes from the television set.

• *Wonderful books that are "hard to get into" are more accessible when read aloud.* The first few pages of an unfamiliar book usually determine whether a child reading independently will go on or give up and look for another book. In some books the reader immediately knows what's going on and is almost instantly swept up in the events of the story. Fairy tales, for example, signal in the first few sentences who the characters are, whether they are good or bad, and what their predicament is. A formula story of a less exalted sort, like a Nancy Drew mystery or a Spider-Man™ comic, also makes the reader feel right at home in familiar territory. But some of the richest, most rewarding books are the unconventional ones, the ones that don't fit a formula. Such books may defer gratification of the reader's curiosity in order to first establish a scene and mood; they are original rather than predictable. These books profit immensely from being read aloud. Your captive audience may be a bit restless until they get oriented, but they will soon be deep in the world of story with you if you have selected well.

- *For the poor student whose inability to read has barred her or him from access to stimulating material in every subject, including literature, there is no substitute for reading aloud.* The attempt of publishers to be responsive to the needs of poor readers by providing high-interest/low-level-of-difficulty books is praiseworthy, but the fact is that many literary experiences that would be moving and meaningful to a fifteen-year-old reading at a third-grade level simply cannot be conveyed in simple sentence structure and vocabulary. Reading aloud is a way to be sure these students aren't deprived of their rich literary heritage.

- *A significant number of children will always grasp material better through their ears than through their eyes.* When asked in a class, one student said he had no early memory of books. He didn't remember ever enjoying a book and doesn't read anything now except required assignments—not even the newspaper. He did recall with pleasure, however, records of stories that he owned as a child—folktales, Hans Christian Andersen stories, and the like. "Words on the page somehow come between me and the story" is the way he described his problem.

He was envious of his classmates' memories of their parents reading to them. He was sure that would have been even better than the records.

There are others like this young man who may never find pleasure in reading, even if they have been read to in childhood. Is reading to such youngsters a waste of time, then? Not at all. Ideally, they should have occasional opportunities to listen to literature all their lives, so that they, too, can savor the unique pleasures of the written word.

- *Studies have shown that reading aloud to children significantly broadens their reading interests and tastes.* Children and adolescents who tend to limit themselves to one author's books or one type of book in their independent reading—mysteries or sports stories or romances, for instance—will often be led to more challenging books and greater variety in their reading by hearing a book chosen by a knowledgeable adult.

- *Exposing children to good literature, presented for enjoyment, will increase the chances that their reading life doesn't end with high school graduation.* A major goal of the schools should be to turn out people who not only are able to read but find enough pleasure in reading that they will actually read a book now and then after they've left school. We know that many American adults simply never read books; of these, only a small number are actually unable to read. In all likelihood, the adults who can but do not read books were once students who read only what was required of them at school. Once the assignments stopped, so did the reading. A few good books read aloud solely for the students' enjoyment could have made a difference.

- *Seeing adults reading with enjoyment increases the chances that children will become lifelong readers.* This means that the parent, teacher, librarian, grandparent, or other adult who finds time to read to a child and does it with enthusiasm is providing a model as well as a story. Observing adults who are

eager to read and are engaged in reading is more effective in making readers of children than any number of lectures on the importance of reading.

And it's important to recognize that, though the parent makes a very effective model, children whose parents have never discovered the pleasures of reading need not be left out. Any adult or older child can fill this role. By providing regular reading-aloud sessions to children who do not get that experience at home, the school or day-care center or library can break through the cycle of illiteracy that victimizes many young people. Then when these children who have enjoyed hearing stories grow up, they may very well pass on the pleasure by reading to the children in their lives.

IV/Fitting It In:

FINDING OR MAKING TIME TO READ ALOUD

"I don't have time to listen to stories."
"Are you kidding? Only babies get read to."
"What about my TV shows?"

In the Home . . .
From time to time we all run across a nostalgic description of family reading sessions in bygone years—cheerful, cozy scenes painted by adults looking back on their happy childhood days. One of the most vivid occurs in "Recipe for a Magic Childhood," written some years ago by the distinguished novelist and educator Mary Ellen Chase for the *Ladies' Home Journal.* She described the kitchen in which the winters of her Maine childhood were spent—warm black wood stove, red-and-white-checked table-cloth, red geraniums at the window, and her young mother cooking and baking, washing and ironing while the four children played or read nearby (school didn't meet during January and February in Maine). "My mother usually somehow managed, at eleven, to sit down for half an hour in the red rocking chair by the window," she related.

She called this half hour her "respite," a word which early charmed me; and . . . she would allow us to sit upon our red stools while . . . she herself would read aloud to us. Here was the very doorsill to complete enchantment, for she was seemingly as lost as we in whatever she was reading. The iron teakettle simmered . . . , the red geraniums glowed with life; smells of our approaching dinner filled our noses from stewpans or baking dishes; while my mother's voice brought trooping into our kitchen all those with whom we rejoiced or suffered, admired or feared, loved or hated.

(Reprinted in Phyllis Fenner,
Something Shared: Children and Books
[New York: John Day Co., 1959],
pp. 15–16)

Who can read that without a moment's pang of envy, followed by an impulsive resolution to provide such "a magic childhood" for the children in our lives, too. Then the chilly breath of reality reminds the mothers among us that they don't spend the entire day in the kitchen (thank heaven). Whether their daily work is pursued in the home or outside it, they do not spend long hours every day with their school-age children, as Mary Ellen Chase's mother did. And for both parents, the time when the family is all together at home is likely to be when the parents are tired and needing a bit of time to themselves.

Yet today's parents can learn from this woman. Notice that she called the reading-aloud ritual her "respite." She, too, was tired from all that cooking on the wood stove and laundering without benefit of automatic washer and dryer. Her use of the term "respite" suggests that reading to her children was for her a valid excuse for letting the housework wait. And it still is—just as valid for the factory-worker or bank-executive parent who returns from a full day's work to a messy house as it was for the Maine housewife decades ago. "Respite" also implies rest, and reading aloud does take less of a weary parent's energy than refereeing the arguments of cranky children or listening to the shrieks and racing around of overexcited ones.

A mother recently recalled the years when her children were little. "I remember feeling guilty at the time that I wasn't a better housekeeper," she said. "I'd let the dishes pile up in the sink and ignore the dirty kitchen floor while I read book after book to my toddler and infant." Now her children are nearly grown and her kitchen immaculate, and she reflects: "We survived the sinkfuls of dishes and the dirty floors, and I wouldn't trade anything for my memory of the sweet weight of the baby in my arms and my toddler snuggled up against my side as we shared the delights of those wonderful books."

A note of thanks for the first edition of this book from the mother of two young children included the words "It's nice to be reminded that when I don't accomplish anything all day, I have accomplished a lot by reading to my sons."

Now, if your children are under six, you won't have any trouble persuading them to listen while you read. Children as young as eighteen months will bring you book after book to read once they have discovered the fun of this activity. But if you haven't started early or if you did read to them when they were little but stopped when they started school, you may find that one of the major obstacles to regular family reading aloud is the children's own resistance. You should be prepared to encounter these reactions:

- Suzy (twelve years old, good reader): "But I baby-sit on weekends and school nights I have to do my homework, and practice the piano, and—oh, yes—wash my hair. I don't have time to listen to stories."
- Joe (a ten-year-old who never picks up a book voluntarily and suffers agonies over reading assignments): "Are you kidding? Only babies get read to."
- Mary Ann (eight years old; she loved being read to until recently): "What about my TV shows? I have to watch *Who's the Boss* and the reruns of *The Bill Cosby Show* and . . . and . . . and . . ."

Let's start with the last problem. *To make time for reading aloud in the home, you are going to have to take a stand against unlimited television viewing.* Some would argue that television can take the place of reading; print will soon be obsolete, they say. Children can get lots of stories just by flipping on the TV—why fight it?

The differences between reading and watching television are many and complicated, and numerous books and articles have been written to explore them (see, for example, the Singer entry in the Bibliography, Appendix B). For our purposes, a few brief points will suffice:

- Television watching is less personal and more passive than listening to a family member read a story. When listening to someone reading, a child automatically creates mental pictures of the scenes and actions described. With television, nothing is left to the visual imagination. In addition, the television narrative cannot be stopped for questions or discussions and started again (at least, with the equipment in most homes). Thus it gives children no practice in using language.

- Television segments are often so short that children who watch a great deal are unable to sustain their interest and stick to an activity for more than a few minutes. Teachers complain that schoolchildren today have short attention spans long after they should have outgrown them. Read-aloud sessions, short for young children and extended (usually by popular demand) as they grow older, can remedy this problem.

- Watching television is not a shared experience in most families; reading aloud is. Even when children's viewing time is limited, they probably do much of their watching when the parent is busy—fixing dinner, for instance—and not present. Using *Sesame Street* for a baby-sitter while you get the meal on the table doesn't make you a negligent parent, but we all know about the powerful temptation to leave the kids in front of the set while you pay bills, talk on the phone, catch up on work, take a bath, or watch *your* favorite program on the second TV set. We have to resist that temptation. And there's no time to lose: experts estimate that children of elementary school age average four and one half to five hours of television watching a day (see Singer book referred to in Appendix B). That doesn't leave time for much reading of any sort!

Although it's hard to change established household patterns, it can be done . . . even when the issue is limiting television viewing. When local teachers went on strike, a woman we know foresaw that her children would begin watching television around the clock. So on the first day of the strike she announced to her seven- and nine-year-olds that they would be limited to two hours of television a day—one hour in the daytime and one in the evening. She then braced herself, expecting howls of outrage. Instead, her children dashed off to find the newspaper so that they could decide what programs would make up their quota for that day. Could it be that children would welcome more leadership in such matters than we think?

As for son Joe's reaction to the prospect of family reading sessions, if you never *stop* reading to your children, you may avoid the charge of babyishness. Otherwise, we recommend asking Joe to give you a trial period. Then choose that first book *very* carefully with Joe's interests in mind. (The listing of surefire books in Chapter VIII is a good starting point.)

It's especially important to break down the resistance of a child like Joe to being read to, precisely because of his difficulties as an independent reader. Having a parent sit down with him and read aloud the first chapter of a dreaded assigned novel can give a considerable boost to Joe's understanding and enjoyment of the book. And if his parents show him that reading aloud and listening are pleasurable for adults as well as small children, half the battle is won.

With children as old as Suzy—junior high and high school age— increasing activities outside the home may make frequent reading sessions difficult. We know one family with teenagers, though, who managed family reading nearly every day. One person read aloud while the others did the dinner dishes (shades of the cigar makers!). If something like this won't work, perhaps you could manage a regular session once a week—Sunday evening might be a good time.

Don't give up on the idea, however, if you can't manage a regular time. Watch for those serendipitous moments. The reading aloud of an appropriate story can become a family tradition at holiday celebrations. This, of course, is already a ritual for many— the Gospel story of Jesus' birth on Christmas Eve; reading the story of Queen Esther and wicked Haman on Purim. Many wonderful secular stories exist as well that the whole family will enjoy: *Mister Corbett's Ghost,* for example, on New Year's Eve, *Zlateh the Goat* during Hanukkah, a favorite ghost story to spook Halloween guests.

Take along a book when you anticipate a long wait somewhere —the dentist's or doctor's office, for instance. You'll probably attract other children as you read, earning the gratitude of their parents as a bonus.

Another occasion for reading aloud arises when a child is too sick to go out but well enough to enjoy a story. Elizabeth remembers her bout with measles at ten: "I itched and had horrible feverish nightmares that I still remember, but the worst part was that the shades were drawn and I wasn't allowed to read. One of my fondest memories of my father is of him reading to me then. Even at the time I appreciated what a labor of love it must have been, for he read all the way through a book that was my favorite but probably would not have been his choice—*Little Women*."

Sometimes family vacations are a perfect time for reading aloud. With no television (if you're lucky), no homework, and no job demands, it's not difficult to find time for reading. If you're traveling, try to choose a book that is related to the area you're visiting. Take along a sea story if you're heading for the shore, or a historical novel that will make a stop at a national landmark more meaningful. One year the Segel family read *Across Five Aprils* driving to Gettysburg and back. This story of the Civil War as experienced by a young farmboy in southern Illinois brought to life the events of the distant past, peopling the quiet, grassy vistas with ghostly men and boys who had been, the family realized, the children and brothers and fathers of others suffering all across the country. Our list of book-places in Chapter IX is designed to help you coordinate reading choices with a travel itinerary.

If you can read in the car (the trick is to shield your eyes so you don't see the countryside whizzing by), you'll find that reading aloud makes the time pass more quickly for children—and for the driver, too.

A graduate student we know pointed out that the pleasures of vacation reading need not be limited to families with children. When she and her husband were vacationing together, she heard him chuckling over a book. "What's so funny?" she asked. That was the beginning of four summers of seashore vacations with Mark Twain. And when a friend of ours became ill on her honeymoon, it prompted her husband to devote himself to reading Sherlock Holmes stories to her—something they both remember fondly.

Finally, parents who are away from home and their children a good deal can maximize the benefit of the time they can devote to reading aloud by taping each reading session on a portable tape recorder (it need not be a fancy one for adequate voice reproduction). The child who has access to a simple tape player can then hear a mother's or dad's voice reading the story again and again while the parent is at work or on a trip. Quite a library of taped literature can be built up this way, and when the children of a family outgrow particular stories, they can be passed on to friends. Listening to a tape is no substitute, of course, for actual reading sessions with their sharing and cuddling, so be sure to continue with "live" reading sessions whenever possible.

In the Schools . . .

> *Literature itself is a survival tool, "equipment for living," as Kenneth Burke says. It must not be elbowed aside.*

As we have noted, despite all the research evidence and expert opinion establishing the value of reading aloud to children, teachers who make oral book sharing of this sort a regular feature of the school day are in a minority. Why aren't more teachers using this simple, inexpensive, and effective educational practice?

For one thing, although the push for accountability by the schools has its good points, it discourages teachers from reading to their students. Accountability rests on testing and test results. When a school's success is judged by its students' performances on standardized tests, testable skills take priority in teaching; teachers understandably "teach to the tests" and are expected to do so. Tests, unfortunately, are limited in what they can measure. A student's warm memory of a story shared with classmates and teacher can't be quantified on a test, even if that memory will last sixty years. A test won't indicate which children will turn to books for pleasure and for continued learning in the years after graduation and which ones will never open a book from one year of their adult lives to the next.

The emphasis on learning programs—such as sets of materials, audiovisual sequences, or computer-based learning programs—also reduces the opportunities for reading to children in the classroom. Once the school system has bought expensive kits, workbooks, dittos, and videotapes, they must be used, and little time is left for activities developed by the teacher. A great advantage of reading aloud is that one teacher or aide and one book can provide thirty or forty children at once with a rich learning experience. This alone should recommend it in these cost-conscious times. But the very fact that it costs nothing for a teacher to read aloud from a library book entails a serious handicap as well—namely, that there are no salesmen or advertising budgets devoted to convincing educators of the virtues of this activity.

Another serious consequence of these skill-based learning programs is that they separate the process of learning to read from the child's experience of the value of reading. As Frank Smith has pointed out: "All programs fractionate learning experience. . . . With their inevitably limited objectives, programs teach trivial aspects of literacy and they can teach that literacy is trivial" ("Demonstrations, Engagement and Sensitivity: The Choice Between People and Programs," *Language Arts* [September 1981], 637, 640). At the very least, learning programs should be supplemented by the experience of hearing first-rate literature read aloud, giving children a better reason for learning to read than to pass a test.

The "Back to Basics" mood that has characterized public opinion in recent years also has not been conducive to reading aloud in the schools. This is surprising, since reading aloud was a standard feature of the traditional classroom that proponents of this approach look to as a touchstone. Besides, reading aloud is surely one of the most basic of educational practices. The explanation seems to be that this view of education stems in part from a dismay at what was considered an overemphasis on the child's enjoyment of learning, that is, "learning through play." There was some truth to the criticism that the less appealing but necessary hard work of learning was neglected in some schools—the memorization needed to master English grammar or acquire a working vocabulary in a foreign language, for instance. Unfortunately, this criticism was generalized to a suspicion of any classroom activity that smacked of "fun." The very fact that children enjoy being read to works against its acceptance by Back to Basics enthusiasts.

In the face of all this, what can individual teachers do? First, they can tactfully challenge the assumption that enjoyment and learning are mutually exclusive. Using the material in this book and the Bibliography, they can spread the word that tests themselves confirm the important educational benefits of reading aloud. Above all, they can resolve to supplement their required materials with frequent reading sessions.

We know it isn't easy to find the time in a hectic school day. Time and again teachers tell us that they'd like to read to their students, but the curriculum allows no time for it. The state or school district mandates so many hours and minutes a day for this subject and that. The middle schools in one district, we are told, are committed to "survival skills"; time that once was available for reading is now assigned to vocational/technical education. This may well be useful, but we believe that literature itself is a survival tool, "equipment for living," as Kenneth Burke says. It must not be elbowed aside.

Each teacher knows the time that might best be set aside in her or his classroom for reading aloud. A regular time is preferable, of course: after lunch to settle children down? twice a week in language arts or reading periods? first thing in the morning with the "homeroom" group? or that traditional slot, the last few minutes of the school day? The possibilities are limited only by your ingenuity.

Teachers who want to promote reading aloud might meet as a group with the school librarian to brainstorm schoolwide plans. On inclement days when children can't go out at lunchtime, a reading-aloud session might be held in the library for those children who wished to come (no compulsory attendance). For older children it might be called a "fantasy club" or "mystery club" and books be chosen accordingly. If your school, like some we know, devotes the afternoon before a holiday to showing mediocre films ("because the kids are too wound up to work"), you might suggest that, instead, pairs of teachers take turns reading to their combined classes. That way teachers' "housekeeping" chores get done and students have a worthwhile experience, too. (Just be sure to pick an exciting story that will grab the attention of those "wound-up" children.)

Be ready, too, for the unexpected bit of time. If you always have a collection of good stories at hand, the bus breakdown that dumps thirty-five rowdy kids on you after a long day won't be a total disaster.

Teachers can extend their effectiveness by encouraging parents to read aloud at home. Polls and studies indicate that the great majority of parents want to help their children become good readers. You can give them guidance in how to do this. Stress the benefits of reading to children at a parent conference or in a letter home, and let parents know what books you will be reading to their child's class. Then suggest other suitable titles at your library for reading to the child at home. Occasionally read the first book in a series in class and let parents and children know that the story continues, suggesting that they get the sequel for home reading (see the list of books with sequels in Chapter VIII).

Suggest to administrators and parent-teacher organizations that they schedule a parent and staff workshop on reading aloud to children.

If a school newsletter goes home with students, offer to contribute a brief review of a book or two for family reading. And if your school draws up a list of suggested or required summer reading for pupils, indicate books families might share through reading aloud.

Ideally, parents and teachers can join forces to introduce the child to all the varieties of book pleasure. Yet many parents aren't comfortable with books or teachers and may not be receptive to your efforts. If this happens, don't be discouraged. For the child whose parents have never been turned on to reading, it takes just one committed teacher to transform books from symbols of frustration to cherished objects. We realize that such a commitment

adds to the burdens of a demanding job, but look at it this way:
How else can you make as great an impact on a student's life and
mind as through a year's worth of books, selected with intelligence and shared with infectious enthusiasm?

V/Casting a Spell:

HOW TO READ ALOUD EFFECTIVELY TO A GROUP OF CHILDREN

*You will be well rewarded for polishing your skills—
by the clamor for "just one more" or the nearly silent sigh of satisfaction.*

Essentially these suggestions on how to read aloud are directed to
readers outside the home, because family members and guests
need not be skilled readers to hold even the most restless listener
spellbound. Keeping the attention of a group of children is more
of a challenge, however. We offer here a few tips that will help the
more reluctant or inexperienced reader to gain confidence and
the veteran reader to perfect his or her technique.

A word about the audience. Reading aloud, although not a
theatrical experience, is a performance. The reader must be
aware of audience reaction; of creating a mood that allows the
listener to respond to the story. This interaction between reader
and listener, between story and audience, is a key to success. This
doesn't mean that one needs a stage, or even a fireplace and deep
leather chair, but it does mean that the reader has to pay attention to the atmosphere and physical setting of the session as well
as the interpretation of the story. Too much heat or polar cold
may distract listeners. With a little thought about which corner of
the room to use, a quiet place can be created in a busy classroom
or library. One librarian found that merely seating a group with
their backs to the main activity of the room helped enormously
with the problem of distraction. One teacher sat in front of a
window that looked out on a pleasant hill but found that the class,
facing the bright light, was restless and uncomfortable. The wiggling decreased when she merely switched her chair around and
sat the group at an angle from the window.

If the children will be sitting on the floor, try to mark out in
some way where they are to sit. Otherwise, all through your
reading children will be inching forward, each jockeying for the

best position, closer to you and the book. Tape or other marks on the floor can be helpful, or place carpet squares (often obtainable from rug stores) in a semicircle at the right distance. Tell each child to sit on her or his bottom on a square. This will rule out sprawling or kneeling for a better view, which blocks other children's view, of course.

Timing is important, too. Experienced day-care and nursery-school staff know that reading a story following a strenuous play-time allows everyone a chance to simmer down.

Make sure that listeners can hear you. Volume control is often difficult for a beginner to regulate, but a simple question like "Can everyone hear me?" does much to reassure fidgety listeners. Since reading out loud is a shared experience, one must look at the audience now and then. Besides confirming the bond between reader and listener, this helps to gauge audience response and thwart rebellion in the back of the room.

Sometimes an epidemic of wiggling is your clue that you have reached the end of children's attention spans, the point at which they cannot keep still, no matter how much they like the story. When this happens, it's best to break off (without scolding) at the next lull in the action, saving the rest for another time. If you are within a page or two of the chapter's end, however, you might just let your audience know that the story is almost over. This often helps the wigglers muster a bit more patience. Then plan to cover less material in subsequent sessions. Groups of toddlers or inexperienced listeners may need to begin with sessions as short as five or ten minutes. Ten- to fifteen-minute sessions suit most preschoolers, fifteen to twenty minutes is a reasonable length for primary school groups, and thirty minutes is about right for middle-graders.

Some preschoolers and even children of five, six, and seven can't sit still for anything. Don't assume that such children aren't enjoying being read to. If you can let these active ones move around (something that is admittedly more feasible at home than in school groups), you will probably find that they never wander out of earshot and are, in fact, taking it all in. In many cases they are enjoying the story as much as the child who sits motionless and clearly enthralled.

When you finish reading, don't break the spell by asking trivial questions ("What was the pig's name who won first prize at the county fair?" or "How long was Abel stranded on the island?"). Children get plenty of reading for information in their school careers. For the greatest benefit, most reading aloud should not be associated with testing of any sort; its goal should be simple pleasure.

If children have been moved by a story, they often do not want to discuss it at all right away. Later they may be happy to talk about it—or sing or dance or paint something that expresses how they feel about the story. The important word is "feel." Young children are not equipped to analyze literature. To press for such a response can reduce a complex and deeply felt experience to a chore.

Purists may be shocked, but we have been known to skip sentences, paragraphs, even an occasional chapter, that we judged would lose us the children's attention. Sometimes this means simply omitting a few nonessential phrases in order to reach the end of a chapter before a restless six-year-old's attention span expires. Or one may find that an author has indulged in digressions that spin out too long a book that otherwise has great appeal for children. Even adults who read *Watership Down* silently may find themselves skipping over some of the discursive essays that begin certain chapters, and we recommend doing so when reading the book to children (unless you have very philosophical listeners and all the time in the world).

Occasionally you may want to omit a whole chapter that you judge dull or offensive. This kind of omission can be made only if the narrative is episodic with one adventure following another but not depending on it for plot development. Such omissions of paragraphs or chapters must be carefully planned, so skim the material in advance and mark what you want to skip. You don't want to discover later that you've left out a piece of information that's essential to understanding the book's conclusion.

We have suggested a few such omissions of nonessential material in our annotations of the recommended titles. Most children are bored, we have found, by "The Lobster Quadrille" chapter of *Alice in Wonderland,* with its several long parodies of poems unfamiliar to children today, and by the inane recitations in chapter twenty-one of *The Adventures of Tom Sawyer.*

This kind of editing has a long and distinguished history from the days when oral storytellers, passing on the old tales, left out what didn't please their audiences and elaborated on what did. It should be sparingly used but is a legitimate expression of a good reader's sensitivity to the needs of her or his audience.

Many of the books we recommend have illustrations that you will want to share with your listeners. The illustrations of picture books are in fact an essential component of the story, so try to hold a picture book facing the children as you read. This means that you have to crane your neck a bit to read from the side or develop the ability to decipher upside-down print, but these are talents that can be mastered. For books that are mostly text with occasional pictures, we suggest that you wait to show the illustrations until you have read aloud at least part of the book. (Of course, this won't be possible when you are reading to one or two listeners who are sitting right next to you.) We make this suggestion because children in this age of television have many fewer opportunities to form their own mental images than earlier generations did. Experts feel that this impoverishment of the visual imagination is one of the most serious penalties of television viewing. By oral reading, we can provide children with the chance to create their own stormy seas or king's palace. They can collaborate with Stevenson in imagining the terrifying blind pirate Pew and the ingratiating yet treacherous Long John Silver. N. C. Wyeth's illustrations for *Treasure Island* are classics, loved by generations of readers, but they are Wyeth's images, his interpretations. Children can enjoy them all the more if they have first developed their own vivid mental pictures with which to compare them.

Children will probably object to this strategy. Their experience with picture books as well as with television has persuaded them that they can't follow the story if they can't see the pictures. But the illustrated book—unlike the picture book—is not dependent on the picture for meaning, and children can be led to understand this. If you don't train them, you'll find yourself having to interrupt your reading frequently to hold the book up for inspection. And nothing breaks the spell of a story faster than impatient squirms and cries of "I can't see," "Hey, teacher, I can't see!"

How dramatic should your reading be? Some readers are very straightforward. Others sway with the blowing wind and gasp in awe as the heroine saves the day. One bit of advice—keep it simple. Sometimes one is tempted to change the quality or pitch of the voice with different characters. In a short book with one or two characters, this isn't too difficult, but in a book like *Queenie Peavy* it would be a mistake to attempt voice characterizations for the many people Queenie encounters. Even the most experienced reader can mistake one character's tone for another when the reading involves several sessions. Furthermore, such voice characterization often complicates the listening process. On the other hand, one does not want listeners to fall asleep—at least, not usually. A soothing, almost monotonous tone that would be fine at bedtime may lose an audience in the middle of the day.

An overly dramatic reading can frighten very small children or those new at listening to stories. Elizabeth was once reading *Caps for Sale* to a group of preschoolers. She doesn't think of this as a scary book, but when she got a bit carried away reading the peddler's part— "You monkeys, you! You give me back my caps" —one adorable little boy burst into tears. He seemed to think that the reader was angry at him!

For older children, whether or not the reading is a dramatic rendition is partly a matter of taste and experience. A more experienced reader can sense when a moment demands a grand gesture or a bellow of rage and perform accordingly. Do be careful with such actions, however. Just such a "bellow" once brought both the principal and the school nurse to the library on the run, and an exuberant father we know knocked a bowl of buttered popcorn sky-high with a sweeping gesture. Dramatization should sound spontaneous but needs to be carefully planned, especially by beginners. In the annotations for each book, we have tried not only to indicate possible difficulties for the reader, but sometimes to suggest occasions where one might wax eloquent.

Gauging the proper pace of a story is another essential ingredient. If the reading is too slow, the listeners may lose track of the action and become fidgety. "Get on with it, Dad" was one family's complaint. Too fast has some of the same problems—the listener simply can't keep up, can't savor the story. While the reader has some control of the overall pace, there are often parts of the narrative that have an internal rhythm of their own. For instance, Lucinda's pell-mell flight to find Policeman McGonegal and save Tony Coppino's fruit stand from bullies in *Roller Skates* is a breathless race, and Ruth Sawyer built that breathlessness into her phrases and sentences. In *Tuck Everlasting*, Mae Tuck's violent confrontation with the man who is after the water of immortality is a dramatic scene that moves as swiftly as the blink of an eye. The pace of life in the humid, hot days suddenly quickens for both reader and listener. The beginning of *The Iron Giant*, on the other hand, unfolds at a slow and dignified—even portentous—

pace, dictated by Ted Hughes's careful choice of word and syntax. Many of our recommended books were chosen in part because the accomplished writers have such control of their material that the reader can't go wrong.

Yet it is through your voice that the author's words reach the listeners. Its tone and pitch color the experience. Music teachers coach their voice students to breathe from the diaphragm, and this admonition certainly applies to those who read aloud—whether just beginning or with hours of experience. Good breathing technique gives substance to a voice that otherwise may be light or high-pitched. It supports the voice and builds the listeners' confidence that you know what you're doing. A breathless quality may be all right when you're reading about the Elephant's Child, breathless with curiosity, as he approaches "the banks of the great grey-green, greasy Limpopo River." A group may get nervous, however, if you periodically appear to be in danger of falling off your chair because you haven't "caught your breath."

Above all, aim for an understandable delivery. Some regional accents, for instance, can confuse listeners not used to hearing such patterns. A high- or very low-pitched voice sometimes accents regional differences and makes it hard to listen. A reader may be unaware of such voice qualities, but a session or two with a tape recorder will certainly identify problem areas. More careful enunciation will modify most problems. Clear enunciation, in fact, helps with all aspects of reading aloud. This does not mean such exaggerated pronunciation that words "hang like ice cubes in the air," as critic Aidan Chambers describes it. Careful attention to the endings of words and sentences, however, helps the listeners to pay attention to the story, not to your reading style.

Finally, there is that bit of polish that makes reading sessions something special. It is the confidence that comes with practice and experience. There is no substitute for enthusiasm and preparation—but it does get easier with practice. One gradually becomes more aware of a story's possibilities and of an audience's subtle reactions. The experienced reader knows that a pause just before Hobberdy Dick makes his choice between the green suit of antic mirth and the red suit of humanity heightens the drama and allows the audience just that second to anticipate the satisfaction of the "right choice." The skilled reader knows that a lowered voice can emphasize the foreshadowing of events as Old Da tells Robbie the legend of the Great Selkie in *A Stranger Came Ashore*.

You will be well rewarded for polishing your skills—by the clamor for "just one more" or the nearly silent sigh of satisfaction.

VI/Queries and Quandaries:

FREQUENTLY ASKED QUESTIONS ABOUT READING TO CHILDREN

You advise parents to read to children. Should children sometimes read to parents?

If your child wants to be a reader in family read-aloud sessions and is a good reader, that's great. By all means, let him or her take a turn. A problem can come up, though, if other children who are listening object because that child isn't a fluent reader. There is something to be said for getting on with the story when your listeners are breathlessly waiting to find out "what happens." One mother told us that family reading at her house often deteriorated into arguments because of this problem.

If this happens in your family ask the child who wants to read aloud to do it at some time when just the two of you are together. Perhaps she or he would read from a favorite book, or from the newspaper or a magazine, while you make a salad or knit or polish shoes. That will allow the child to feel proud and can give you an idea of how that child's reading ability is progressing. Reading to others will help children improve their skills, but until they are able to read clearly and "with expression," their reading won't provide the same benefits to young listeners that they obtain when an adult reads.

I read to my children, but I can't get my husband to read to them. What do you suggest?

It's surprising how many mothers have asked us this question. The answer depends on the reason the father doesn't read to his children. In some cases, one parent is a poor reader and is ashamed to reveal this to his or her children. If such a parent provides the children with other kinds of stimulating experiences —takes them to the park, helps them build block-towns or plastic models—then we wouldn't push that parent to do something that he or she doesn't enjoy. (Remember that part of why reading aloud works is that the parent who enjoys the activity provides a positive model.)

If, however, a husband doesn't read to his children because he figures that's a woman's job, then it's worth trying to persuade him otherwise. One reason so many more boys than girls have reading problems in our society seems to be that reading is viewed by many as a feminine activity. In one study, 63 percent of women identified themselves as book readers, and only 47 percent of men. Jim Trelease, a father himself, has spoken eloquently on this subject: "There's always a shortage of men in the groups I talk to on reading aloud, but I'll tell you where there's no shortage of males in this country—in the remedial reading class. . . . And I propose that an enormous percentage of those boys are in those classes not because of learning disabilities but because of father or male disabilities. They have been convinced by their fathers and males on TV that the really important things in life are the things we throw and the things we catch" (*U.S. News & World Report,* March 17, 1986, 65). It's essential that children, especially sons, see their fathers reading. And reading together is too special to be monopolized by one parent.

I know you recommend that a parent sometimes make a tape of read-aloud sessions, for the child's enjoyment when the parent can't read to her. What do you think of the prerecorded audiotapes of children's books that one can buy?

Many excellent books for children are now marketed with a recording of the story, so that children can turn pages on cue and follow the printed words as they listen to them. Several parents have told us that their child learned to read this way. This is a fine *supplement* to the activity of individual adults reading to children, but we suspect that the breakthrough to reading for these children was preceded by many years of one-on-one book sharing. For the toddler and preschooler, hearing a story works best as an interaction between reader and listener. A tape and tape player cannot answer questions; nor can it provide the security of a hug when the story gets scary.

Excellent adaptations of picture books are now available on videotape also. For families who own a VCR, they are a welcome alternative to the hours of violent and sexist cartoon shows and to the commercials on children's network television that usher children into the "gimme" culture. Yet they, too, are not as valuable as reading aloud, which is more active and interactive, and which guarantees an adult's availability when questions arise. If you want to invest in videotapes, try the episodes of public television's *Reading Rainbow* programs. Each includes an adaptation of a children's book, plus capsule reviews by children of other books. The enthusiasm of these young readers is contagious and will go far toward whetting other children's appetite for books.

My son's school sends home a summer book list. He's supposed to read at least three books from the list, but he puts it off and puts it off. Then I have to nag him about it and we're all miserable. How can I get him to read the required books?

"No more pencils, no more books, / No more teacher's dirty looks!" was what we used to chant at the beginning of summer when we were children. No doubt children today have similar sentiments. The summer book list that the teacher and school librarian see as a guide to exciting and liberating reading, many children view as one more dreaded assignment. You as a parent are caught in the middle. It *is* important that a child read during the summer; children who don't do so lose ground educationally over those months. But nagging is rarely effective. How about instead reading some of those books, or the first chapter or so, *to* your child? We encourage those who draw up summer reading lists to star titles that are particularly good for family reading.

When I read to my children, should I ask questions to see if the children listening understand what they are hearing?

Tiny children who are just learning to listen benefit from questions that relate what they see in a book to similar things in the world around them. "See the bicycle in the picture? Who do you know who rides a bicycle?" for example. When children are a bit older, however, refrain from asking factual questions that could prevent them from "getting lost in the story," for that experience of absorption is what the story aims to give. Discussion can sometimes clarify or even extend a story, but specific questions about who said or did what can cut off the emotional impact of a tale. Asking about children's reactions—what character they liked, or what was scary, for instance—will at the same time let you know whether your listeners understood the story or not.

My children have so much homework, even the one in second grade, that most nights we have no time to read aloud. What can we do?

We know that nothing parents can do for their children does more to help them succeed in school than simple daily reading aloud. Unfortunately, the message hasn't yet reached all educators. One kindergarten teacher, when she was told that her five-year-olds had to do homework every night, sent home notes saying that for homework, children should listen to someone read a story. Her principal stopped that, saying that listening to stories was not real "work," and so would not build the necessary habits of discipline. Now, we understand the value of homework assignments, but five seems unnecessarily young to require out-of-school work. And we remain convinced that simple reading aloud by parents in the home is more beneficial than having parents play homework policeman, which tends to set up schoolwork as a parent-child battleground. Furthermore, reading aloud is something parents can do a better job of than helping with homework assignments. (After all, even those parents who know where the commas go haven't tried to define a subordinate clause in twenty years.) Besides, family reading is so much more rewarding. While monitoring homework too often turns parent and child into adversaries, the special shared experience of a story draws them closer together.

We urge that you get your parent-teachers organization to sponsor a talk on reading aloud by an enthusiastic children's librarian or educator—someone who can persuade teachers and parents *and administrators* of the value and rewards of this activity. After the talk, the group might have a brainstorming session to generate ways of encouraging reading aloud at home and school. You'll probably need an incentive to get people to attend. Door prizes and refreshments help, and we know one group that always schedules a simple performance by students as part of such meetings. Even parents whom wild horses can't drag to school ordinarily will often come out to see their offspring sing, dance, or recite.

Until you're able to get the school to support this activity by adjusting homework requirements, it's worth extending bedtime fifteen minutes if those fifteen minutes are spent listening to a story.

VII/What to Read?

> *We offer these lists of books with something of the*
> *pleasure that a matchmaker must feel when she or*
> *he brings together the perfect couple. . . .*

All right. You're sold on the value of reading aloud; you *will* make time to read to the children in your life, by hook or by crook. And you've picked up some tips that will make you an effective reader-aloud. Just one question remains: *what to read?* You've heard of a few books that are rousing successes when read aloud—E. B. White's *Charlotte's Web,* for instance. But beyond *Charlotte's Web,* a blank.

Perhaps you have tried books you remember from your own childhood and have been dismayed to discover how dry many passages of *The Leatherstocking Tales* seem now or how syrupy-sweet *The Five Little Peppers.* Even the fondly remembered *Beautiful Joe* turns out to be too sentimental for today's tastes. We know one father whose attempt to read *Robinson Crusoe* to his ten-year-old was abandoned by mutual consent after about twenty minutes, for though children still love survival tales, they no longer have to wade through hundred-word sentences and pious moralizing to get them. In short, your good intentions are frustrated by not knowing which of the old books retain their appeal or what good books for children have been published since you were a child.

Or it may be that as a teacher you chose to read a book by an author you know to be popular with children. When you got into it, you discovered that the book is written from a child's point of view and expressed in a child's voice. You felt like a phony reading: "This kid who moved into my building is unreal, I tell you—I mean *weird.*" Besides, the language gained nothing by being read aloud—in fact, oral reading probably revealed that the language and style were the book's weakest elements. Pell-mell plot and appealing characters can often sustain a silent reading but are unlikely to prevent a book that lacks other qualities from falling flat when read aloud.

For this part of the guide, then, we have culled from hundreds of titles those we believe will be successful when read aloud, and rewarding to both reader and listener.

For your convenience we've divided the books into two parts: the Booklist for Younger Listeners, for infants to five-year-olds, and the Booklist for School-Age Listeners, for children roughly six to twelve. If you have a five- or six-year-old, however, be sure to scan both lists, for some books that we judged will appeal to children four to six, we put on the first list; others, which seemed right for five- to eight-year-olds, ended up on the second list.

We resisted dividing the books into a list of picture books and a list of novels, though that would have made it much easier to decide where to place books. We didn't want to reinforce the assumption many people have that picture books are only for children who don't yet know how to read. More and more challenging and beautiful picture books are being published with an audience of older children in mind, and we included a generous sampling of these in our Booklist for School-Age Listeners.

The criteria on which our recommendations are based are strict. The books on this list differ from most lists of recommended titles in that they *read well aloud*—except for a few baby books with no words or very few words that were chosen because they stimulate the dialogue that precedes real listening. Many of the books we ourselves have read to living, squirming children and found that they worked. The squirmers became still, the next installment was eagerly awaited, and children frequently went on to reread the book or to read others by the same author.

We tried to include a good number of *books that children might not pick up and read for themselves.* We agree with Aidan Chambers's principle that the limited time available for reading aloud should be weighed "in favor of those books that children need help with in order to find the pleasure they offer" *(The Horn Book Magazine* [February 1981], 107). This doesn't mean that there aren't many readily accessible books on the list, however, and these are good choices to start with. (They have been listed as "Surefire Books" in Chapter VIII.)

The books we have chosen *work well with groups* as small as a family of three and as large as an entire class. They are also books that lend themselves to being shared between adults and children. Many books that are popular with preadolescent children in particular explore experiences and feelings that are private and not intended to be shared with an adult or even with a group of children. The atmosphere of intimacy on which their appeal hinges is violated by having an adult reader stand between the story and the child, so to speak. Judy Blume, whose books are obvious examples of this type, confided to an interviewer: "I shudder sometimes when a teacher or librarian tells me that she's reading these books out loud because I really feel they're personal books. They're personal experiences, just between me and the child who's reading them" (James A. Smith and Dorothy M. Park, *Word Music and Word Magic* [Boston: Allyn and Bacon, 1977], 280).

The books on our list are titles that we judge to be *high in literary value.* Some would assume that this means we have simply produced yet another list of the standard classics, but we do not agree with those who see the classics of the past as superior to anything written in our own day. Our recommendations include both the literature of the past and recent books that we judge outstanding. This emphasis on literary quality means that no book made the list on the strength of its message alone, whether it be teaching children native American customs, showing them the value of honesty, or warning of the dangers of peer pressure. The recommended titles may communicate many sorts of information and values to children, of course, but they earn a place on the list only if they are outstanding literature, shaping and communicating human experience in such a way as to illuminate, move, or delight the listener.

One of the qualities of outstanding literature is that it enhances one's sense of human possibility in some way. We have recommended no book that we think would injure the self-esteem of a child or reinforce a biased view of those in some way different from the listener. Some books with strong stories and definite reader appeal were not included because the bias of another time seems to pervade them. That does not mean, however, that we rejected any book that depicts a prejudiced character or idea. When racist or sexist attitudes are expressed in dialogue or situation as a way of characterizing a person or a whole society, but do not represent the attitudes of the author (as deduced from the book as a total experience), we have no objection to the book. One criterion of good historical fiction, after all, is that it be an accurate depiction of past ideas and attitudes; such stories can help children understand the roots of prejudice in the past.

In reading aloud, when you come upon prejudiced remarks used to characterize a person or time, you may want to make clear that this is not your view. For instance, several of our otherwise unobjectionable books portray young boys as thinking or saying, "Oh, she's only a girl!" Children are smart enough to know that the author's intention isn't to denigrate females but to create a specific and believable boy who is at the stage where he has to bolster his own confidence by putting down the other sex. A shake of the head and a roll of the eyes may be sufficient to let listeners know that you view such a remark as silly.

More discussion may be needed when reading aloud a book like *Sounder.* With the stark simplicity of traditional folklore, this poignant tale relates the sufferings of a poor black sharecropper's family decades ago. The cruelties of the bigots and the courage of the protagonist and his family are depicted in their actions, but the narrator does not explicitly condemn the one and praise the other. Talking about the story can assure that all the children clearly perceive where the author's sympathies and respect lie. Young listeners also need to be reminded that in the early part of the twentieth century, black Americans had fewer avenues by which to protest against and resist injustices. We need to supply historical perspective lest today's children unfairly dismiss these heroic characters as unduly passive.

Some outstanding books do not appear on the list because we felt they might be too painful or upsetting for a sensitive child (Paula Fox's *The Slave Dancer* is one such book). While we believe that most children, especially from about the age of ten on, are able to deal with harsh truths of life as well as (or better than) many adults, and while we applaud writers courageous enough to explore these subjects, we see a difference here between the experience of independent reading and that of listening to a book as a member of a group. Children are very good judges of what their psyches can handle. If a book that they have chosen and are reading to themselves makes them uncomfortable, they will stop reading it. But children being read to—particularly in the school situation—are a captive audience. They can't leave; most are reluctant to admit that they are scared or upset by the story. Thus, in selecting books to be read aloud to a group, we have been more cautious than we would be in recommending books for independent reading. In general, we suggest that the larger or less familiar the audience, the more conservative one should be when it comes to selecting potentially disturbing material.

Other fine books that we omitted don't lend themselves to oral presentation because they cannot be appreciated unless the reader has the page right in front of her or him. In some such cases, detailed illustrations must be examined simultaneously with the text. In others, charts, diagrams, or handwritten notes play a major part in the book's meaning (Ellen Raskin's engaging puzzle-mysteries fall into this category).

Although availability of books was an important consideration, we have mentioned a few books that are currently out of print, noting that fact in the heading of that listing. These books, which were too good to leave out, should be available in many libraries.

We decided to include only one entry on each list for each author so that we could provide a broader selection of writers. If you have had great success with a book, by all means seek out additional titles by the same author.

You will find on the lists books to suit different ages, tastes, and situations. Although we encourage regular repeated sessions for sharing "chapter books" with older children, we know that sometimes a reader can't be sure of getting an audience back again soon, or just may feel like reading a complete story in one sitting. For such occasions we have included "thin books," just right for

one reading session, picture books, and collections of ancient folktales and contemporary short stories, any one of which can provide a complete literary experience in a few minutes. On the
other hand, if you or your listeners hate to have a good thing come
to an end, there are a few novels that will stretch over weeks.

The list is balanced between stories featuring female characters
and those focusing on male characters. We strongly discourage
teachers from choosing only "boys' books" for reading to a mixed
group of girls and boys. In the past many teachers and librarians
were advised to do this because of the antiquated notion that girls
will read about boys but boys won't read (or listen to) a book about
girls. This may have been true when so-called boys' books were
much more exciting than the insipid volumes labeled "girls'
books," but with the lively and interesting books published in
recent years featuring female protagonists, it is no longer the
case. Both boys and girls will enjoy and profit from imaginatively
sharing the experiences of a member of the other sex.

Comedy, romance, adventure, biography, historical fiction, and
fantasy are all represented in our listings, as well as a few informa-
tional books of outstanding literary qualities. We encourage you to
build a similar variety into your reading-aloud plans.

We offer these lists of books with something of the pleasure that
a matchmaker must feel when she or he brings together the
perfect couple: we believe you'll find books here that will become
a cherished part of your and your listeners' lives.

A Note on Suggested Listening Levels

The "Suggested Listening Level" that precedes each book's
annotation is a rough estimate of the age or grade span for a
potential audience. For children between the ages of four or five
to about seven, parents and teachers should check both lists. (We
have used age designations in the list for younger readers and
grade levels in the one for school-age listeners.) Children who
have been read to a great deal and are eager listeners may be
ready for a particular book much earlier than we've indicated.
Our estimates refer to the typical child and can be applied more
directly when reading to children in the school than in the home.

The better you know the child or children to whom you will be reading, the more you can substitute your own judgment for ours.

Our suggested age or grade levels tend to be lower than the reading levels publishers or reviewers use to indicate how much difficulty a book will pose to the child reader. Because these books are to be read *to* children, we have aimed at matching books to the interests and general understanding of children at particular ages, not to reading skills.

For family reading, we recommend choosing a book geared more to the older children's level and interests. Parts of the book may be over the head of a younger child in the family, but she or he will take from the story that which is meaningful and feel proud to be offered a more grown-up story, while an older child won't stay around long for a book that is aimed at younger children. (A list of books we think will hold the interest of children of different ages, headed "Wide Age-Range," appears in Chapter VIII.)

BOOKLIST FOR YOUNGER LISTENERS

Abiyoyo BY PETE SEEGER. *Illustrated by Michael Hays.* New York: Macmillan Publishing Co., 1986.

Suggested Listening Level: 4–7 years

Based on a South African lullaby, *Abiyoyo* has been a highlight of Pete Seeger concerts for decades. Now a handsome book, this rousing tale tells of a giant who had "stinkin' feet 'cause he didn't wash 'em" and "slobbery teeth 'cause he didn't brush 'em . . ." Hays's striking illustrations place the trick-playing father and musical son who overcome the giant in a wonderfully diversified community.

Airport WRITTEN AND ILLUSTRATED BY BYRON BARTON. New York: Thomas Y. Crowell, 1982.

Suggested Listening Level: 2–4 years

This is a straightforward account of what happens from the time one arrives at an airport until that glorious moment when one feels the plane lift off into the sky. The pictures are simply drawn, using black outline and bright, flat colors, and the book has been commended for outstanding design. Adults may feel that there's not much story here, but many preschool children love this book, which both informs and, in its last spread, captures the wonder of flight.

Alexander and the Terrible, Horrible, No Good, Very Bad Day BY JUDITH VIORST. *Illustrated by Ray Cruz.* New York: Atheneum Publishers, 1972. Paperback: Atheneum.

Suggested Listening Level: 4–7 years

Everyone has days when events begin badly and grow worse. Pictures and text provide just the right touch of empathy so that listeners can share Alexander's dismay about all the things that have gone wrong in his day and yet see the humor, too. Another favorite is Viorst's *The Tenth Good Thing About Barney,* a sensitive story mourning the death of a pet cat.

Amelia Bedelia BY PEGGY PARISH. *Illustrated by Fritz Siebel.* New York: Harper & Row, Publishers, 1963. Paperback: Harper.

Suggested Listening Level: 4–7 years

When she went to work for Mr. and Mrs. Rogers, Amelia Bedelia did exactly what the list of chores said to do: She drew a picture of the window drapes instead of closing them; she put dusting powder on the furniture to "dust" it; and she decorated the steak with bows to "trim the fat." Fortunately, she also made the best lemon meringue pie the Rogerses had ever tasted, so they kept her—and so will you. Be sure to use this funny book and its sequels with only one or two listeners so that everyone can see the illustrations: several of the puns are visual ones. Beginning readers can enjoy this one on their own, too.

Anansi the Spider: A Tale from the Ashanti RETOLD AND ILLUSTRATED BY GERALD MCDERMOTT. New York: Holt, Rinehart & Winston, 1972. Paperback: Holt.

Suggested Listening Level: 4–7 years

Brilliant colors and stylized figures from the Ashanti tradition add dramatic intensity to the tale of the spider, Kwaku Anansi, his six sons, and how the moon came to be in the sky.

Andy and the Lion WRITTEN AND ILLUSTRATED BY JAMES DAUGHERTY. New York: The Viking Press, 1938.

Suggested Listening Level: 4–6 years

Timeless as the original fable of Androcles and the lion is this retelling of how a good deed is rewarded. Daugherty's robust drawings dramatize the tale, adding vigor and authority.

Are You My Mother? WRITTEN AND ILLUSTRATED BY P. D. EAST-MAN. New York: Random House, 1960. Paperback: Random House.

Suggested Listening Level: 3–5 years

If his mother isn't there when the egg hatches, how's a baby bird to know his mother? Designed for those just beginning to read, this is wonderful to share with even younger children who may have lost their mother sometime—in the grocery store or shopping mall or park.

Avocado Baby WRITTEN AND ILLUSTRATED BY JOHN BURNING-HAM. New York: Thomas Y. Crowell, 1982.

Suggested Listening Level: 3–5 years

All the Hargraveses were weak, even the new baby, until Mrs. Hargraves mashed up an avocado pear. And then . . . outrageous humor tickles even solemn three-year-olds, who will be delighted that a *baby* can defeat the bullies of the world.

The Baby's Bedtime Book COLLECTED AND ILLUSTRATED BY KAY CHORAO. New York: E. P. Dutton, 1984.

Suggested Listening Level: 1–3 years

Twenty-seven lullabies and poems are gathered here for young families to share. The pastel colors and comfortable figures make a pleasing combination for end-of-the-day quiet time.

The Baby's Catalogue WRITTEN AND ILLUSTRATED BY JANET AND ALLAN AHLBERG. Boston: Little, Brown & Co., 1983. Paperback: Little, Brown.

Suggested Listening Level: 1–3 years

All the things that babies do, play with, see, feel, and like are depicted in soft, detailed illustrations which picture each item or activity with six different families.

Bedtime for Frances BY RUSSELL HOBAN. *Illustrated by Garth Williams.* New York: Harper & Row, Publishers, 1960. Paperback: Harper.

Suggested Listening Level: 3–5 years

Frances may *look* like a badger, but her bedtime ritual is so similar to a young child's that you may not notice. Frances also has other funny and warm family adventures; *Bread and Jam for Frances* is one of our favorites.

The Biggest Bear WRITTEN AND ILLUSTRATED BY LYND WARD. Boston: Houghton Mifflin Co., 1952. Paperback: Houghton Mifflin.

Suggested Listening Level: 4–6 years

Brown-and-white illustrations enhance this story of Johnny Orchard, who raised a bear much too big for the farm where his family lived. Through much of the book Ward shows the reader only the results of the bear's destructive action at the farm, so children are astonished when they finally see just how large the bear has grown.

Bringing the Rain to Kapiti Plain BY VERNA AARDEMA. *Illustrated by Beatriz Vidal.* New York: The Dial Press, 1981. Paperback: Dial.

Suggested Listening Level: 4–7 years

Rhythmic verse accumulates in a tale from Kenya reminiscent of "The House That Jack Built." Both preschool and primary-grade children will enjoy hearing about Ki-pat, "who watched his herd . . . as they mooed for the rain . . . from the cloud overhead— the big, black cloud, all heavy with rain, that shadowed the ground on Kapiti Plain." This was a favorite on *Reading Rainbow* and it is a favorite of ours.

Brown Bear, Brown Bear What Do You See? BY BILL MARTIN, JR. *Illustrated by Eric Carle.* New York: Holt, Rinehart & Winston, 1967, 1983.

Suggested Listening Level: 1–4 years

Rhythmic verse and vivid colors combine to capture the attention of the youngest with simple text that is based on an old call-and-response game. As it progresses from red bird and yellow duck to mother and children, two-year-olds soon join the chant.

Cakes and Custard: Children's Rhymes COLLECTED BY BRIAN ALDERSON. *Illustrated by Helen Oxenbury.* New York: William Morrow & Co., 1975.

Suggested Listening Level: 3–7 years

Nursery rhymes, both familiar and unusual, have been selected by a noted British critic. Black-and-white sketches alternate with full-color in the humorous, sometimes lyrical, illustrations.

Caps for Sale WRITTEN AND ILLUSTRATED BY ESPHYR SLOBODKINA. New York: W. R. Scott, 1947. Paperback: Scholastic.

Suggested Listening Level: 3–5 years

A peddler loses his caps to a tree full of monkeys, cleverly retrieves them, and makes his way out of town. The echoes of street cries and the images of the peddler and monkeys imitating each other make this perfect for the time when your audience demands, "Just one more, pleeease."

The Carrot Seed BY RUTH KRAUSS. *Illustrated by Crockett Johnson.* New York: Harper & Row, Publishers, 1945.

Suggested Listening Level: 3–5 years

Very simple text and pictures capture a small boy's persistent faith that a seed will grow when nurtured.

A Chair for My Mother WRITTEN AND ILLUSTRATED BY VERA B. WILLIAMS. New York: Greenwillow Books, 1982. Paperback: Greenwillow.

Suggested Listening Level: 3–5 years

Vibrant colors fill the pages as a little girl tells the story of how a loving single-parent family, after all their furniture is lost in a fire, saves enough to buy a comfortable chair for her hardworking mother.

The Chalk Doll BY CHARLOTTE POMERANTZ. *Illustrated by Frané Lessac.* New York: B. Lippincott Co., 1989.

Suggested Listening Level: 4–7 years

Rose has a cold and has to stay in bed. To keep her mother by her bedside, she asks questions about when "you were a little girl in Jamaica." She hears about the homemade rag doll Mama had, the "chalk" (store-bought) doll she longed for, the birthday when she had three whole pennies, and her high heels made from mango pits that went "clickety click clack" as she walked home from school. At the end, Rosie wonders if she herself, with all her toys, has as much fun as Mommy did. As the story ends, Rosie and her mother are making Rosie a rag doll. Lessac is a Caribbean artist whose colorful primitive paintings reinforce the warmth and vitality of the story.

Clean-up Day CREATED BY KATE DUKE. New York: E. P. Dutton, 1986.

Suggested Listening Level: 2–3 years

One of several board books depicting a mischievous guinea pig in everyday activities. We like best this one where a small guinea pig "helps" mother clean house. Even very little ones will notice with amusement that the helper creates more mess than she or he cleans up.

Cloudy with a Chance of Meatballs BY JUDITH BARRETT. *Illustrated by Ron Barrett.* New York: Atheneum Publishers, 1978. Paperback: Macmillan.

Suggested Listening Level: 4–7 years

Grandpa's tall tale at bedtime tells of the wonderful village of Chewandswallow, where no one shopped for food because it came in with the weather. Although it is a bit long, four- and five-year-olds who have listened to stories, and to the weatherman, find this really funny. So do their older sisters and brothers.

Come a Tide BY GEORGE ELLA LYON. *Illustrated by Stephen Gammell.* New York: Orchard Books, 1990.

Suggested Listening Level: 4–8 years

As this book begins, we see a family picnic getting under way, but a few stray raindrops warn us of a storm coming. Soon everyone is running for shelter and Granny calmly makes her forecast: "It'll come a tide." Indeed a flood does hit the Appalachian hollow where the story is set, and we see how the family and their neighbors cope with the danger. Granny's calm acceptance strikes the dominant note, from her first prediction to her day-after advice: time to "make friends with a shovel." Lyon and Gammell do not deny the danger and dirt brought by the flood, but coping with such disasters is obviously a tradition in these hills. As a result, the child in the story and the children listening to it can enjoy the excitement without being overly frightened. Rarely have watercolors been used to such advantage as in Gammell's illustrations to this watery tale.

Corduroy WRITTEN AND ILLUSTRATED BY DON FREEMAN. New York: The Viking Press. 1968. Paperback: Penguin.

Suggested Listening Level: 2–4 years

Some teddy bears are perfect even without the button on their overalls. Corduroy finally finds the little girl who had loved him at first sight and with her, the home of which he has dreamed. Other favorites by Freeman include *Mop Top* and *Norman the Doorman.*

The Crack-of-Dawn Walkers BY AMY HEST. *Illustrated by Amy Schwartz.* New York: Macmillan Publishing Co., 1984.

Suggested Listening Level: 4–6 years

Sadie and Ben take turns having Grandfather to themselves on alternate Sunday mornings. Detailed black-and-white illustrations depict loving, ritual-laden strolls in this story of sibling rivalry.

Curious George WRITTEN AND ILLUSTRATED BY HANS A. REY. Boston: Houghton Mifflin Co., 1941. Paperback: Houghton Mifflin.

Suggested Listening Level: 3–5 years

Curious monkeys and curious children sometimes get in trouble, but aren't they lucky to have a man in a yellow hat to save them from their mischief. George is as appealing to today's children as he was to their parents and grandparents.

David and Dog WRITTEN AND ILLUSTRATED BY SHIRLEY HUGHES. Englewood Cliffs, N.J.: Prentice-Hall, 1978. Paperback: Prentice-Hall.

Suggested Listening Level: 3–5 years

David's big sister Bella has seven teddy bears to sleep with, and his baby brother has hard toys to cut his teeth on, but David needs only shabby old Dog for comfort. When David loses Dog, kind Bella comes to the rescue. Big sisters and middle brothers will understand the loyal, loving relationship that these two share.

Dr. De Soto WRITTEN AND ILLUSTRATED BY WILLIAM STEIG. New York: Farrar, Straus & Giroux, 1982. Paperback: Scholastic.

Suggested Listening Level: 4–7 years

A clever fellow was the dentist De Soto, even if he was a mouse. After taking pity on a suffering fox (in spite of a policy never to treat animals dangerous to mice), Dr. De Soto and his equally clever wife fool the hungry fox and win the day. As with all of Steig's books, a witty, urbane style and brightly colored, detailed cartoons provide a pleasure for all.

Drummer Hoff BY BARBARA EMBERLEY. *Illustrated by Ed Emberley.* Englewood Cliffs, N.J.: Prentice-Hall, 1967. Paperback: Prentice-Hall.

Suggested Listening Level: 3–5 years

Brightly colored woodcuts add a twist to this sprightly cumulative nursery rhyme about the firing of a cannon that ends its days as a nesting place for birds and flowers.

The Elephant and the Bad Baby. BY ELFRIDA VIPONT. *Illustrated by Raymond Briggs.* New York: Coward-McCann, 1969, 1986. Paperback: Putnam.

Suggested Listening Level: 2–5 years

"Rumpeta, rumpeta, rumpeta" trumpets the elephant as he and the bad baby race through town causing trouble and creating chaos. Told with gusto, this is great fun for all who like to be occasionally rambunctious.

The Fairy Tale Treasury. COLLECTED BY VIRGINIA HAVILAND. *Illustrated by Raymond Briggs.* New York: The Putnam Publishing Group, 1980. Paperback: Dell.

Suggested Listening Level: 3–7 years

This large-format volume contains thirty-two enduring folktales for young children, from "The Three Bears" and "The Three Billy Goats Gruff" to less familiar ones, like a West Indian Anansi tale. Families will return to it again and again for satisfying stories and eye-catching pictures.

Father Fox's Pennyrhymes BY CLYDE WATSON. *Illustrated by Wendy Watson.* New York: Thomas Y. Crowell, 1971. Paperback: Scholastic.

Suggested Listening Level: 3–5 years

The rhymes and jingles here are reminiscent of the centuries-old Mother Goose nursery rhymes. These are fresh and fun and the detailed illustrations add to the play. "What you say is what you are, now what do you think of that?"

Five Hundred Words to Grow On WRITTEN AND ILLUSTRATED BY HARRY McNAUGHT. Paperback only: Random House, 1973.

Suggested Listening Level: 6 months–5 years

This inexpensive paperback will give hours of pleasure to a child, starting at five or six months and continuing for years. Clearly drawn colorful pictures of familiar objects are grouped on each set of pages: toys, kitchen words, animals, things that go, and many more. Babies will ask "whazzat" repeatedly and proudly pipe up with the words they know; five-year-olds can use the pictures as clues to the words printed beneath.

The Fox Went Out on a Chilly Night ILLUSTRATED BY PETER SPIER. New York: Doubleday & Co., 1961.

Suggested Listening Level: 3–5 years

An old folk song is illustrated with meticulous line drawings and watercolors as clear and crisp as the New England evening when the fox went out on the town-o. This award-winning artist has created so many delightful picture books that selection was difficult. Be sure to seek out others.

Frederick WRITTEN AND ILLUSTRATED BY LEO LIONNI. New York: Pantheon Books, 1966. Paperback: Pantheon.

Suggested Listening Level: 4–6 years

Unlike the other mice, Frederick failed to store grain and nuts and straw for the winter. Instead he stored words and colors and became a poet for his friends. If you like Lionni's strong design and gentle morals, many of his fine picture books are collected in *Frederick's Fables*.

Freight Train WRITTEN AND ILLUSTRATED BY DONALD CREWS. New York: Greenwillow Books, 1978. Paperback: Penguin.

Suggested Listening Level: 2–4 years

Bold design and bright colors chase each other across the pages as the train roars its way in and out of tunnels, over trestle bridges, and through cities. Details pull the reader and listener back again and again with something new to see each time one looks.

Frog and Toad Are Friends WRITTEN AND ILLUSTRATED BY ARNOLD LOBEL. New York: Harper & Row, Publishers, 1970. Paperback: Harper.

Suggested Listening Level: 4–7 years

"It's spring!" shouts the exuberant Frog. "Blah!" says Toad. So listeners are introduced to the companions whose friendship provides much quiet humor. This book for beginning readers is only the first of several about the duo who find themselves in ordinary situations that require extraordinary solutions. There are many other Lobel favorites. Ours include *Prince Bertram the Bad* and *The Book of Pigericks.*

The Funny Little Woman BY ARLENE MOSEL. *Illustrated by Blair Lent.* E. P. Dutton, 1972. Paperback: Dutton.

Suggested Listening Level: 4–7 years

The Japanese folktale about a rice dumpling that rolls into the underworld and the giggling little woman who went after it is told with vigor and good humor.

George and Martha One Fine Day WRITTEN AND ILLUSTRATED BY JAMES MARSHALL. Boston: Houghton Mifflin Co., 1978. Paperback: Houghton Mifflin.

Suggested Listening Level: 4–6 years

Five very short funny encounters between "two fine friends" who just happen to be hippopotamuses. Sample others in the series too: *George and Martha, George and Martha Rise and Shine,* and *George and Martha Encore.*

Geraldine's Blanket WRITTEN AND ILLUSTRATED BY HOLLY KELLER. New York: Greenwillow Books, 1984.

Suggested Listening Level: 2–4 years

Geraldine loves her blanket and takes it with her wherever she goes. When Mother, Father, and Aunt Bessie try to distract her with a doll, "Geraldine knows what to do." Anyone who has ever had a favorite toy or blanket or doll will cheer as Geraldine triumphantly dresses the doll in the scrap of blanket and calmly goes out to play.

Good Morning, Chick RETOLD BY MIRRA GINSBURG. *Illustrated by Byron Barton.* Greenwillow Books, 1980.

Suggested Listening Level: 1–3 years

A little chick explores the limits of his world while mother hen stands by to keep him safe. This is a wonderful book to read with a venturesome toddler.

Goodnight Moon BY MARGARET WISE BROWN. *Illustrated by Clement Hurd.* Harper & Row, Publishers, 1947. Paperback: Harper.

Suggested Listening Level: 6 months–3 years

Here is a never-fail favorite that recounts with a few words and stylized illustrations the ritual of going to bed. "Goodnight stars, goodnight air, goodnight noises everywhere."

Growing BY FIONA PRAGOFF. New York: Doubleday & Co., 1987.

Suggested Listening Level: 4 months–2 years

Between us, we have bought stacks of this captivating book for new baby gifts. The stiff laminated pages with spiral binding display photographs of babies crying, sleeping, splashing, and engaging in all the other familiar activities of infancy. Special touches include the "growing" of the infants as the pages turn, the babies' ethnic diversity, and the vibrant primary color scheme.

The Gunniwolf EDITED BY WILHELMINA HARPER. *Illustrated by William Wiesner.* New York: E. P. Dutton, 1967.

Suggested Listening Level: 4–7 years

The little girl promises her mother that she won't go into the woods, but when she sees such beautiful flowers there, her promise is forgotten. Then up pops the Gunniwolf, and the little girl has to sing him to sleep to get away. Rhythmic chants and nonsense songs enliven this favorite cautionary tale.

Harry the Dirty Dog BY GENE ZION. *Illustrated by Margaret B. Graham.* New York: Harper & Row, Publishers, 1956. Paperback: Harper.

Suggested Listening Level: 3–5 years

Harry's story is perfect for all those who ever balked at a bath. This and other Harry stories have long been nursery school favorites.

Have You Seen My Duckling? WRITTEN AND ILLUSTRATED BY NANCY TAFURI. New York: Greenwillow Books, 1984. Paperback: Penguin.

Suggested Listening Level: 2–4 years

Early one morning a mother sets out to search for her eighth duckling, who has wandered off, hiding among rushes, inside a water lily, under a dock, and behind a tree. Lovely full-color pages show the microcosm of a small pond where birds and beavers, turtles and other small creatures, live. Small listeners will be eager to help the mother duck as she swims from one side of the page to the other searching for her small adventurer.

Horton Hatches an Egg WRITTEN AND ILLUSTRATED BY DR. SEUSS. New York: Random House, 1940.

Suggested Listening Level: 4–7 years

"I meant what I said and I said what I meant. . . . An elephant's faithful one hundred per cent!" Rhymed verse and zany illustrations depict Horton's classic egg-sitting in this vintage Dr. Seuss.

How Do I Put It On? BY SHIGEO WATANABE. *Illustrated by Yasuo Ohtomo.* New York: The Putnam Publishing Group, 1980. Paperback: Putnam.

Suggested Listening Level: 1–3 years

Toddlers chortle as the young bear tries to dress himself and gets it all wrong. The pictures show that he tries his pants on his head, his cap on his foot, and so on, as he says: "Do I put it on like this?" A student of ours reported that developmentally disabled four-year-olds in her class loved the book, shouting out "No! No! No!" at the bear's mistakes, and "Yes! Yes! Yes!" when a turn of the page showed him getting it right.

Huge Harold WRITTEN AND ILLUSTRATED BY BILL PEET. Boston: Houghton Mifflin Co., 1961. Paperback: Houghton Mifflin.

Suggested Listening Level: 4–7 years

A story in verse
About a huge rabbit.
More tales by Peet
Make reading a habit.

Hush Little Baby ILLUSTRATED BY ALIKI. Englewood Cliffs, N.J.: Prentice-Hall, 1968. Paperback: Scholastic.

Suggested Listening Level: 1–3 years

Adapted from an English lullaby, this version of a favorite song for babies has appealing American folk-motif illustrations.

I Touch CREATED BY HELEN OXENBURY. New York: Random House, 1986.

Suggested Listening Level: 6 months–2 years

One of three board books that portray sense experiences of the small child's world. On the left-hand page Oxenbury pictures water, on the right, a toddler being splashed; on the left, a cat, who is next shown rubbing against the leg of a delighted child. All three are good choices for early book sharing.

If You Give a Mouse a Cookie WRITTEN BY LAURA JOFFE NUMER- OFF. *Illustrated by Felicia Bond.* New York: Harper & Row, Pub- lishers, 1985. Paperback: Scholastic.

Suggested Listening Level: 3–7 years

If you give a mouse a cookie, he'll want a glass of milk, of course, then a straw, and on and on. Felicia Bond's engaging illustrations show a willing but increasingly worn-out little boy cheerfully complying with the requests of his jaunty mouse friend until the story comes full circle. Kids cannot resist the charm of this origi- nal picture book.

Ira Sleeps Over WRITTEN AND ILLUSTRATED BY BERNARD WABER. Boston: Houghton Mifflin Co., 1972.

Suggested Listening Level: 4–6 years

No matter *what* your sister says, staying at someone else's house overnight without your teddy bear is difficult. It's nice to know that friends have teddy bears too. Hilarious true-to-life dialogue alternates with touching moments in this tour de force for dra- matic reading.

Is This a House for Hermit Crab? BY MEGAN MCDONALD. *Illus- trated by S. D. Schindler.* New York: Orchard Books, 1990.

Suggested Listening Level: 3–6 years

Hermit crab has outgrown his house, and must quickly find an- other before the pricklepine fish finds *him.* In beautifully ca- denced prose, McDonald shows hermit crab's quest as he "stepped along the shore, by the sea, in the sand . . ." looking for the right home. He tries out different places—a rock, a tin can, a child's pail—but each is too hard, or too noisy, or too deep. After a scary moment, he happens upon just what he needs. As in all the best stories of adventure, the dangers of the big world give way to a safe homecoming. Schindler's cleverly textured faithfully rendered illustrations make reading this book the next best thing to a day at the shore.

It Could Always Be Worse: A Yiddish Folk Tale WRITTEN AND ILLUSTRATED BY MARGOT ZEMACH. New York: Farrar, Straus & Giroux, 1977. Paperback: Scholastic.

Suggested Listening Level: 4–7 years

With a mother, a wife, and six children in a one-room hut, what's a poor husband to do? The rabbi's solution to bring in more and more animals was noisy and smelly at first, but when they're removed the hut seems spacious. Children love both the boisterous noisy doings and the peaceful end.

Jamaica's Find WRITTEN BY JUANITA HAVILL. *Illustrated by Anne Sibley O'Brien.* Boston: Houghton Mifflin Co., 1986.

Suggested Listening Level: 3–6 years

A lonely little girl finds a stuffed dog at the playground and decides to keep it instead of turning it in at the Lost and Found desk. After her mother observes that "it probably belongs to a girl just like Jamaica," Jamaica wrestles with her conscience. Her honesty is rewarded when she can restore the much-loved toy to its rightful owner, and she makes a friend in the process. This story teaches values without being heavy handed, and the illustrations of a loving African American family are exceptionally expressive.

Jambo Means Hello: Swahili Alphabet Book BY MURIEL FEELINGS. *Illustrated by Tom Feelings.* New York: The Dial Press, 1974. Paperback: Dial.

Suggested Listening Level: 3–6 years

Although there is little text, just enough to explain each word, we like this for reading aloud to one or two or a small group, because the warmth and joy of the illustrations echo the lovely Swahili words presented.

Jesse Bear, What Will You Wear? BY NANCY WHITE CARLSTROM. *Illustrated by Bruce Degen.* New York: Macmillan Publishing Co., 1986.

Suggested Listening Level: 2–4 years

A repetitive rhyme takes Jesse Bear through the day wearing pants that dance, with rice in his hair, stars in his eyes . . . and dreams in his head. Substitute your own toddler's name for Jesse's and make this a never-fail winner.

Jim and the Beanstalk WRITTEN AND ILLUSTRATED BY RAYMOND BRIGGS. New York: Putnam, 1980. Paperback: Putnam.

Suggested Listening Level: 4–7 years

Here's what happened a long time *after* Jack had climbed the beanstalk. Be sure that your listeners know the old nursery tale and then join in the laughter as Jim fits the giant with eyeglasses and false teeth and a wig.

The Last Puppy WRITTEN AND ILLUSTRATED BY FRANK ASCH. Englewood Cliffs, N.J.: Prentice-Hall, 1983. Paperback: Prentice-Hall.

Suggested Listening Level: 2–4 years

A puppy, last of the litter, last at feeding time, last to be chosen, is the *first* puppy of his new owner. Softly rounded figures and pastel tones complement this gentle story.

Little Bear's Visit BY ELSE H. MINARIK. *Illustrated by Maurice Sendak.* New York: Harper & Row, Publishers, 1961.

Suggested Listening Level: 4–6 years

A day of dancing and playing and telling stories with Grandma and Grandpa Bear finally wears out even an energetic Little Bear. Comfortable text and illustrations capture the warmth of a loving family in this and other easy-to-read books about Little Bear.

The Little Engine That Could BY WATTY PIPER. *Illustrated by George and Doris Hauman.* (The original classic edition) New York: Platt & Munk, 1930, 1961.

Suggested Listening Level: 3–5 years

Parodied by television comics and imitated by countless other stories, this story about the persistent, hardworking little engine has chugged its way into contemporary folklore and should not be missed by a new generation.

Little Gorilla WRITTEN AND ILLUSTRATED BY RUTH BORNSTEIN. Boston: Houghton Mifflin Co., 1976. Paperback: Ticknor & Fields.

Suggested Listening Level: 2–4 years

Everyone loved Little Gorilla. Although he grew and grew and grew until he was *enormous,* his family and friends kept on loving him.

The Little House WRITTEN AND ILLUSTRATED BY VIRGINIA LEE BURTON. Boston: Houghton Mifflin Co., 1942. Paperback: Houghton Mifflin.

Suggested Listening Level: 3–5 years

"This Little House shall never be sold for gold or silver and she will live to see our great-great-grandchildren's great-great-grandchildren living in her." The city grew up around her, however, until one of the descendants found the Little House buried by tall buildings and subways and hurrying people and moved her back to the country. Changing seasons and the changing environment do *not* change the enduring appeal and continuity of this story. *Mike Mulligan and His Steam Shovel* by the same author vies with *The Little House* as an all-time favorite.

The Little Red Hen WRITTEN AND ILLUSTRATED BY PAUL GALDONE. Boston: Houghton Mifflin Co., 1973. Paperback: Houghton Mifflin.

Suggested Listening Level: 3–5 years

Clear, uncluttered illustrations enliven this timeless nursery tale of the ultimate independent workaholic. Galdone has retold and illustrated other old favorites such as *The Gingerbread Boy* and *The Three Billy Goats Gruff.*

Little Tim and the Brave Sea Captain WRITTEN AND ILLUS-TRATED BY EDWARD ARDIZZONE. Henry Z. Walck, 1955. Paperback: Puffin.

Suggested Listening Level: 4–6 years

Little Tim who loves the sea stows away on a steamer. After a fierce storm he and the brave sea captain are rescued just before their ship "goes to Davy Jones's locker." First published in 1936, this classic saga of running away from home has delighted generations. Black-and-white ink drawings alternate with color pages so clear and lifelike that you can smell the briny English Channel. Other adventures of Little Tim are also vividly appealing.

Lost in the Museum BY MIRIAM COHEN. *Illustrated by Lillian Hoban.* New York: Greenwillow Books, 1979. Paperback: Dell.

Suggested Listening Level: 4–6 years

For anyone whose class has ever been on a field trip—whether to a museum, library, or even a farm—this captures both the excitement of a new adventure and the bewilderment of new places. Try some of the other books by this sensitive team: *No Good in Art, Will I Have a Friend?*, and *See You Tomorrow, Charles.*

Madeline WRITTEN AND ILLUSTRATED BY LUDWIG BEMELMANS. New York: The Viking Press, 1939. Paperback: Penguin.

Suggested Listening Level: 3–5 years

Intrepid adventurers will recognize a counterpart in the brave Madeline who is daunted by nothing—including the removal of an appendix! Rhymed verse and Paris street scenes are equally pleasing.

Make Way for Ducklings WRITTEN AND ILLUSTRATED BY ROBERT MCCLOSKEY. New York: The Viking Press, 1941.

Suggested Listening Level: 3–5 years

Both Bostonians and those who have never been there love this classic tale of the perils of city life for a family of young mallards. *Blueberries for Sal* is another favorite picture book by McCloskey that has great child-appeal.

Mama Don't Allow WRITTEN AND ILLUSTRATED BY THACHER HURD. New York: Harper & Row, Publishers, 1984. Paperback: Harper.

Suggested Listening Level: 4–6 years

Exuberant text and illustration tell the story of Miles and his Swamp Band, who play for the Alligator's Ball and nearly become the main course at dinner. Dialogue is lively, and be sure to sing "Mama don't allow no . . ." Text and music are included at the end of the story.

Marguerite de Angeli's Book of Nursery and Mother Goose Rhymes COLLECTED AND ILLUSTRATED BY MARGUERITE DE ANGELI. New York: Doubleday & Co., 1954. Paperback: Doubleday.

Suggested Listening Level: all ages

Safe, warm, friendly, appealing, cozy—all these terms apply to this standard collection of more than 376 nursery rhymes. Smiling children and adults in old-fashioned dress move across pages decorated with small sketches of birds, flowers, dancing dogs and cackling hens. Lavish full-color pages are interspersed with the black-and-white illustrations carefully placed on the double-page spreads to give the book a light, uncluttered look. This is a special collection for families, to be shared with babies and then pulled out again and again for renewed acquaintance with favorite rhymes.

May I Bring a Friend? BY BEATRICE S. DE REGNIERS. *Illustrated by Beni Montresor.* New York: Atheneum Publishers, 1964. Paperback: Macmillan.

Suggested Listening Level: 3–5 years

Imaginative verse and colorful drawings set the stage for a tea party with the King and Queen. Young listeners will envy the child in the story who has as friends monkeys and lions and elephants and seals. Much depends on surprise illustrations when the page is turned, so use this with listeners who can sit close to you.

Millions of Cats WRITTEN AND ILLUSTRATED BY WANDA GÁG. New York: Coward, 1928. Paperback: Putnam.

Suggested Listening Level: 3–5 years

Rhythmic text with lots of repetition has kept this tale of an old couple's search for a pet popular for what seems like hundreds of years, thousands of years, millions and billions and trillions of years.

Miss Nelson Is Missing! BY HARRY ALLARD. *Illustrated by James Marshall.* Boston: Houghton Mifflin Co., 1977. Paperback: Houghton Mifflin.

Suggested Listening Level: 4–7 years

Room 207 was the worst-behaved class in the school until Miss Viola Swamp replaced the lovely Miss Nelson. Extra lessons and no story hour convince the class (and your listeners) that Miss Nelson is worth behaving for. This very funny story ends with a surprise.

Miss Rumphius WRITTEN AND ILLUSTRATED BY BARBARA COONEY. New York: Viking–Penguin, 1982. Paperback: Penguin.

Suggested Listening Level: 4–7 years

Miss Alice Rumphius had two goals: to go to faraway places and then come home to live by the sea. And her grandfather gave her a third: to do something to make the world more beautiful. Lovely luminous pictures complement this gentle story of just how Miss Alice Rumphius did all three.

Mr. and Mrs. Pig's Evening Out WRITTEN AND ILLUSTRATED BY MARY RAYNER. New York: Atheneum Publishers, 1976. Paperback: Macmillan.

Suggested Listening Level: 4–6 years

Mrs. Wolf promised to be careful with the ten piglets in her care, but Garth was too tempting a morsel. His nine brothers and sisters had to rescue him, and then Father Pig dumped that Wolf in the river. Not to be read if children are anxious about being left with a baby-sitter, nonetheless this is great good fun, as is a sequel, *Garth Pig and the Ice-Cream Lady.*

Mr. Rabbit and the Lovely Present BY CHARLOTTE ZOLOTOW. *Illustrations by Maurice Sendak.* New York: Harper & Row, Publishers, 1962. Paperback: Harper.

Suggested Listening Level: 3–5 years

How to choose the absolutely perfect birthday present for one's mother? The little girl asks Mr. Rabbit for help and, in spite of his sometimes outlandish suggestions (which will make your listeners smile), together they find red apples and blue grapes and yellow bananas and green pears for an absolutely perfect fruit basket. Sendak's full-page watercolors are a feast in themselves. Parents and small boys will enjoy another of Zolotow's sensitive picture books, *William's Doll.*

Morris's Disappearing Bag: A Christmas Story WRITTEN AND ILLUSTRATED BY ROSEMARY WELLS. New York: The Dial Press, 1975. Paperback: Dial.

Suggested Listening Level: 3–5 years

Victor and Betty and Rose told Morris he was just too little to play with their new presents. But when Morris opened *his* box to find a disappearing bag and used it—everyone wanted a turn. A dollop of reward for the too-littles provides just the right note of humor. A board book by Wells, *Max's First Word,* is especially successful with the very youngest. Their parents will appreciate Wells's humor.

The Most Amazing Hide-and-Seek Counting Book CREATED BY ROBERT CROWTHER. New York: Viking–Penguin, 1981.

Suggested Listening Level: 3–5 years

All children love pop-up books, and this is one of the best. Each large page does double-duty: the first shows *one* toadstool; when the child pulls a tab, *two* spiders appear on the toadstool. Similarly, a tab sends *six* goldfish jumping around *five* water lilies. Each number up to twenty has its own illustration, but at thirty the figures incorporate multiples of ten up to ninety. The last page creates a veritable stage-setting as layers rise to display "100 little creatures." Though sturdier than many manipulation books, this one will last longer if an adult is present to remind the small counter to pull *gently*.

The Mother Goose Treasury ILLUSTRATED BY RAYMOND BRIGGS. New York: Coward-McCann, 1966. Paperback: Dell.

Suggested Listening Level: all ages

An oversize Mother Goose anthology with 408 rhymes and 897 illustrations (although *we* didn't count them), this colorful, vigorous collection presents a lively setting for traditional favorites and unfamiliar rhymes. The size may make it awkward to hold both book *and* baby, so be sure to have adequate room to prop up one or the other.

Mother, Mother, I Want Another BY MARIA POLUSHKIN. *Illustrated by Diane Dawson*. New York: Crown Publishers, 1978. Paperback: Crown.

Suggested Listening Level: 2–4 years

A plea for "just one more" brings Mrs. Duck, Mrs. Frog, Mrs. Donkey, and Mrs. Pig to the bedside of baby mouse to sing another good-night song. But what the baby really wanted was another kiss, and that he got.

Much Bigger Than Martin WRITTEN AND ILLUSTRATED BY STEVEN KELLOGG. New York: The Dial Press, 1976. Paperback: Dial.

Suggested Listening Level: 3–5 years

Like all younger siblings, Henry hates it when his big brother Martin tells him he's too little. He hopes to grow bigger than Martin by eating lots of apples, and imagines terrorizing him and his mean friends. All Henry gets is a stomachache, but Martin makes an effort to be nicer, and when he backslides, Henry figures out a way to have his own fun. The illustrations of real and imagined scenes are full of funny and endearing details.

My Noah's Ark WRITTEN AND ILLUSTRATED BY M. B. GOFFSTEIN. New York: Harper & Row, Publishers, 1978.

Suggested Listening Level: 4–6 years

Goffstein has the ability to intrigue young viewers with simple black-and-white line drawings and a few words, as in this story of a ninety-year-old woman remembering a toy ark made for her by her father. The ark and its animals were added to over the years, giving pleasure to her and her children, and they still hold memories. Though young children find concepts of time difficult to grasp, they can certainly enjoy the sense of sharing something very special that pervades this gem.

The New Baby BY FRED ROGERS. *Photographed by Jim Judkis.* New York: The Putnam Publishing Group, 1985. Paperback: Putnam.

Suggested Listening Level: 2–4 years

The New Baby is one of a series called First Experience Books, issued by Family Communications, Inc., the production company for the *Mister Rogers* series. The books show the same caring and sensitive approach to children's feelings that parents have appreciated in the award-winning TV program. A quiet text and unusually attractive photographs of two families (one black, one white) address feelings of jealousy, frustration, and pride in two preschoolers who are adjusting to new siblings.

Nobody Asked Me If I Wanted a Baby Sister WRITTEN AND ILLUS-
TRATED BY MARTHA ALEXANDER. New York: The Dial Press,
1971. Paperback: Dial.

Suggested Listening Level: 4–6 years

Oliver is tired of hearing grown-ups admire his baby sister, so he
puts her in his wagon and sets out to give her away. He's not
successful, but when the baby prefers him to anyone else, he
decides she's not so bad. The book's small size and delicate, humorous illustrations make this, like all of Alexander's books, good
for sharing with one or two lucky children at a time.

Noisy WRITTEN AND ILLUSTRATED BY SHIRLEY HUGHES. New
York: Lothrop, Lee & Shepard Books, 1985.

Suggested Listening Level: 1–3 years

All kinds of noises—loud clangy ones, soft splashy ones—are described in lilting verse. The appealing antics of a little girl and her
family are just the right length for a bedtime tale. Other titles of
this series are equally successful: *Bathwater's Hot* and *When We
Went to the Park.*

1,2,3 CREATED BY TANA HOBAN. New York: Greenwillow Books,
1985.

Suggested Listening Level: 6 months–2 years

An award-winning photographer here designs a first-rate counting book for the youngest viewers. Each bright, indestructible
page of this board book shows a numeral and the appropriate
number of dots in red, plus familiar objects—one birthday cake,
two shoes, three blocks, up to ten. Hoban's photography graces
dozens of books for children of all ages. Look in your library for
others as your baby grows.

Our Animal Friends at Maple Hill Farm WRITTEN AND ILLUS-TRATED BY ALICE AND MARTIN PROVENSEN. New York: Random House, 1974. Reissued, 1984.

Suggested Listening Level: 2–5 years

People live at Maple Hill Farm and so do two dogs, a pig, and five horses. There are also "geese, lots of chickens, a few goats, several sheep, and four special cats," all lovingly and humorously described as they grabble and grouch and butt and play their ways through the days and nights at Maple Hill Farm. Small details highlight the personalities of the animals: we like Max the cat, who is fierce and clever but likes children, Pola Negra the rooster, and even Evil Murdoch the gander. We like the quiet corner where an old hound and three cats are buried. We'd like to visit Maple Hill Farm. These talented artists have also fashioned a lively, lovely book of nursery rhymes, *The Mother Goose Book.* Their work *Glorious Flight Across the Channel with Louis Bleriot* was awarded the Caldecott Medal in 1984, but the creatures at Maple Hill Farm make it our favorite.

Over in the Meadow ARRANGED BY JOHN LANGSTAFF. *Illustrated by Feodor Rojankovsky.* New York: Harcourt Brace & World, 1967. Paperback: Harcourt Brace Jovanovich.

Suggested Listening Level: 1–5 years

" 'Sing,' said the mother. 'We sing,' said the three. So they sang and were glad in their nest in the tree." Even nonsingers will enjoy this old song, and babies begin to repeat "their part" with great delight.

Owl Moon BY JANE YOLEN. *Illustrated by John Schoenherr.* New York: Philomel Books, 1987.

Suggested Listening Level: 4–7 years

You have to be very quiet when you go owling, quiet and careful to listen to the sounds of the night and the woods. These are the words that guide a father and child as they set off on an evening's walk, hoping to find an owl. The wonderful use of white space sets off the dark woods and snow-covered clearings lit by moonlight as the pair finally spy the great owl. This Caldecott winner is a compelling blend of text and illustrations that can easily be used in a group. The text sings of that special bond between father and child that sharing such a moment can bring.

The Ox-Cart Man BY DONALD HALL. *Illustrated by Barbara Cooney.* New York: The Viking Press, 1979. Paperback: Penguin.

Suggested Listening Level: 4–6 years

Words of a poet, spare and lean words, chronicle the life of an industrious nineteenth-century New England farm family. Rich, prize-winning illustrations complete the image of a loving family in a changing countryside.

Pat the Bunny WRITTEN AND ILLUSTRATED BY DOROTHY KUNHARDT. New York: Western Publishing Co., 1942.

Suggested Listening Level: 6 months–2 years

For years this small book has invited babies and their parents to explore sensory play by touching soft "fur" or a "whiskery" face, smelling flowers or putting a finger through a "ring" that is a hole in the page. Although the spiral binding falls apart quickly, it offers such pleasure to families that we think it worth the little bit of extra care.

Peace at Last WRITTEN AND ILLUSTRATED BY JILL MURPHY. New York: The Dial Press, 1980. Paperback: Dial.

Suggested Listening Level: 3–5 years

Mr. Bear couldn't sleep because of a loud clock and dripping water and snoring, until it was just about time to get up. Children will love the repeated "Oh no, I can't stand THIS." It's a story for Mother and Father Bears who want just one more wink of sleep, as well as for their children.

Petunia WRITTEN AND ILLUSTRATED BY ROGER DUVOISIN. New York: Alfred A. Knopf, 1950.

Suggested Listening Level: 3–5 years

This silly goose believes that merely holding a book will make her wise, until in her vanity she nearly destroys her barnyard friends. Cleverly droll, Duvoisin presents a gentle lesson about the wonder of words in a beautifully designed format.

Pig Pig Grows Up WRITTEN AND ILLUSTRATED BY DAVID MC-PHAIL. New York: E. P. Dutton, 1980.

Suggested Listening Level: 4–6 years

Pig Pig, the baby of the family, simply refuses to grow up. This pudgy porker eats pabulum, wears a too-tight sleep suit in a too-short crib, and insists that his poor mother push him in a stroller. But one day Momma loses her grip on the stroller and it careens downhill straight at a *real* baby. Pig Pig saves the day and decides he likes being a hero so much that he'll grow up after all. You might think that parents would like the story's not-so-hidden message more than children, but the little ones we know are ardent fans of Pig Pig.

Piggybook WRITTEN AND ILLUSTRATED BY ANTHONY BROWNE. New York: Alfred A. Knopf, 1986.

Suggested Listening Level: 4–6 years

Mr. Piggott and his sons Simon and Patrick allow, even demand, that Mrs. Piggott wait on them hand and foot. One day she departs, leaving a note: "You're PIGS." And they are. Everything in the house becomes piggish. With high good humor and loads of funny details, this not so subtle story should please the entire family—pigs or not.

Play with Me WRITTEN AND ILLUSTRATED BY MARIE HALL ETS. New York: The Viking Press, 1955. Paperback: Penguin.

Suggested Listening Level: 2–4 years

A little girl is lonely and pleads with the animals to play, but not until she sits quietly do they come to join her on the bank of a pond. Black-and-white line drawings with soft yellows, browns, and grays capture the gentle spirit of the story. *In the Forest* is another book by Ets that has had wide audience appeal.

Reading WRITTEN AND ILLUSTRATED BY JAN ORMEROD. New York: Lothrop, Lee & Shepard Books, 1985.

Suggested Listening Level: 6 months–2 years

As father reads, a very appealing baby climbs over his legs and in and out of his lap until the baby, too, is "reading." The other books in this series, *Messy Baby, Sleeping,* and *Dad's Back* present the same father and baby, giving a charming glimpse into ordinary family activities.

The Real Mother Goose *Illustrated by Blanche Fisher Wright.* Chicago: Rand McNally & Co., 1916.

Suggested Listening Level: all ages

For many families the title says it all. The flat pastel drawings and variety of rhymes have made this a standard collection for more than seventy years.

The Relatives Came BY CYNTHIA RYLANT. *Illustrated by Stephen Gammell.* New York: Bradbury Press, 1985.

Suggested Listening Level: 4–7 years

When the relatives came to visit, there was "so much laughing and shining faces and hugging in the doorways. You'd have to go through at least four different hugs to get from the kitchen to the front door." An exuberant reunion is celebrated in text and illustration.

Richard Scarry's Best Word Book Ever (revised edition) WRITTEN AND ILLUSTRATED BY RICHARD SCARRY. New York: Western Publishing Co., 1980.

Suggested Listening Level: 1–4 years

Detailed humorous illustrations identify hundreds of household objects and commonplace activities to intrigue even the youngest.

Rosie's Walk WRITTEN AND ILLUSTRATED BY PAT HUTCHINS. New York: Macmillan, 1968. Paperback: Macmillan.

Suggested Listening Level: 2–4 years

The words tell us only that Rosie the Hen takes a walk, where she goes, and that she gets back for dinner. But it doesn't take toddlers long to notice the fox lurking in the background of each picture, trying with comical results to catch Rosie. The result is a wonderful introduction to cause and effect. Another outstanding picture book by Hutchins is *Good-night, Owl!*

Sam BY ANN H. SCOTT. *Illustrated by Symeon Shimin.* McGraw-Hill Book Co., 1967.

Suggested Listening Level: 3–5 years

Soft, textured drawings show lonely Sam, whose busy family finds him just too little to take part in what's going on. The quiet story is perfect for anyone who has had sad feelings put right by a bit of loving attention. Also try Scott's *On Mother's Lap.*

Sam Who Never Forgets WRITTEN AND ILLUSTRATED BY EVE RICE. New York: Greenwillow Books, 1977. Paperback: Penguin.

Suggested Listening Level: 2–4 years

Comfortable, rounded figures detail Sam the zookeeper's zealous care of all the animals, even the anxious elephant. This is one of several appealing picture books by an accomplished young artist.

Sam's Car BY BARBRO LINDGREN. *Illustrated by Eva Eriksson.* New York: William Morrow & Co., 1982.

Suggested Listening Level: 1–3 years

Sam hasn't learned to share, so he and Lisa quarrel tearfully over his toy car. Fortunately, wise Mother provides another so that the two can play together happily. Soft tones and pictures offer a story that toddlers and their mothers understand.

She's Not My Real Mother WRITTEN AND ILLUSTRATED BY JUDITH VIGNA. Niles, Ill.: Albert Whitman & Co., 1980.

Suggested Listening Level: 4–6 years

Two homes and a new wife for Daddy create a time of confusion for any youngster. All is resolved by patient understanding in this sensitive story of contemporary family life.

Sloppy Kisses BY ELIZABETH WINTHROP. *Illustrated by Anne Burgess.* New York: Macmillan Publishing Co., 1980. Paperback: Puffin.

Suggested Listening Level: 3–6 years

Emmy Lou's family loved to kiss and hug and Emmy Lou loved sloppy kisses, until her friend Rosemary told her such behavior was only for babies. So Mother and Father merely patted her shoulder when she went to school or to bed. Emmy Lou soon decided *that* was an awful way to begin or end a day. A book that invites hugs and kisses, this is one that the whole family will enjoy.

The Snowy Day WRITTEN AND ILLUSTRATED BY EZRA JACK KEATS. New York: The Viking Press, 1962. Paperback: Penguin.

Suggested Listening Level: 3–5 years

Bright collages define the cityscape as Peter explores the pleasure of a fresh snowfall. Other adventures of Peter, playing with his dog in *Whistle for Willie* or attempting to deal with a new baby in *Peter's Chair,* are equally appealing.

Some of the Days of Everett Anderson BY LUCILLE CLIFTON. *Illustrated by Evaline Ness.* New York: Holt, Rinehart & Winston, 1970. Paperback: Holt.

Suggested Listening Level: 4–7 years

In gentle, reassuring verse, Clifton helps us get inside the skin of a small African American child. Everett Anderson feels the joy of being a boy, is frightened by a siren, dreams of Mama staying home from work to play with him, and misses his daddy. Children will be glad to know that they can learn more about Everett Anderson in other fine books by Clifton.

Squawk to the Moon, Little Goose BY EDNA M. PRESTON. *Illustrated by Barbara Cooney.* New York: Viking-Penguin, 1984.

Suggested Listening Level: 3–5 years

"Good's good and bad's bad" learns Little Goose, as she finds that listening to her mother is a good way to avoid being eaten by a fox in this rollicking tale.

Stone Soup RETOLD AND ILLUSTRATED BY MARCIA BROWN. New York: Charles Scribner's Sons, 1947. Paperback: Macmillan.

Suggested Listening Level: 4–7 years

A very old tale with variations in many cultures, *Stone Soup* in Brown's retelling retains the flavor of France and the appeal of letting the listener in on the trick. In her long and distinguished career, Marcia Brown has created many other outstanding picture books for children.

A Story, a Story WRITTEN AND ILLUSTRATED BY GAIL HALEY. New York: Atheneum Publishers, 1970. Paperback: Macmillan.

Suggested Listening Level: 4–7 years

Bold colors and evocative language ensnare your listeners, just as the leopard was caught by the binding game, just as the hornets were lured into the calabash to help Ananse the Spider man pay the price asked by the Sky God for his stories. This version of an African tale will delight children and give them a very different spiderman hero than the one they see on television.

The Story About Ping WRITTEN AND ILLUSTRATED BY MARJORIE FLACK. New York: The Viking Press, 1933.

Suggested Listening Level: 3–5 years

Although Ping lives with his mother and father and sisters and brothers and aunts and uncles and forty-two cousins on a wise-eyed boat on the Yangtze River, this little duck will be recognized by anyone who has wanted to stay up all night—just to see what happens. *Ask Mr. Bear,* in which Danny tries to find the perfect birthday present for his mother, is another favorite Marjorie Flack story for younger children.

The Story of Babar WRITTEN AND ILLUSTRATED BY JEAN DE BRUNHOFF. New York: Random House, 1937.

Suggested Listening Level: 4–6 years

The life of Babar the elephant is chronicled from birth through his crowning as King. Simple language and a mix of ordinary family life with the fantasy of a gentle talking elephant have made this Gallic tale popular for more than fifty years.

The Story of Ferdinand BY MUNRO LEAF. *Illustrated by Robert Lawson.* New York: The Viking Press, 1936. Paperback: Penguin.

Suggested Listening Level: 3–6 years

For more than fifty years this tale of a bull who was brave enough to sit and smell the flowers has been a favorite. Lawson's humorous details of pastures and Madrid crowds and pompous bullfighters are a counterpoint to the touching story of peaceful Ferdinand.

Strega Nona WRITTEN AND ILLUSTRATED BY TOMIE dePAOLA. Englewood Cliffs, N.J.: Prentice-Hall, 1975. Paperback: Prentice-Hall.

Suggested Listening Level: 4–7 years

Big Anthony couldn't resist trying out Strega Nona's magic pasta pot, but not knowing the secret of how to stop it, he nearly buried the town in pasta. Stylized figures illuminate this variant of an old folktale that will tickle your listeners whether they like pasta or not.

The Tale of Peter Rabbit WRITTEN AND ILLUSTRATED BY BEATRIX POTTER. New York: Frederick Warne & Co., 1902. Paperback. Many editions.

Suggested Listening Level: 4–6 years

Peter is a reckless explorer who nearly comes to a bad end when he ventures into Mr. McGregor's garden, but generations have taken comfort, with him, in a dose of camomile tea and a safe homecoming. This nearly perfect book is just the right size for small hands to hold.

Tales of Oliver Pig. BY JEAN VAN LEEUWEN. *Illustrated by Arnold Lobel.* New York: The Dial Press, 1979. Paperback: Dial.

Suggested Listening Level: 4–6 years

Designed as a book for those just beginning to read for themselves, these and other tales of Oliver Pig and baby sister Amanda present everyday situations with deft touches of humor and a loving tone. They make shared reading between adult and child or older and younger siblings both pleasant and easy.

The Tall Book of Nursery Tales ILLUSTRATED BY FEODOR ROJANKOVSKY. New York: Harper & Row, Publishers, 1944.

Suggested Listening Level: 3–6 years

Feodor Rojankovsky has just the right style to illustrate the twenty-four favorite nursery tales in this timeless collection. His people are homely countryfolk, his furniture hand-hewn, and the pictures often seem to dance on the page. This ideal collection for preschoolers at home or school has the added fun of a table of contents that consists of pictures, not titles, so that children can choose the next story "all by themselves."

Tell Me a Mitzi BY LORE SEGAL. *Illustrated by Harriet Pincus.* New York: Farrar, Straus & Giroux, 1970. Paperback: Scholastic.

Suggested Listening Level: 4–6 years

Mitzi had a mother and a father and a baby brother named Jacob and she liked "Mitzi" stories because they were about the things that happened or might have happened to Mitzi and her mother or her father or her baby brother Jacob. Told at a breathless pace, these read aloud much like the stories a four- or five-year-old might tell.

Ten, Nine, Eight WRITTEN AND ILLUSTRATED BY MOLLY BANG. New York: Greenwillow Books, 1983. Paperback: Penguin.

Suggested Listening Level: 1–3 years

Counting down for the night from "ten small toes all washed and warm" through hugs and kisses, this is a lovely bedtime book for the youngest. Illustrations show a loving black daddy and his daughter.

This Is the Bear BY SARAH HAYES *Illustrated by Helen Craig.* Philadelphia: J. B. Lippincott Co., 1986. Paperback: Harper.

Suggested Listening Level: 3–5 years

Here's what happened to a favorite bear who, tossed in a sack, went to the dump, all grumpy and cross, but came back home denying he'd been lost. The illustrator's use of white space gives an airy, lighthearted feeling to this cumulative tale in verse.

Through Grandpa's Eyes BY PATRICIA MACLACHLAN. *Illustrated by Deborah Ray.* New York: Harper & Row, Publishers, 1980.

Suggested Listening Level: 4–7 years

Though Grandpa is blind, he teaches John how to see in a different way. Patient and gentle, this sensitive story will allay some of the fears blindness stirs in children, but more than that, it celebrates the bond between young and old.

Thy Friend, Obadiah WRITTEN AND ILLUSTRATED BY BRINTON TURKLE. New York: The Viking Press, 1969. Paperback: Penguin.

Suggested Listening Level: 3–5 years

Old Nantucket is the setting for a small Quaker boy's trials and tribulations with a seagull who follows him everywhere, prompting teasing from big brothers and sisters. When the gull needs help, however, Obadiah discovers he does care for the pesky bird.

The Tub People BY PAM CONRAD. *Illustrated by Richard Egielski.* New York: Harper & Row, Publishers, 1989.

Suggested Listening Level: 3–7 years

At bathtime, little wooden Tub People—father, mother, grandmother, policeman, doctor, child, and dog—ride the soap and bob along in water races. One sad evening, however, the child of the Tub People disappears down the drain. The others search and call in vain for the lost child, until much later the drain clogs and big people come to fix it. Not only is the child found, but the reunited group is moved to the safety of a bed, where they devise new games. This simple tale proves to be remarkably moving, perhaps because it touches on the common childhood fear of separation. For most children, it will not be too frightening, since the adventure befalls dolls, not people. At certain stages, though, it might be scary. Egielski's vibrant illustrations beautifully complement Conrad's understated text.

Umbrella WRITTEN AND ILLUSTRATED BY TARO YASHIMA. New York: The Viking Press, 1958. Paperback: Penguin.

Suggested Listening Level: 3–5 years

Soft mixed-media illustrations enhance small Momo's excitement with a special birthday gift, an umbrella of her own. Japanese words and characters are used to highlight some of the pages.

The Very Hungry Caterpillar WRITTEN AND ILLUSTRATED BY ERIC CARLE. New York: World Publishing Co., 1969, 1981.

Suggested Listening Level: 2–5 years

A simple story about the metamorphosis of a caterpillar into a butterfly is a vehicle for Carle's vivid artwork. Shapes and colors intrigue four- and five-year-olds while younger children are captivated by the ingenious design of the book. The book, complete with holes, is now available in a miniature version as well.

We're Going on a Bear Hunt BY MICHAEL ROSEN. *Illustrated by Helen Oxenbury*. New York: Macmillan Publishing Co., 1989.

Suggested Listening Level: 4–7 years

"Going on a Bear Hunt," that favorite activity at library storytimes, is transformed here into a captivating picture-book experience. The repeated refrain and accompanying noises (like swishy, swashy, and splash, splosh) invite rousing audience participation, while Oxenbury's artistic genius has never been so clear as in the extra-large illustrations of the adventurous family and the *enormous* bear.

What Will the Weather Be Like Today? BY PAUL ROGERS. *Illustrated by Kazuko*. New York: Greenwillow Books, 1990.

Suggested Listening Level: 2–5 years

A book about weather may sound dull, but this one will quickly enthrall young children and those who read to them. A lilting rhyme lists the possibilities—windy, warm, snow, storm—while paper collage illustrations contain much for young eyes to spy.

What's Under My Bed? WRITTEN AND ILLUSTRATED BY JAMES STEVENSON. New York: Greenwillow Books, 1983. Paperback: Penguin.

Suggested Listening Level: 4–6 years

Mary Ann and Louie are convinced something is under the bed, but when Grandpa tells about *his* childhood fears, the children have prosaic, commonsense explanations. Children will giggle over pictures of Grandpa as a little boy, still sporting his moustache.

Where the Wild Things Are WRITTEN AND ILLUSTRATED BY MAU-
RICE SENDAK. New York: Harper & Row, Publishers, 1963. Paperback: Harper.

Suggested Listening Levels: 4–6 years

Angry, mischief-making Max in his wolf suit found the Wild
Things, but in the end he wanted to be where someone loved him
best of all. Wild Things and their parents should share this adventure where Max is always in charge and where dinner is waiting
when the wild impulses have been tamed. Be sure to try the four
wonderful stories in Sendak's small Nutshell Library also. Although it is hard to choose just one favorite, we are partial to
Pierre . . . because we care.

Where's Spot? WRITTEN AND ILLUSTRATED BY ERIC HILL. New
York: The Putnam Publishing Group, 1980.

Suggested Listening Level: 1–3 years

Mother Dog searches for Spot in the piano and the clock and the
cupboard. She finds many unlikely animals (a bear and a snake, for
instance) before she finds her own puppy. Doors and lids open so
that small investigators can search with Spot's mother. The bold
shapes and uncluttered pages invite even the youngest to partici-
pate in this best seller for babies.

Whose Mouse Are You? BY ROBERT KRAUS. *Illustrated by José
Aruego.* New York: Macmillan Publishing Co., 1970. Paperback:
Macmillan.

Suggested Listening Level: 3–5 years

One of the simplest of picture books, *Whose Mouse Are You?* is a
rhyming tale of a lonely mouse who rescues mother, father, and
sister from danger and reunites them as a loving family. Deeply
satisfying, the story will be asked for again and again.

The Wolf's Chicken Stew WRITTEN AND ILLUSTRATED BY KEIKO KASZA. New York: G. P. Putnam's Sons, 1987.

Suggested Listening Level: 3–5 years

Although this wolf is always thinking about food, the idea of chicken stew is especially appealing to him. Instead of trapping the chicken that crosses his path, however, he decides to fatten her up with one hundred scrumptious pancakes, doughnuts, and a cake. Her many children are delighted with the wolf's gifts and give "Uncle Wolf" hundreds of kisses. Just the right length for a bedtime story, this is worth hundreds of goodnight hugs.

BOOKLIST FOR SCHOOL-AGE LISTENERS

Abel's Island WRITTEN AND ILLUSTRATED BY WILLIAM STEIG. New York: Farrar, Straus & Giroux, 1976. Paperback: Farrar, Straus & Giroux.

Suggested Listening Level: Grades 4–8

Abel's Island recounts the harrowing adventures of a mouse who, in the midst of a picnic, is swept away from his beloved bride by a sudden storm. He ends up on an uninhabited island in the middle of a river. The dangers Abel encounters in the months that follow —near-drowning, owls, starvation, despair—are sometimes scary, sometimes comical, but always interesting. Steig eloquently chronicles the stages of Abel's transformation from a dandified and somewhat shallow city fellow to a self-sufficient individual who has confronted the fundamental philosophic questions as well as the practical issues of life.

The author is a cartoonist for *The New Yorker* magazine and the book's illustrations are outstanding, but clearly Steig has been influenced by *The New Yorker*'s distinguished prose stylists as well, for all his children's books are polished and original in expression with cadences tailor-made for reading aloud.

As one might guess from the loving mouse-husband's full name, Abelard, there are many allusions in the book that will amuse well-read adults and older children. Yet the story is equally satisfying to those who experience it simply as a Crusoe tale of intrepid victory against great odds. Thus it is a good choice for a family with a wide range of ages.

The book's twenty chapters average five minutes reading time, so the total book can be read aloud in just under two hours. Steig's shorter animal fantasies are good choices for younger children, five to eight years old. *The Amazing Bone, Sylvester and the Magic Pebble,* and *Caleb and Kate* are our favorites.

About Wise Men and Simpletons: Twelve Tales from Grimm TRANSLATED BY ELIZABETH SHUB. *Illustrated by Nonny Hogrogian.* New York: Macmillan Publishing Co., 1971, 1986.

Suggested Listening Level: Grades K–6

This attractive volume contains some of the best known of the folktales collected by the Grimm brothers: "The Elves and the Shoemaker," "Briar Rose" (a Sleeping Beauty tale), "Hansel and Gretel," and "The Bremen Town Musicians." Here, too, are a few less familiar but deeply appealing stories, especially in the section "About Simpletons." The language throughout is spare, the rhythm flowing, and, as the introduction points out, "the storyteller's voice is omnipresent."

These are translations without the embellishments that other adaptations offer, short and to the point of the story. They provide easy reading for bedtime or for the last ten minutes before the bus comes. Primary grades will enjoy every minute, and older listeners usually don't mind being reminded of their old favorites.

(Readers should know that the "Rapunzel" in this volume is not the familiar toned-down version. Here the witch finds out about the prince's visits to the tower when Rapunzel wonders out loud why her clothes are getting tight and the witch sees that she is pregnant.)

Across Five Aprils BY IRENE HUNT. Chicago: Follett Publishing Co., 1964. Paperback: Ace Books.

Suggested Listening Level: Grades 5–8

In April 1861, all the talk in rural southern Illinois is of imminent war—talk that makes Ellen Creighton fearful that her grown sons will be lost as were her three little boys in an epidemic years before. But to her youngest child, nine-year-old Jethro, war means loud brass music and men on shining horses—and he's impatient with President Lincoln's wavering. When war comes, it brings to the farm pain Jethro never imagined. By the next April, one brother is among the Union dead at Pittsburg Landing. Another brother, Jethro's favorite, follows his conscience and joins the Confederate Army. This provokes a gang of rowdies to contaminate the Creighton well and burn the barn. Jethro must take on a man's work, his childhood snatched away long before the armistice is signed. The book ends on a comforting note as Jethro's dream of an education promises to come true, but it is a sober rejoicing indeed.

Through the skillful use of authentic detail, Irene Hunt depicts the scene and characters so vividly that *Across Five Aprils,* set far from any battlefield, provides a clearer sense of the meaning and impact of the Civil War than any other book for children. Each of the twelve chapters supplies ample material for one reading session.

The Adventures of Tom Sawyer BY MARK TWAIN (PSEUD. OF SAMUEL LANGHORNE CLEMENS). 1876. Many editions.

Suggested Listening Level: Grades 4–8

The Adventures of Tom Sawyer still has great vitality and appeal to children, though weighted down a bit with nostalgia and satire of bygone institutions. Twain's account of boyhood in an earlier era has lavish amounts of two surefire ingredients: humor and suspense. Whether Tom is playing with a pinch-bug in church, dosing Aunt Polly's cat with painkiller, or collecting valuables from his friends for the privilege of whitewashing the fence, his shenanigans amuse listeners of all ages. The suspense begins to build when Tom and Huck witness a murder and culminates when Tom and Becky Thatcher discover that they are lost in the great cave with Injun Joe, the murderer.

Some sections are digressions from the exciting plot and you may want to do some slight editing—shortening the examples of "youthful eloquence" (i.e., school recitations) in chapter twenty-one, for instance. The stereotyping of Injun Joe should be pointed out to children as a common, but unfortunate, attitude in nineteenth-century America. The thirty-five chapters vary in length; we recommend taking a cue from your audience's interest when deciding how many chapters to include in a particular reading session.

The Alfred Summer BY JAN SLEPIAN. New York: Macmillan Publishing Co., 1980. Paperback: Scholastic.

Suggested Listening Level: Grades 5–8

Told by Lester, whose cerebral palsy makes him look "like a puppet whose manager has been goosed by lightning," this is a remarkable story of determination and the ability of the human spirit to rise above limiting circumstances. Tied to his mother by invisible strings, Lester is friendless and ignored, an object of pity or scorn, considered unable to do anything on his own. Then he meets Alfred, a skinny kid with black curls, dark eyes, and "nothing going on inside or outside." But Alfred accepts Lester as he is, makes no demands, and when Lester helps rescue Alfred at the beach, a friendship is begun.

These two are joined by lumpy, red-faced Myron, who is also beleaguered by mother, sisters, assorted relatives, and neighbors. Myron has a secret dream that he finally shares with Lester and Alfred: He is building a boat in the basement of his Brooklyn apartment house. Claire, a fast talker who is also a sympathetic listener, completes the group, and the four begin building not only a boat but relationships that provide a sense of independence and a realization that each one has something special to contribute.

The hope and tough-mindedness of these characters will allow young listeners to understand the feelings locked in an uncooperative body. While the story can be read in about two and a half hours, the characters remain unforgettable.

Alice's Adventures in Wonderland BY LEWIS CARROLL (PSEUD. OF CHARLES L. DODGSON). *Illustrations by John Tenniel.* 1865. Many editions.

Suggested Listening Level: Grades 1–5

Lewis Carroll's classic is a book that we recommend with reservations. Without question it was a historical milestone in the development of children's books. And many adults have reported that they were deeply and happily affected by it as children. Yet we know more than a few children who intensely dislike the book— *and* its celebrated Tenniel illustrations.

We can only guess at the reasons for such different responses, but it seems likely that some children are upset by Alice's confusion and anxiety through much of the story. Her adventures in Wonderland are not a pleasant experience for her, by and large, even though her awakening at the end shows that the threats were not real. Children who like the book seem to respond to its humor and to the wonder of a world in which one can shrink as well as grow, of babies that turn into pigs, and of just plain nonsense. They notice that Alice is really superior to all those zany adult figures and relish her eventual rebellion against their endless rules.

Even children who enjoy the book do not enjoy every episode equally, though. The size-changing bits fascinate children of five and six, while appreciation of the parody of Victorian educational practices requires a more mature listener. And then the humor of some episodes loses its point because it depends on a knowledge of English history or of songs and events of Carroll's own day.

We recommend, then, that you read aloud the early chapters, "Down the Rabbit Hole" and "The Pool of Tears," and then continue only if the reception has been enthusiastic. If you do read on, continue to gauge your listeners' interest and omit sections that seem tedious. Even if you read only the opening chapters, you will have introduced children to a work of literature that has permeated our culture, and stretched their imaginations. For those children who become Carroll devotees, *Through the Looking Glass* offers more adventures of Alice. Each book consists of twelve chapters.

All-of-a-Kind Family BY SYDNEY TAYLOR. *Illustrations by Helen John.* Paperback: Dell, 1966.

Suggested Listening Level: Grades K–3

In this book, Sydney Taylor chronicles the everyday life of a Jewish family on Manhattan's Lower East Side in the early twentieth century. The episodes have the homey warmth and gentle humor that primary-grade children love in family stories. Each of the five sisters, ranging from four to twelve, has a different personality; most children find the dramatic, headstrong Henny especially interesting.

The episodes revolve around situations all children experience —losing a library book, trying to spend one's allowance wisely at the candy store, feeling left out when one's siblings are sick. At the same time, the author faithfully re-creates the distinctively Jewish ambience of her childhood. Holiday customs, foods, and the colorful world of pushcarts and little shops are described clearly and provide a good introduction to immigrant life for both Jewish and non-Jewish children.

The thirteen chapters vary in length, but each is a self-contained episode and should be read in one session. This book has several sequels.

All Times, All Peoples: A World History of Slavery BY MILTON MELTZER. *Illustrated by Leonard Everett Fisher.* New York: Harper & Row, Publishers, 1980.

Suggested Listening Level: Grades 4–8.

"White, black, brown, yellow, red—no matter what your color, it's likely that someone in your family, way back, was once a slave." From this first sentence, Milton Meltzer pulls the young listener into his succinct history of the ten-thousand-year-old institution of slavery. In carefully shaped, eloquent prose he informs us that slavery was at first a step forward for humankind, allowing war captives who would formerly have been slaughtered a chance to live. Tracing slavery's form in different cultures, Meltzer demonstrates that slaves did all kinds of work, from the most intellectual to the most menial. He shows that until the pernicious doctrines of racial superiority were developed about three hundred years ago, slavery was a manifestation not of racism but of power, pure and simple. By the end of the book, we know that slavery still exists today and have been given ideas of what we can do to help eradicate it. Chapters on escapes from slavery and on slave revolts contain powerful vignettes of memorable figures and events, and by providing a fine bibliography of books for children and adolescents, the author makes it possible for listeners to find out more about Toussaint, Harriet Tubman, the biblical Joseph, and other real and fictional slaves. Nonfiction tends to be overlooked when people are giving out prizes. This book is a good introduction to one of the most reliable, prolific, and skilled writers of nonfiction for children.

The book itself is handsomely produced, with powerful black-and-white illustrations by a distinguished artist lending their own strength and drama to the compelling words. Social studies teachers will find it well worth a few minutes of class time over several days. Total reading time is under ninety minutes.

American Tall Tales BY ADRIEN STOUTENBURG. *Illustrated by Richard M. Powers.* New York: The Viking Press, 1966. Paperback: Penguin.

Suggested Listening Level: Grades 4–7

Here are the stories of eight brave men, strong and true: Paul Bunyan, Pecos Bill, Stormalong (Alfred Bulltop Stormalong, that is), Davy Crockett, Johnny Appleseed, John Henry, and Mike Fink. They lived in the days when America was new and "trees were there, stretching in tall, wind-shining rows"; when Texas had "so much sky that it seemed as if there couldn't be any sky left over for the rest of the United States." And each one of these heroes was mighty big. Davy Crockett was never *quite* as tall as the Great Smoky Mountains, but nearly so. Stormalong, they say, was nearly two fathoms high by the time he was ten. Since a fathom is about six feet, "Stormy was pretty tall." And Mike Fink spoke for all of them when he said, "I'm second cousin to a hurricane, first cousin to a seven-day blizzard and brother to an earthquake!"

The author has handled the folklore material with the ease of a scholar and the ear of a storyteller. The language reflects a time when gigantic tasks challenged the ingenuity and taxed the stamina of men and women. These exaggerations are most appreciated by listeners of at least fourth-grade level. Too many of these tales read in succession could wear thin, however, so we recommend interspersing them with other stories.

Anastasia Again! BY LOIS LOWRY. *Illustrated by Diane De Groat.* Boston: Houghton Mifflin Co., 1981. Paperback: Dell.

Suggested Listening Level: Grades 5–8

Anastasia is afraid that when her family moves from Cambridge, Massachusetts, to the suburbs (ugh!) her mother will take to wearing big pink curlers and worrying about wax buildup. But when the family sees their new house, they fall in love with it because it has everything: a study with bookshelves floor to ceiling for her English-professor father; a solarium for her painter mother; plenty of closets for two-year-old Sam (he likes standing in them); and for Anastasia—a tower! Even with the move finished, however, Anastasia must begin the difficult task of finding new friends.

Another ordinary move-into-the-new-neighborhood-find-a-friend story? Wrong. There is absolutely nothing ordinary about Anastasia Krupnik—from father to friends. And rarely will you find a funnier party than the one Anastasia arranges with the local senior citizens' "Drop-in Center" for her next-door neighbor, Mrs. Stein. For families who also read *The New York Review of Books,* for classrooms who don't mind a bit of irreverent hilarity, *Anastasia Again!* will provide approximately three and a half hours of sidesplitting delight. To get through the party scene, though, the reader *must* prepare—otherwise your audience will never be able to hear the story through your own laughter. *Anastasia Krupnik* is an earlier book about the Krupnik family. It is appealing but not quite as funny as *Anastasia Again!*

The author sets a completely different mood in her Newbery

winner *Number The Stars*. Here the terror of war and the courage
of the Danish resistance are told through the perspective of ten-
year-old Annemarie Johansen as she helps to save her friend Ellen
Rosen.

. . . and Now Miguel BY JOSEPH KRUMGOLD. *Illustrated by Jean
Charlot.* New York: Thomas Y. Crowell, 1953. Paperback: Apollo
Editions, Harper Junior.

Suggested Listening Level: Grades 4–6

This coming-of-age story focuses on Miguel Chavez, an often
overlooked child in the middle of a large family of sheep ranchers.
Twelve-year-old Miguel wants passionately to go to the Sangre de
Cristo mountains in the summer with the men and the flocks but
is told he's too young. He decides to work so hard and well that his
father will change his mind. The book is narrated from Miguel's
point of view, and his desperate longing is convincingly rendered,
as is the close relationship between Miguel and his adored older
brother. Krumgold succeeds in creating a touching portrait that
all children will understand.

The story depicts in detail the culture of New Mexican sheep
ranchers, a fascinating way of life that goes back centuries to
Spain. Each of the fourteen chapters is an interesting episode in
Miguel's ultimately successful campaign, but the narration is leisurely and contemplative. This is not a book for wigglers or easily
distractible children. The distinguished illustrations by a noted
muralist and painter add authenticity to the story.

And Then What Happened, Paul Revere? BY JEAN FRITZ. *Illustrated by Margot Tomes.* New York: Coward, McCann & Geoghegan, 1973. Paperback: Coward, McCann & Geoghegan.

Suggested Listening Level: Grades 2–4

Paul Revere was a man of many talents. When he took over his
father's silversmithing business, he made everything from beads
to candlesticks. He even made a silver collar for a pet squirrel. But

more than that, he rang church bells, went off to fight in the French and Indian War, and became a leader in the secret Sons of Liberty.

This is a spirited biography, full of the life and times of an active man and his exciting Boston-town. The style is lively and the questions posed by the author—"What could be done?" "So what happened?" "And *then* what happened?"—serve to point up the action. This could be read in one long session (probably about forty minutes) for primary grades but would break easily about midway through as Paul Revere is declared the Number One express rider between Boston and Philadelphia (p. 23). The book should be made available to children after it is read aloud so that they can enjoy the details of Margot Tomes's vigorous illustrations. Many of the author's other witty biographies are also good for reading aloud.

Homesick: My Own Story is a fictionalized autobiography of Jean Fritz's first twelve years, spent in China, as the daughter of missionary parents. The book recounts her longing for the far-off Pennsylvania she has never seen but thinks of as home. Her life in Hanchow was one of contrasts: of political turmoil and family events; riots and going to school; gunboats on the river and Christmas celebrations—and the birth and inexplicable death of a longed-for baby sister. *Homesick . . .* is longer than the historical biographies; the seven chapters can be read in four or five sessions. The story will intrigue listeners of all ages, and if you know a family living outside the United States, this will be a special gift from home.

The Animal Family BY RANDALL JARRELL. *Illustrated by Maurice Sendak.* New York: Pantheon Books, 1965, 1985.

Suggested Listening Level: Grades 3–8

The hunter lived in a cabin that he had made, surrounded by the skins of animals that he had caught for cap and coat and rug. But in the spring when "the beach was all foam-white and sea-blue with flowers" and in the winter "when a great green meteor went

slowly across the sky," there was no one to tell what he had seen.
Then one summer evening the hunter heard the song of the
mermaid and he waited and watched and courted her, patient as
the animals he knew so well. They taught each other words and
spent time in the meadow, and in the fall she went into the house.

A bear cub, a lynx, and finally a baby boy join the hunter and
the mermaid in their lyrical life. The images are so vivid that both
reader and listener will want to savor every word. Maurice
Sendak's delicate line drawings depict only the physical setting of
this special place, leaving one with the impression that the characters are just off the edge of the page. Don't make this a first
choice and don't rush the experience. "Plot" and "action" are
terms that don't apply, but "poetry," "music," "imagination" do.
Find a place where the forest runs down to the ocean, for "say
what you like, but such things do happen—not often, but they do
happen."

Annie and the Old One BY MISKA MILES. *Illustrated by Peter
Parnall.* Boston: Little, Brown & Co., 1971.

Suggested Listening Level: Grades 2–5

Annie, a Navajo child, could not accept her beloved grandmother's announcement: "My children, when the new rug is taken
from the loom, I will go to Mother Earth." So each night after the
family was asleep, Annie would go out and unravel the weaving
that had been done that day. If the rug was never finished, Annie
reasoned, her grandmother would not die. The Old One at last
realized what Annie was doing and explained to her that death
was a part of life, not to be feared but accepted.

In this brief picture book, Parnall's simple black-and-white lines
outline a place and a time and a small family, Everyfamily, that
are warmed by the gold and brown tones of Earth, "Earth, from
which good things come for the living creatures on it. Earth, to
which all creatures finally go." The prose is also simple, but rich in
detail and loving in tone, moving at a majestic pace. It provides
both reader and listener with a quiet, reflective moment to

rejoice in life, to consider death, and, like Annie, to be ". . . breathless with the wonder of it."

April Morning BY HOWARD FAST. New York: Crown Publishers, 1961. Paperback: Bantam.

Suggested Listening Level: Grades 6–8

The frontispiece in one edition of this book, seeking to catch the reader's attention, trumpets *"April Morning:* a novel about one of the most glorious days in American history," but the true achievement of Howard Fast's book is to reveal the total absence of glory at Lexington and Concord on April 19, 1776. This first-person account of that day and the preceding one does much more than depict a historical event. It explores the nature of courage, of grief, and of the fear of death, as experienced by a fifteen-year-old boy who faced the British on Lexington green, saw his father shot, fled in panic, and then sniped at the Redcoats as they marched back to Boston. Adam's physical and emotional states are tellingly captured, making this an honest and eloquent addition to American coming-of-age fiction.

Readers must be prepared to encounter unpleasant descriptions of what wounds actually look like, but none are gratuitous and to omit them from realistic battle accounts would be dishonest. Unlike some historical novelists writing for the young, Fast does not suggest an easy distribution of right and wrong. His faithfulness to life's complexities anticipates the carefully documented fiction of the Collier brothers (especially *My Brother Sam Is Dead*), but *April Morning* is better suited to reading aloud.

The novel is divided into eight sections; if you can devote a half hour or so at a stretch to reading, we recommend completing one section at a sitting.

Auks, Rocks and the Odd Dinosaur: Inside Stories from the Smithsonian's Museum of Natural History BY PEGGY THOMSON. New York: T. Y. Crowell, 1986.

Suggested Listening Level: Grades 3–7

The Smithsonian often has been called the nation's attic because only a fraction of its holdings are on display. Here in twenty short chapters, one is introduced to some of those holdings and the collectors, researchers, and other specialists who have gathered such a splendid array. Items like the great auk, the fossilized bones of the ferocious Antrodemus, and the Komodo Dragon, are displayed in short episodes that present a fascinating look at the work of the Natural Science division of the museum. Take the Riftia pachyptila, for instance. This is a "whopping, pasty-looking worm, as big around as a garden hose, floating upright in a bottle. . . . The worm is even more peculiar than it looks. It has no mouth and no gut—no way, or so it seems, to take in food or digest it." The chapter describes how it was collected, why the scientists want to know more about it, and how the research is carried out.

Individually the chapters can be read in about fifteen minutes. They can be used on their own or with other, longer, books so that listeners might gain additional insight. Try this with *From the Mixed-Up Files of Mrs. Basil E. Frankweiler* to provide another view of museum life, or the chapter on the Komodo Dragon before or after Margaret Hodges' *Saint George and the Dragon*. Any way you read this, your audience will be intrigued.

Babe, the Gallant Pig. BY DICK KING-SMITH. *Illustrated by Mary Rayner.* New York: Crown Publishers, 1983.

Suggested Listening Level: Grades 3–6

Ho-hum, you say, just another pig story? Not at all, for Babe is a *most* unusual pig. Babe is a sheep-pig. He didn't start out as a sheep-pig, of course, but when he found himself adopted by Fly, Farmer Hogget's sheepdog, it just seemed a natural thing to do. And Fly didn't mind at all that, after training, Babe could move the sheep more efficiently than Fly had ever done. It was all because Babe spoke politely to the sheep. They were tired of being called stupid and harassed and chased up hill and down dale. So eventually Farmer Hogget took Babe to the sheepdog trials, where that pig, a "proper little gennulman" to the sheep, won the day.

All the familiar ingredients are here: the verbose farmer's wife, laconic farmer, a cast of sheep with the good, the bad, and the silly represented, a major event with lots of media coverage, and the hero, will-he-or-won't-he-win-the-day. Somehow, King-Smith has raised this above the trite, however, into a truly delightful reading event. *Magnus Powermouse* and *Pigs Might Fly* are also entertaining and funny books by King-Smith, but you can't beat Babe in the field, or the classroom. The twelve chapters read in four twenty-minute sessions.

Badger on the Barge and Other Stories BY JANNI HOWKER. New York: Greenwillow Books, 1985.

Suggested Listening Level: Grades 5–8+

This collection of five short stories, each about a momentous encounter between a young person and an elderly one, marked the debut of a brilliant young English writer. The stories seem as dense and fully realized as novels, and because each can be read in an hour, they would be an excellent choice for reading aloud in a middle school, where schedules make it difficult to fit in read-aloud sessions regularly. In a home, parents and grandparents as well as older children will find the stories both gripping and thought-provoking. We have recommended them for intergenerational programs; they are ideal for adolescents to read to the elderly, and vice versa, turn and turn about.

"Reicker" would be a good choice for a start. In it, two bored boys taunt "Nazi Reicker," a prisoner of war who stayed on in England as a farm laborer. Hours later, they take part in a manhunt on the dark mountainside, a manhunt of which Reicker proves the hero. The action is full of suspense, but Sean's wrestling with the meaning of war and the nature of prejudice is so urgently described that it will hold listeners' interest also. In the title story, a lonely girl, whose parents are too busy mourning the death of her favored older brother to notice her, finds an unlikely friend in a sharp and cranky old lady who keeps a badger on a barge in the river. Another story, "The Egg-Man," shows a sensitive girl that an old recluse who both fascinates and frightens her is a real person with a sad past.

Most of the book's English colloquial expressions, such as "any road up" for our "anyway," are clear from their context. Don't worry about them; it would be a shame to miss this remarkable collection because of a few unfamiliar terms.

A Bear Called Paddington BY MICHAEL BOND. *Illustrated by Peggy Fortnum.* Boston: Houghton Mifflin Co., 1960. Paperback: Dell.

Suggested Listening Level: Grades K–4

Mr. and Mrs. Brown found the bear in Paddington Station "a very unusual kind of bear. It was brown in colour, a rather dirty brown, and it was wearing a most odd-looking hat, with a wide brim." The bear claimed that he was a stowaway from Darkest Peru, where he had been taught to speak English by Aunt Lucy before she went to the home for retired bears. Because he'd been discovered in the Station, the Browns called their bear Paddington. Things are never quite the same again in their London household, for Paddington in his shy, diffident way causes one disaster after another. Although *his* feelings are always soothed by some extra marmalade—Peruvian bears love marmalade—it is not as easy to calm the ruffled feelings of cooks or clerks or cabbies.

Paddington has become something of a celebrity, as his stuffed likeness appears in department stores and toy shops around the country. Anyone who has a replica of this jam-loving bear, however, should have the opportunity to meet the *real* Paddington in this first of the series. Two and a half hours reading time should suffice, but those who have strong feelings about bears may demand repeats.

Beat the Story-Drum, Pum-Pum RETOLD AND ILLUSTRATED BY ASHLEY BRYAN. New York: Atheneum Publishers, 1980.

Suggested Listening Level: Grades 2–8.

If you have heard Ashley Bryan read these African tales in person or on record, you may feel you can never match his theatrical and resonant style. Don't be discouraged. He has shaped these stories so that they make the most of any spoken voice. Just loosen up and have fun with them. The opening of "How Animals Got Their Tails," a lighthearted creation story, shows how Bryan succeeds in capturing the sense of an oral storyteller:

"If you're talking about the beginning of things, you've got to go back, way, way back, back to the time when the animals had no tails. That's right! In the beginning Raluvhimba, god of the Bavenda, created the animals without tails. Uh-huh! He never even gave tails a thought, uh-uh! not in the beginning."

In "Hen and Frog," which is a close cousin to "The Little Red Hen" but with more serious results for the lazy frog, children will appreciate your imitating the respective voices of the clucking hen and croaking frog. They'll like, too, the scat-talk of the scatter-brained monkey in "Why Bush Cow and Elephant Are Bad Friends." "Why Frog and Snake Never Play Together" is a parable of sorts that can generate thoughtful discussion. Frogchild and Snakeson have a wonderful time playing together one day until their mothers tell them that snakes *eat* frogs. That ends their friendship, but they both remember that glorious day and wonder: "What if we had just kept on playing together, and no one had ever said anything?"

Ashley Bryan is professor of fine arts at Dartmouth College, and his woodcuts greatly enrich this volume. He has written that his goal in retelling these and other African stories from scholarly sources was to function as "a tender bridge" connecting us across "distances of time and space." Most children would not discover the pleasures of this volume on their own, however, so you, too, are needed to complete the bridge of story.

Ben and Me WRITTEN AND ILLUSTRATED BY ROBERT LAWSON. Boston: Little, Brown & Co., 1939. Paperback: Dell.

Suggested Listening Level: Grades 2–4

Amos, the oldest in a large family of poor churchmice, grows tired of nibbling at tough sermons and ventures out into the world, where he finds a warm refuge in the lining of Ben Franklin's fur cap. From this vantage point he finds he can advise the famous but rather inept Dr. Franklin on everything from inventions to statecraft to mud puddles that lie in the path. According to Amos, his ideas lead to the invention of the Franklin stove, although he lets Ben take the credit in return for supplying the comforts of life to Amos and his needy family. Amos's life from then on is never dull. He is nearly electrocuted as an unwilling subject in Ben's electricity experiments. Accompanying Ben to France, Amos organizes the daring rescue of a lovely French Mouse aristocrat.

Funny and irreverent, *Ben and Me* has long been a popular choice for reading aloud. Though it presupposes some knowledge of Benjamin Franklin's life, it is geared to the primary grades. We recommend in this case sharing Lawson's illustrations with the children as you go along; they add a great deal and are bold enough to be seen by a group. The adventures of Amos and Ben are recounted in fifteen chapters, each requiring about six to eight minutes of reading time.

The Best Christmas Pageant Ever BY BARBARA ROBINSON. *Illustrated by Judith Gwyn Brown.* New York: Harper & Row, Publishers, 1972. Paperback: Avon, Tyndale.

Suggested Listening Level: Grades 2–5

Everyone figured the mean Herdman kids were "headed straight for hell by way of the state penitentiary." They were always doing things like setting Fred Shoemaker's toolhouse on fire with a stolen chemistry set and then stealing all the doughnuts that were sent over for the firemen. They had never set foot in church until they heard they could get cake and candy there. Once they had invaded the Sunday school, however, they hogged all the best parts for the Christmas pageant; no other kid was going to risk the bruises that came when you had something the Herdmans wanted. Everyone is aghast at the thought of cigar-smoking

Imogene Herdman as Mary, and her ruffian brothers as Joseph and the Wise Men, but it turns out to be "the best Christmas pageant ever." These incorrigible kids have never heard the Christmas story, and in their outrage about the inhospitable inn-keeper and the bloodthirsty Herod and their fierce protective-ness toward the baby Jesus, everyone else rediscovers the power of the familiar Gospel story.

Barbara Robinson is a very funny writer and your listeners will interrupt you many times with irrepressible laughter before you reach the touching conclusion. Even allowing for such pauses, though, you can read the book's seven chapters in about an hour and a quarter.

Blackberries in the Dark BY MAVIS JUKES. *Illustrated by Thomas B. Allen.* New York: Alfred A. Knopf, 1985.

Suggested Listening Level: Grades 3–5

Summer visits to his grandparents' farm have always been special for Austin. This summer, his grandfather was to have taught him how to fly-fish, but Grandpa is dead, and Austin's visit to the farm is painful. He doesn't want to learn fly-fishing from Wayne, a neighbor from the next farm, and between Austin and his grand-mother things are awkward. Grandmother sends Austin off to pick some blackberries from the patch by Two Rock Creek. Later, she surprises him by turning up dressed in Grandpa's old hip boots and fishing hat, and after struggling with the fishing gear, they finally catch a lovely brook trout. Then they let it go for good luck, just as Grandpa always said. Grandmother and Austin help each other back to the house, missing Grandpa but somehow stronger and closer to each other.

The story is quiet and restrained but resonant with summer sounds and memories. Although the death of a beloved grandfa-ther and husband creates a poignancy, the story's internal strength will fortify listeners and readers alike. This is a story about beginnings, not endings, and can be read in one sitting of about thirty minutes. If this one works well, try *Like Jake and Me,* about a warm, loving relationship between a boy and his stepfather as they wonder about the birth of a new baby.

A Blue-Eyed Daisy BY CYNTHIA RYLANT. New York: Bradbury Press, 1985.

Suggested Listening Level: Grades 5–8.

One of the pleasures of revising this book has been the chance to include wonderful new read-alouds that have been published since the first edition went to press, like this one by Cynthia Rylant, a young writer of considerable talent. Her book *A Blue-Eyed Daisy* is an appealing Appalachian story of Ellie, youngest of five sisters, and her twelfth year. Ellie's love for and growing closeness to her dad, who drinks too much after his mine accident, run through each understated episode. Few books capture the feel of contemporary rural mountain culture as deftly as this one. Ellie's problems will be familiar to many children not born to affluence: the tensions that breed with seven people confined in a small house; her longing for a room of her own and a bedspread with roses on it; her self-consciousness about her rotting teeth. The predominant mood is happy, however. To the delights of a goofy shopping trip with a best friend and a dreaded boy-girl party that turns out to be fun, are added moments when Ellie's flawed parents come through with understanding and love to help her through a year of growing up.

This small, ninety-nine-page book is organized into four sections, one for each season. Within the sections, each short chapter stands on its own. Total reading time is less than ninety minutes, with frequent breaks possible.

Don't miss Cynthia Rylant's collection of very short and very special stories, each centering on an animal: *Every Living Thing*.

The Borrowers BY MARY NORTON. *Illustrated by Beth and Joe Krush.* New York: Harcourt Brace & World, 1953. Paperback: Harcourt Brace.

Suggested Listening Level: Grades 3–6

Have you ever misplaced a needle, some stamps, a pencil or two, or a thimble? If these items or others unaccountably disappear, it is possible that the Borrowers are nearby. Borrowers are tiny people who live out of sight in old houses, subsisting on what they can "borrow" from "human beans." Cats or noisy children make life distinctly uncomfortable for them, and Routine and houses deep in the country are safest, but even in such circumstances there may be trouble. It certainly surprised Homily, Pod, and their daughter Arriety to find a Boy in the old house when none had been around for years. The Boy, however, provides the family with treasures beyond their dreams until the terrible day when the Borrowers are seen by Mrs. Driver, the housekeeper.

Listeners are fascinated by the miniature world of the Borrowers, perhaps because they, too, have noticed missing things and heard a rustle that can't be explained by a gust of wind. The reading time for *The Borrowers* is approximately three hours, but be sure that the first session includes both chapters one and two so that the listeners have a chance to meet Pod, Homily, and Arriety and glimpse their world under the floorboards.

Once involved in the adventures of this intrepid family, you may wish to follow the Borrowers to their new homes in four other books. Our favorite of the sequels is the most recent, *The Borrowers Avenged*. Every bit as delightful as the original, it is full of humor and perilous escapes, as Pod, Homily, and Arriety find a home in an old rectory and successfully outwit the greedy human couple who are determined to capture and exhibit them in a glass case.

The Brave Little Toaster BY THOMAS M. DISCH. *Illustrated by Karen Lee Schmidt.* New York: Doubleday & Co., 1986.

Suggested Listening Level: Grades 3–8.

The Brave Little Toaster makes a splendid book for adults and children to share. One of the most original books we know, it is at the same time patterned on a surefire formula: the perilous quest for home. Young listeners will fall right into the spirit of the suspenseful plot, while adults will revel in the sophisticated humor and in the style, which comes right out of the classic adventure tale. The story, which was first published in *The Magazine of Fantasy and Science Fiction,* concerns a group of appliances, abandoned without warning in a summer cottage, who bravely set out to find their master. (We know it sounds bizarre, but if you can enjoy whimsy at all, within minutes you will be happily caught up in the fantasy.) Led by the plucky toaster, these unusual characters rig up a desk chair with an automobile battery. Then they set out, the smaller appliances riding on the chair, the battery-powered vacuum cleaner towing them all. From the lugubrious vacuum cleaner to the well-informed clock-radio, each has a distinct personality which Disch consistently develops. They survive storms and escape from a thief and a junkyard, but their quest is not rewarded in the way that they hoped. Nevertheless, their resourcefulness triumphs at last, winning through to a happy ending that is totally satisfying to both appliances and audience.

The book is divided into seven sections; total reading time is just over one and a half hours.

Bridge to Terabithia BY KATHERINE PATERSON. *Illustrated by Donna Diamond.* New York: Thomas Y. Crowell, 1977. Paperback: Avon.

Suggested Listening Level: Grades 4–7

Jess's life was hard enough, stuck in the middle of four sisters and loaded down with farm chores, without the new girl next door spoiling his dream of being the fastest runner in the fifth grade. In spite of himself, though, Jess begins to like Leslie, and before long they find a secret place that becomes their own private kingdom. Jess discovers he has much to learn about mythical kingdoms; he doesn't even know the proper language. The two youngsters teach each other, however, and Leslie shares with Jess her vivid imagination, her dreams, even her parents, who have left a busy city life for the isolated Virginia countryside. Jess attempts to protect Leslie from taunting classmates who can't imagine anyone living anywhere without television and begins to understand his own artistic talent for catching "the poetry of the trees."

There is much that is "usual" in children's books here: Two loners from different backgrounds find each other, become friends, grow up a bit. It is the author's deft characterization and understanding of the luminous quality of friendship, however, that brings this story out of the ordinary. Both Leslie and Jess are remarkably vivid people, and listeners will suffer with Jess at Leslie's tragic accident. The thirteen chapters are approximately ten to twelve minutes each. Longer sessions toward the end of the book may cushion the impact of Leslie's death with Jess's hopes for the future and the continuation of the kingdom of Terabithia. *The Great Gilly Hopkins,* also by Katherine Paterson, is the story of a feisty unwanted child, and is successful with children who have had a limited exposure to books.

Brothers BY FLORENCE B. FREEDMAN. *Illustrated by Robert A. Parker.* New York: Harper & Row, Publishers, 1985.

Suggested Listening Level: Grades K–4.

Florence Freedman has retold in picture-book form an old Hebrew legend of generosity and brotherly love. Two brothers, each worrying about the welfare of the other in a time of drought, take wheat secretly to the other's threshing floor. Since, to their surprise, neither one's supply of wheat is diminished, they continue the nightly exchange until they happen to meet on the road and embrace. On that spot, it is said, the city of Jerusalem was built. The simple but powerful story is a fine choice for children, and will be welcomed also by adults looking for stories which embody the important values of cooperation and caring. The story is so simply written that many primary-level students will be able to reread it for themselves, while lingering over Robert Andrew Parker's striking illustrations. This would also be a fine story for children to informally act out. Total read-aloud time is only ten minutes.

Buffalo Woman WRITTEN AND ILLUSTRATED BY PAUL GOBLE. New York: Bradbury Press, 1984.

Suggested Listening Level: Grades K–4

A great and brave hunter one day watches while a buffalo turns into a beautiful woman, smelling of wild sage and prairie flowers. She has been sent to the hunter to strengthen the bond between the Buffalo Nation and the human tribe because he is a good and kind man. The hunter and the woman marry and have a son called Calf Boy, but the hunter's family are unkind to the woman and her son. After a time she leaves, and in order to reunite his family, the hunter has to face a trial involving the whole Buffalo Nation.

Goble has re-created this story from several versions told by the Plains Indians. The story has strength and dignity and your listeners will be caught by the intensity of the relationship between man and beast that reflects the respect the Indians gave to the great animals that roamed the plains. Try this with Carl Sandburg's poem "Buffalo Dusk." The book can be read in one twenty-minute session, but be sure to give your listeners time to look at the handsome illustrations that enhance the story. You might try some of Goble's other retellings. We like *The Girl Who Loved Wild Horses* and *Star Boy*.

The Bully of Barkham Street BY MARY STOLZ. *Illustrated by Leonard Shortall.* New York: Harper & Row, Publishers, 1963. Paperback: Harper & Row.

Suggested Listening Level: Grades 3–6

Martin Hastings, big for his grade, overweight, belligerent and a liar, is always in trouble. He picks on smaller kids, sasses adults, and drives away with his mean remarks anyone who tries to be friendly. We've all known a Martin Hastings, but Mary Stolz helps us see the world through his eyes. To Martin it seems that everyone is against him: his parents, who give away the dog who is his only friend; the kids who taunt him with names like Plump Pudding and Fatso; the teacher who ignores his imaginative composition to jump on spelling mistakes and inkblots. Gradually and believably over the course of the book, however, things improve for Martin, and we are left with that gift of good fiction—increased sensitivity to another person's experience.

The book is a companion volume to *The Dog on Barkham Street*, in which Mary Stolz recounts exactly the same events from the viewpoint of the younger boy next door, who is often the target of Martin's bullying. Both books display a rare understanding of children's feelings. If you can read both, begin with *The Dog on Barkham Street*. If you have time for only one, *The Bully of Barkham Street* is the more original and successful of the two books. The eight chapters run between twenty and thirty minutes each when read aloud.

In 1985, Mary Stolz published a sequel to *The Bully of Barkham Street*. Entitled *The Explorer of Barkham Street*, it tells of Martin, the former bully, at thirteen. Still getting into trouble and escaping into fantasies of heroism, Martin continues to be a "problem child," but he is again viewed sympathetically. The happy ending as he begins to find acceptance is credible and satisfying. Finally, if you're a fan of pig books, try Stolz's *Quentin Corn*. Q's successful escape from being butchered for barbecue involves impersonating a young man. This may be farfetched, but the escapades provided many chuckles to children we know.

Burnish Me Bright BY JULIA CUNNINGHAM. *Illustrated by Don Freeman.* New York: Pantheon Books, 1970. Paperback: Dell.

Suggested Listening Level: Grades 4–8

In a small French village a mute boy endures a miserable existence of frequent beatings and scanty food. Then he meets Monsieur Hilaire, who, though he is now old and ill, was "a few yesterdays ago" the greatest mime in the world. When the old man discovers that Auguste has the gift of mime, he teaches him in secret all that he can, and the boy's misery blossoms into happiness. Monsieur Hilaire dies, however, after warning the boy that to the suspicious villagers "the enemy is anyone who is different."

As this delicate tale unwinds the villagers come to fear Auguste's gift as witchcraft and he becomes the victim of mob violence. He survives, however, to keep alive the gift he has received from the old mime. In this story the author offers a parable about art and prejudice in a hostile world at a level children can understand. She creates the narrow society of a provincial village in deft strokes, and listeners will be swept up in the current of impending tragedy. Fortunately, the love between Auguste and his mentor plus the friends he finds among the children soften the story's harsh events. Even so, this is not recommended fare for primary grades.

The entire book can be read in approximately an hour and thirty minutes. The last two chapters, seven and eight, are very short and should be read in the same session. Don Freeman's graceful ink-and-wash sketches capture the story's essence.

By the Great Horn Spoon! BY SID FLEISCHMAN. *Illustrated by Eric von Schmidt.* Boston: Little, Brown & Co., 1953.

Suggested Listening Level: Grades 3–5

Twelve-year-old Jack, an orphan, and Praiseworthy, the family butler, stow away in potato barrels on a vessel sailing around Cape Horn from Boston to California. The time is the height of the gold rush; their object—to restore the family fortunes, of course. The ingenuity and pluck of this delightful pair enable them to extricate themselves and others from all sorts of difficulties—they are becalmed, robbed, and bamboozled, among other things. Our heroes do strike it rich, but then lose their gold. In the end, they manage to solve the family's problems in an unexpected way. You'll read many a book before you find one with as satisfying an ending as this one. Though the story smacks of the tall tale in its narrative style, it conveys interesting and authentic information about gold rush days, showing the rampant inflation in the gold fields, for instance, and vividly describing the rotting ships that fill

San Francisco harbor (they've been deserted by their gold-hungry crews).

This rollicking adventure yarn is a good choice for reading aloud. It is bound to please children and keep them clamoring for the next installment, but they might not choose it themselves because of its odd title. The book contains eighteen short chapters.

Another surefire read-aloud by Fleischman is *The Whipping Boy,* which in 1987 won the Newbery Medal as the best children's book by a United States author.

Calico Bush BY RACHEL FIELD. *Illustrated by Allen Lewis.* New York: Macmillan Publishing Co., 1931, 1966.

Suggested Listening Level: Grades 4–7

Calico Bush, a book written more than half a century ago (it was runner-up for the Newbery Medal in 1932), holds up remarkably well. It was reissued in 1966 and is still attracting a good many enthusiastic readers.

Marguerite Ledoux, who immigrated to America from France with her grandmother and uncle, found herself in the poorhouse after their sudden deaths. She had no choice but to become a "bound girl." The book opens in 1743 as she is traveling by boat to Maine from Marblehead, Massachusetts, with a poor family that has purchased her services for six years in return for giving her board and keep. Marguerite deals bravely with loneliness, endless chores, and the general prejudice against anything French, in addition to the hardships inherent in pioneering life. Her competence and courage through all sorts of crises make her a worthy and memorable heroine.

One needs to have a bit of French to do justice to this one in oral reading, for Marguerite frequently finds a French phrase slipping out at moments of emotion. Also, the words of a French lullaby play a part in a poignant episode.

Charlotte's Web BY E. B. WHITE. *Illustrated by Garth Williams.*
New York: Harper & Row, Publishers, 1952. Paperback: Harper &
Row.

Suggested Listening Level: Grades K–4

"Where's Papa going with that ax?" Fern's horror at her father's
plans to kill the newborn runt pig rings out on the first page of
Charlotte's Web. Fern prevails on her father to spare the pig,
names him Wilbur, and raises him on a bottle until he's too big
and must go to live in her uncle's barn down the road. The barn is
a wonderful place, full of pleasant sounds and smells, but Wilbur is
lonely until he makes a friend, a spider named Charlotte. In spite
of her bloodthirsty way of life, Charlotte proves a loving and wise
companion. It is she who conceives and executes the plan that
saves Wilbur from being butchered in the fall.

If a vote were taken for the best-loved read-aloud book in
America today, *Charlotte's Web* would win hands down. It has
everything: humor, vivid characters, pathos (Charlotte, like all
her kind, dies after laying her eggs), and wisdom. Though Charlotte's death will draw tears, White's sensitive handling of the
subject provides reassurance on a level that children can grasp.
Written by one of the finest prose stylists of our time, the book is a
model of eloquent, yet simple, English language. Each of the
twenty-two chapters makes a good read-aloud session for younger
children; we strongly recommend, though, that you do not stop
after chapter twenty-one (which ends with Charlotte's death), but
read on as White describes the ways that Charlotte's spirit lives
on.

Cheaper by the Dozen BY FRANK B. GILBRETH AND ERNESTINE
G. CAREY. New York: Thomas Y. Crowell, 1948. Paperback: Bantam.

Suggested Listening Level: Grades 4–8

The antics of the Gilbreth family keep children in stitches today just as they have for over forty years. Life is never dull in a family of twelve children and two efficiency-expert parents. Much of the humor centers on Mr. Gilbreth, portly and a bit pompous but with a marvelous sense of humor. His trials include not only governing a crew of red-haired Irish kids who have inherited his gift for practical jokes, but coping with a temperamental Pierce-Arrow (when cars were still a novelty). Mrs. Gilbreth is his foil—capable and serene through all the chaos. The Gilbreths' unconventional strategies for educating their brood, decades ahead of their time, give the book added substance.

Cheaper by the Dozen is ideal for family reading, as even young children can enjoy the slapstick elements, while mature listeners (and the reader) will appreciate the more subtle, irreverent touches.

The insensitivities of an earlier era crop up in two brief passages that you may want to edit or omit: a short minstrel-show routine near the end of chapter sixteen and the depiction of a stereotyped Chinese cook in chapter nine.

Child of the Silent Night: The Story of Laura Bridgman BY EDITH FISHER HUNTER. *Illustrated by Bea Holmes.* Boston: Houghton Mifflin Co., 1963. Paperback: Dell.

Suggested Listening Level: Grades 2–3

Laura Bridgman had been blind and deaf since she had scarlet fever at the age of two. Her friend Mr. Asa Tenney, called Uncle Asa by the Bridgmans, helped Laura and gave her the special love and attention she needed by taking her for long walks in the woods so that she could touch and smell the life around her. He explained it this way: "It is as though Laura is living in a room without windows or doors. I must make windows and doors into that room." Uncle Asa's windows and doors were opened even wider for Laura at the Perkins School for the Blind in Boston, and she thrived in the environment provided her. This biographical account does not minimize the hard work and long hours spent by both Laura and her teachers in mastering skills taken for granted by so many of us.

Primary grades listen and understand with sympathy much of Laura's struggle. Total reading time is about two hours, with chapters providing easy ten-minute sessions. Although the action is minimal, even very young listeners are captivated by the thoughtful Laura, who asked what the wind was made of, and why a waterfall doesn't stop.

Childtimes: A Three-Generation Memoir BY ELOISE GREENFIELD AND LESSIE LITTLE. New York: Thomas Y. Crowell, 1979.

Suggested Listening Level: Grades 5–8

Children who like to hear about "olden days," who beg a parent or grandparent to "tell me about when you were little," will enjoy this memoir. The book consists of reminiscences by Eloise Greenfield—a black writer with many outstanding children's and adult books to her credit—by her mother, and by her grandmother. It is a moving chronicle of change in American childhood over a century and of the continuity provided by love and struggle that spans the generations. As the introductory section puts it: "There's a lot of crying in this book, and there's dying, too, but there's also new life and laughter. It's all part of living." The book's first two sections are set in and around the small hamlet of Parmelee, North Carolina; the third in Washington, D.C., for like many other black families, this one headed on north in 1929 to look for a safer and better life.

Childtimes lacks the suspense of fiction; the first part of the book, especially, consists of fragmented memories, and the events described are mostly undramatic, but they succeed in bringing to life people, involving us in their joys and sorrows. It is not a book to be read to a large group but is wonderful for family reading when children have grown old enough to be interested in learning more about life in the past. The book's design is unusually attractive with charcoal sketches and photographs of the authors' families.

Chimney Sweeps, Yesterday and Today BY JAMES CROSS GIBLIN. *Illustrated by Margot Tomes.* New York: Thomas Y. Crowell, 1982.

Suggested Listening Level: Grades 4–8

James Giblin became interested in chimney sweeps when he sat next to one on an airplane journey. His curiosity led him to research the subject, with this award-winning book as the result. From today's respected professional, with vacuum cleaner and telescoping brushes, to the pauper boys as young as four who were forced by pinpricks to climb up narrow, sooty London chimneys two hundred years ago, the book presents vividly the facts and lore of this unusual work. Did you know why a kiss from a sweep is said to bring luck to a bride? Or why sweeps were respected and paid well in Germany but shamefully exploited in England? In describing the development of this profession and the attempts at reform, Giblin indirectly provides readers and listeners with a good introduction to the links between technology and employment, status and exploitation. Yet the book's eight short chapters are never dull, thanks to the author's skill at selecting striking vignettes and his appealing prose style. Margot Tomes's illustrations enhance the text and should be shared with listeners. The entire book can be read in forty-five minutes.

Commodore Perry in the Land of the Shogun BY RHODA BLUMBERG. New York: Lothrop, Lee & Shepard Books, 1985.

Suggested Listening Level: Grades 5–8

To the Japanese, the American sailors on Perry's ships were bearded barbarians; to your listeners both the Japanese and the Americans are forceful examples of the social context of history. This outstanding work presents the events and individuals involved in opening Japan to U.S. traders in 1853 and 1854. Using letters, diaries, sketches, and photos, the author has created a remarkable sense of time and place. Even more noteworthy, however, is the evenhandedness of her presentation of the two cultures. While a Japanese official filled his glass with olive oil assuming it was wine, an American sailor tasted Japanese hair oil "believing it was good liquor." The juxtaposition of such behavior points up for young listeners the misunderstandings that can come with different cultural experiences.

The book can be read in five or six sessions of about twenty-five minutes. Do show some of the pictures along the way. It will be more successful with audiences used to listening. This volume is perfect for a middle-school class, whether studying Japan or simply working on an appreciation of cultural diversity—or both.

The Courage of Sarah Noble BY ALICE DALGLIESH. *Illustrated by Leonard Weisgard.* New York: Charles Scribner's Sons, 1954. Paperback: Macmillan.

Suggested Listening Level: Grades K–3

The only comfort for eight-year-old Sarah is her father's presence and the warm cloak her mother had fastened under her chin. In the dense forest, strange rustlings, real and imagined, seem almost overwhelming as she accompanies her father to a new homesite in eighteenth-century Connecticut. Most fearsome of all are the thoughts of Indians, until she meets the children of a village not far from the site of the Nobles' cabin. Sarah has need of all her courage, however, when her father leaves to bring the rest of the family back, asking her to remain with the Indian family of the man they call Tall John.

"Keep up your courage, Sarah Noble" was her mother's admonition as the journey began. It was a phrase that Sarah repeated over and over to herself and that listeners will pick up and share as the occasion demands. One youngster muttered it over and over to himself, substituting his own name, as he went to the hospital for a tonsillectomy. It can be read in two or three rather short sessions and is a good beginning for either kindergarten or first-grade listeners. The author's *Bears on Hemlock Mountain,* with its ringing refrain and exciting buildup of suspense, also makes good reading aloud.

The Cricket in Times Square BY GEORGE SELDEN (PSEUD. OF GEORGE SELDEN THOMPSON). *Illustrated by Garth Williams.* New York: Farrar, Straus & Giroux, 1960. Paperback: Dell.

Suggested Listening Level: Grades K–4

Transported unawares after feasting in a picnic basket, a Connecticut cricket named Chester finds himself stranded in the dirt and bustle of Times Square subway station. His chirping attracts friendly help, however, and soon he is snugly settled in the Bellinis' newsstand as the treasured pet of Mario Bellini. Tucker Mouse and Harry Cat, good-natured scavengers who live in a nearby drainpipe, also befriend Chester. When Chester discovers that he can learn and perform any piece of music he hears, Tucker is the one who sees a way to repay the kindness of the struggling Bellini family. In time, Chester's musical talent brings fame and modest fortune to the hardworking Bellinis.

All those who appreciate good music and good food, both younger and older audiences, will delight in the humor and solid sense of Tucker, Harry Cat, and, of course, Chester. This is an excellent choice for primary grades who have developed the ability to listen to longer narratives. We prefer to read the conversations between Mario and the Chinese gentleman Sai Fong without the somewhat exaggerated dialect indicated by the spelling ("Velly, velly good. You got clicket . . . You know stoly of first clicket?"). The author's skillful use of word order and diction are sufficient to characterize Mr. Fong. The fifteen chapters can be combined into about seven sessions, five if audiences can tolerate longer sessions.

Dicey's Song BY CYNTHIA VOIGT. New York: Atheneum Publishers, 1982. Paperback: Fawcett.

Suggested Listening Level: Grades 6–8

If you and your listeners revel in dense novels that paint settings and characters as vividly real as those you inhabit every day, *Dicey's Song* is for you. The story recounts how four abandoned children and the eccentric grandmother who takes them in forge a true family. Dicey, the thirteen-year-old central character, has led her younger brothers and sister from the Connecticut parking lot where their mother disappeared, victim of a mental breakdown, to the old house on the shores of Chesapeake Bay where their grandmother has lived as a recluse. That story is told in Voigt's earlier novel, *Homecoming.* In this sequel, the task changes from bare survival to finding how to get along as a family. Dicey must learn to share the worrying, Gram Tillerman must learn to accept help and to face the pain of the past; together they gradually discover how to help the younger children overcome the scars of their traumatic early life. If nominations were being taken for most interesting and admirable young fictional heroines, Dicey would be high on our list. Also, Voigt's loving descriptions of the Maryland shore make us want to pack up and head there. All in all, this is a wonderful book to live in for a week or two. Each of the book's twelve chapters requires approximately one-half hour to read aloud.

Do Bananas Chew Gum? BY JAMIE GILSON. New York: Lothrop, Lee & Shepard Books, 1980. Paperback: Archway.

Suggested Listening Level: Grades 3–6

Sam Mott has big problems. The other sixth-graders in his new school call him Tinsel Teeth, adults insist on calling him Sammy, and when they learn he reads like a second-grader, everyone will no doubt begin calling him Dumbhead Sam, which is how he thinks of himself. Jamie Gilson has written about a learning disability from the inside, and if you like books that touch the emotions and the funny bone as well, you'll enjoy *Do Bananas Chew Gum?* Sam is miserable when his parents argue about how to handle his reading problem and frustrated that he can't learn about archeology, which fascinates him, from a book. He's sick of lousy tests he'll only fail. But he does in the end get help from a pleasant and capable reading specialist. He also makes a good friend and proves to be a terrific baby-sitter, keeping the job even though he has trouble reading the notes the boys' mother leaves for him.

Only a former junior high school teacher could write so convincingly of sixth-grade craziness (your listeners will howl at Sam and Wally's search through the lunchroom garbage for a lost retainer) or of classroom dynamics as experienced by a poor student. After reading *Do Bananas Chew Gum?* (the title comes from one of the dreaded tests Sam has to take), reader and listeners will have new understanding of kids like Sam. They'll also be eager to read more books by Jamie Gilson. When reading this one aloud, try one or two of the eleven chapters at a sitting. Total reading time approximates three hours. The book contains a couple of examples of Sam's misspelled and messy handwriting. You may want to pass the book around so listeners can see those pages.

The Dollhouse Caper BY JEAN S. O'CONNELL. *Illustrated by Erik Blegvad.* New York: Thomas Y. Crowell, 1976. Paperback: Scholastic.

Suggested Listening Level: Grades 3–6

Now that their home was off the high shelf and set up for the Christmas holidays, Mrs. Dollhouse should have been happy, but she couldn't help worrying. Would the young Humans, Kevin, Peter, and Harry, think themselves too grown up for Mr. and Mrs. Dollhouse and their family? And what about the robbery that the Dollhouse family overheard being plotted? How could the Humans be warned?

Like Father Dollhouse, who spends a lot of time stuffed head-first in the dollhouse toilet by the middle brother, the assumption that doll stories are for girls is turned upside down by this book. The fast-paced account of how the Dollhouse family foil the robbers can't help but amuse both boys and girls, and boys will especially appreciate the author's understanding of the pressures on boys to grow up. The twelve chapters divide into six sessions of about twenty minutes each and provide surefire material for third through sixth grade.

The Doubleday Illustrated Children's Bible BY SANDOL STODDARD. *Illustrated by Tony Chen.* New York: Doubleday & Co., 1983.

Suggested Listening Level: Grades 2–6

This handsome volume contains the chief stories of the Old and New Testaments in clear, simplified versions. Children's favorites, such as David and Goliath, Joseph and his brothers, and Noah's ark, are all here, as are many less-well-known episodes. A particularly welcome feature of the book is an arrangement of Psalms, "brought together . . . so as to remind us of the story we have read thus far." A section bridging the Old and New Testament stories places biblical events in historical context. Tony Chen's intense watercolor illustrations add a rich Mediterranean feel to the pages.

Some vignettes are only a page or two long, but each stands on its own, so you may choose your stopping points. The New Testament stories are, as one would expect, told from a Christian viewpoint, probably with a predominantly Christian audience in mind, but they also could be used to introduce children of different religious traditions to the Christian Bible.

Dragonwings BY LAURENCE YEP. New York: Harper & Row, Publishers, 1975. Paperback: Harper.

Suggested Listening Level: Grades 5–8

Dragonwings is the story of a Chinese immigrant to San Francisco who in 1909 successfully built and flew a biplane. It is based on fact, but nothing beyond this is known of the man. The book is Laurence Yep's attempt to flesh out the life of just one of the anonymous hundreds of thousands of Chinese who came to America in the nineteenth and early twentieth centuries. (Yep reports this in the afterword, but we've found that children prefer to know the story's relation to "real life" at the start.)

Events are described through the eyes of the inventor-flyer's young son, Moon Shadow. Throughout the book the non-Chinese reader is challenged to see Western culture from Moon Shadow's Chinese viewpoint, whether he is revolted by the awful greasy drink, cow's milk, or confronting a drunken mob of "red-and-white faces, distorted into hideous masks of hatred and cruelty." Moon Shadow's father, Windrider, has a dream of flying, however, that takes them both out of Chinatown, and in a "white demoness" and her granddaughter they find a measure of understanding and friendship.

The book does not gloss over unpleasantness: Moon Shadow and his father visit graphically described opium dens in a violent underworld as they search for an addict relative, and the San Francisco earthquake reveals the moral depths to which some people sink in calamity. Moon Shadow and Windrider prevail, however, and the book is a fitting tribute to the unrecognized achievement of a brave and hardworking immigrant group that has greatly contributed to American society.

Child of the Owl, set in San Francisco's Chinese community in the 1970s, is another fine book by Yep about cultural identity and assimilation.

The Ears of Louis BY CONSTANCE C. GREENE. *Illustrated by Nola Langner.* New York: The Viking Press, 1974.

Suggested Listening Level: Grades 3–5

Louis had big ears and small muscles—a bad combination. This warm and funny novel tells how Louis comes to terms with his ears and with the constant teasing they invite. The problem is real but never overwhelming, for Louis has an understanding family, an elderly neighbor who gives him good advice over their fiercely competitive poker games, and a friend named Matthew who is everything a friend should be. "I think your ears are nice," he says. Why? "Well . . . when the sun shines through them, they're all pink and everything."

Constance Greene's own ears must be keen, for she captures just the way kids talk to each other and adults talk to kids, making this short novel great fun to read aloud. The book, which is divided into short sections, can be read in just over one hour.

The Egypt Game BY ZILPHA KEATLEY SNYDER. *Illustrated by Alton Raible.* New York: Atheneum Publishers, 1967. Paperback: Dell.

Suggested Listening Level: Grades 4–7

April and Melanie, two friends with vivid imaginations, discover a chipped replica of the famous Nefertiti statue in an overgrown vacant lot behind a junkshop. Thus begins the Egypt game. They read about ancient Egypt, make costumes, and develop shrines and rituals for their secret world. Melanie's little brother, Marshall, plays too, as the crown prince of the ancient pharaohs, and three other children eventually join the "Egyptians." The murder of a child in the neighborhood, however, brings the Egypt game and all other outdoor play to an abrupt halt. To make things worse, the stern old "Professor" who owns the junkshop is a suspect in the murder. When April and Marshall are attacked by the murderer, however, it is the Professor who saves them and leads to the murderer's capture.

Each of the children in the story comes to life as a distinct and appealing person; that they happen to be of different races and nationalities (quite plausible in the California university-town setting) is a special bonus. The book consists of twenty-three chapters, with a total reading-aloud time of approximately four hours. The first chapter, which sets the scene, is a bit slow, so we recommend that the first reading session include chapter two. Once listeners are introduced in that chapter to April, with her Hollywood airs and great ideas, they'll be hooked.

The Endless Steppe: Growing Up in Siberia BY ESTHER HAUTZIG. New York: Thomas Y. Crowell, 1968. Paperback: Scholastic.

Suggested Listening Level: Grades 5–8

The secure and lovely world of ten-year-old Esther Rudomin was destroyed one morning in June 1941 when Russian soldiers burst into her grandparents' home in Vilna, Poland. Arrested as capitalist "enemies of the people," Esther, her parents, and her grandparents travel in a cattle car with dozens of other prisoners for six miserable weeks to a frontier village on the Siberian steppe. There, under conditions of extreme hardship and deprivation, they work in a gypsum mine and on a farm. In spite of the suffering, the resilient young girl finds small pleasures—a rare American movie, visits to the bazaar in town, and eventually the beauty of the harsh, rugged steppes. She feels a real sense of loss, as well as deliverance, when the family is returned to Poland at the end of the war. There they discover that their exile has, ironically, saved their lives. The rest of the family has perished in Nazi concentration camps.

In this autobiographical account, Hautzig displays an excellent sense of pace, using telling incidents to convey emotion in an understated way. She captures the humanity of the characters so vividly that *their* strength gives us the strength to read on, and the book is ultimately a heartening, not a devastating, experience.

The book has twenty-two chapters. The first is quite long, plenty for one read-aloud session. Subsequent chapters can be read in combinations of two or three. Don't be intimidated by the occasional Russian or Polish place name; just sound them out as you go. Listeners will be so caught up in the story that they won't be critical.

Escape from Warsaw BY IAN SERRAILLIER. Original title: **The Silver Sword.** *Illustrated by C. Walter Hodges.* Paperback: Scholastic, 1972.

Suggested Listening Level: Grades 4–6

When Joseph Balicki, headmaster of a Warsaw school, is imprisoned by the Nazis and his Swiss wife taken away for forced labor, their three children must depend on their own resources to survive the chaos of wartime Europe. They hide in bombed-out cellars in the winter and woods in the summer. Edek provides food and clothes until he, too, is captured and sent to Germany to work on a farm. Ruth and Bronia are joined by a ragamuffin named Jan as they begin their search for Edek and then their parents. It is Jan's "silver sword," a small letter-opener given him by Mr. Balicki, that becomes the symbol of hope that the children take with them all the way from Warsaw to Appenzell, Switzerland.

The story is based on a factual account, and in spite of incredible odds the children manage to find each other, stay together, and finally reach their parents. They experience terror and despair along the way, but this is not a depressing story—there is a degree of security in Ruth's strength and in the resourcefulness of Jan and Edek. The twenty-nine chapters can be read two or three at a time. Total reading time is about five hours.

The Eternal Spring of Mr. Ito BY SHEILA GARRIGUE. New York: Bradbury Press, 1985.

Suggested Listening Level: Grades 5–8

Sara has been sent away from England during the bombings of World War II, to live with her aunt and uncle in Vancouver, British Columbia. She becomes very fond of her uncle's Japanese gardener, Mr. Ito, who is helping her grow a bonsai. After the Japanese attacks on Pearl Harbor and Hong Kong, in which Cousin Mary's fiancé is killed, Mr. Ito is fired and his family interned by the Canadian government. Sara keenly feels the injustice of this edict: why, Mr. Ito fought beside Uncle Duncan in World War I, and all his family are loyal Canadians! Mr. Ito prepares for the death that he prefers to the dishonor of being sent to a camp. Before he dies, however, he passes along to Sara much wisdom and helps her to deal with the losses war brings. Sara, in turn, bravely finds a way to meet with the Ito family and comfort them in their exile.

This beautifully written book, based loosely on the author's childhood memories, alternates tautly paced action with reflective moments that arise naturally from the relationships of her well-drawn characters. The nineteen chapters average eight pages each, making a total reading time of slightly over four hours.

A Fair Wind for Troy BY DORIS GATES. *Illustrated by Charles Mikolaycak.* New York: The Viking Press, 1976. Paperback: Penguin.

Suggested Listening Level: Grades 5–8

Daughter of Zeus, daughter of Leda, Helen was the most beautiful woman in the ancient world. When she chose Menelaus, one of the most powerful men in Greece, as her husband, all her other suitors took an oath swearing to exact no vengeance on the winner and to aid Menelaus should anyone ever abduct Helen. When the Trojan prince Paris stole her away, all of the warriors of Greece gathered under the leadership of Agamemnon to carry out their oath. Because of an offense to the goddess Artemis, however, the Greek ships are becalmed, and a sacrifice must be made to appease the goddess. Iphigenia, daughter of Agamemnon, is the price of "a fair wind for Troy."

The author has carefully chronicled the events leading to the Trojan War in this powerful retelling. You may wish to set the scene for this reading by discussing mythology in literature and by forewarning the listeners of the harsh and bloody events that are a part of this tradition. Gates has handled the story with the dignity and grandeur that it deserves, however, as she does in her other volumes of Greek mythology.

Each chapter has within it natural stopping points; twenty-minute sessions are usually enough, even for older listeners.

Fantastic Mr. Fox BY ROALD DAHL. *Illustrated by Donald Chaffin.* New York: Alfred A. Knopf, 1970. Paperback: Bantam.

Suggested Listening Level: Grades K–4

Take three rich, greedy, and disgusting villains, pit them against a charming, clever fellow whose only crime is trying to feed his engaging family, and you have a story certain to appeal to primary-grade children—and their big sisters and brothers. Dahl's pell-mell plot in which the three farmers Boggis, Bunce, and Bean destroy the countryside in their attempt to exterminate the fox family will capture children's attention immediately. The complete triumph of the fantastic Mr. Fox will leave them cheering.

Adults should be forewarned of Dahl's crude vulgarity. The villains pick their noses with filthy fingers, call each other rude names, and generally serve to set off by contrast the loving and mannerly hero.

This is flamboyant entertainment in the "Perils of Pauline" tradition, and Dahl is a master of it. The eighteen chapters are very short. Plan to read several in each session. Total reading time is under two hours.

Favorite Folktales from Around the World EDITED BY JANE YOLEN. New York: Pantheon Books, 1986.

Suggested Listening Level: Grades 3–8

The 140 folktales contained in this volume will provide you with stories for any occasion—long stories, short stories, love stories, ghost stories, and knee-slapping funny stories, to name but a few types. Jane Yolen, prolific author of children's books and noted storyteller, has selected folktales from more than forty different cultures, some of which will be familiar to you, but most will not. Sharing them is guaranteed to expand the horizons of your young listeners. One feature of the book we especially like is the categories by which Yolen has chosen to group the stories: "The Very Young and the Very Old," "True Loves and False," "Tricksters,

Rogues, and Cheats," and "Heroes: Likely and Unlikely," for instance. Some of the stories may have limited appeal to children, so we particularly recommend with this book that you read to yourself ahead of time any story you are thinking of reading aloud.

The Fighting Ground BY AVI. *Illustrated by Ellen Thompson.* Philadelphia: J. B. Lippincott Co., 1984. Paperback: Harper.

Suggested Listening Level: Grades 6–8

This story about a thirteen-year-old's participation in a trivial skirmish of the Revolutionary War is one of the most gripping books we've found. Jonathan, "hot, dirty, and bored" from working in the fields, hears the alarm bell toll at the tavern in the village, and hopes that it signals fighting nearby that he might join. He disobeys his parents and volunteers to join a small ragtag group assembled by an unsavory corporal to confront a small troop of British soldiers. The British turn out to be fierce-looking Hessians and to outnumber the colonials. After a totally confusing confrontation, Jonathan is captured by three Hessians. Soon he cannot decide whether they are his friends or his enemies, yet he is compelled to become the instrument of their deaths. The writing is full of vivid sensory details—the smell of fresh-turned fields, the nausea of panic. All the action takes place between 9:58 one April morning and 10:30 the next, and the concentrated events indelibly depict the unglamorous realities of war.

This book reminds one of the Civil War story *Across Five Aprils,* for the protagonists are similar, and the suffering of one war repeats that of its predecessors. In that book, however, a lyrical style and the emphasis on loving relationships provides consolation to the listener. Avi's book is more immediate and action-filled, and in it the sense of brutality and loss is nearly overwhelming (though Jonathan does survive). Still, *The Fighting Ground* can help both boys and girls to understand better the sources of masculine fascination with battle and to weigh more accurately the true costs of war.

The book is short overall and composed of brief scenes. Some

German phrases are spoken by the Hessians, but are translated in a glossary at the back of the book.

Five Children and It BY E. NESBIT (PSEUD. OF EDITH BLAND). *Illustrated by H. R. Millar.* London: Unwin, 1902; New York: Dodd, Mead & Co., 1905. Paperback: Penguin.

Suggested Listening Level: Grades 3–6

When five brothers and sisters discover a Psammead while digging in the gravel quarry near their summer cottage, the stage is set for wondrous adventures. A Psammead, you see, is a sand-fairy, and this rather grumpy, Muppet-like creature is obliged to grant wishes that last until sundown. With their parents away, the children envision a perfectly blissful summer. Alas, they find their wishes often entail unpleasant consequences. When they request a quarryful of gold, the suspicious shopkeepers won't take their guineas and instead turn them over to the police. The wish for wings turns out well, as they enjoy a glorious day of flying around the countryside, but they are stranded, wingless, on a church roof at nightfall. Most disconcerting of all is Cyril's offhand wish that the troublesome baby would "grow up now." Before their eyes the two-year-old is transformed into a dapper young gentleman who views them as bothersome tagalongs.

Numerous writers since Nesbit have written similar fantasies, but they cannot duplicate her success, which owes a great deal to her perfectly gauged casual asides to the reader. For instance: "I know this is the second fight—or contest in this chapter, but I can't help it. It was that sort of day. You know yourself there are days when rows seem to keep on happening, quite without your meaning them to."

The slang is a bit dated (i.e., "brekker" for breakfast and pet names for all the children), and the English idiom may prove difficult for those inexperienced at reading aloud; nevertheless, the book retains its special charm across the years and cultures.

There are eleven chapters for the children's eleven adventures. The chapter "Scalps" embodies every dime-novel stereotype of

American Indians, yet it is at heart a satire of the popular romanti-
cized image of the Indian. (Check it out in advance and omit it if
you find it objectionable.) Sequels are *The Phoenix and the Carpet*
and *The Story of the Amulet.*

The Fledgling BY JANE LANGTON. New York: Harper & Row,
Publishers, 1980. Paperback: Harper.

Suggested Listening Level: Grades 3–6

Georgie was nine years old, a spindly wisp of thistledown looking
more like six—or even five. The family was worried because
Georgie wanted to fly; not just an ordinary wanting, but a determined wanting that included three attempts down the front
stairs. And the great Canada goose on the seasonal flight south-
ward wanted to find someone worthy of the special "present" he
had found in Walden Pond. These two loners finally discover each
other. Tucked close and safe on the goose's back, Georgie is at last
flying! Through the night sky they glide—over the fields and
woods, circling down toward Walden Pond. But their secret flying
has not been so secret. Interfering Mr. Preek and Miss Prawn
have seen the two and set out to "rescue" Georgie. The tragic
result of their intervention ends Georgie's flying, but she will
treasure forever the Goose's special present.

Who can say it's impossible? Certainly not the adults in this
story; certainly not Eleanor or Edward, Georgie's cousins; certainly not readers/listeners of all ages. Since the spirits of Emer-
son and Thoreau permeate the story, this would be especially
good for families traveling to the Boston area, but it could enthrall
any group of listeners—third through sixth grades. Airplane travelers are also a natural audience for this book. The reader needs to
be prepared for Langton's sometimes sudden changes of narrator.

Another book about Georgie is *The Fragile Flag.* Intrepid Georgie decides to walk all the way to Washington to persuade the
President not to deploy the so-called Peace Missile. A modern-day
children's crusade develops, which is funny and moving and
leaves listeners with much food for thought.

Flossie and the Fox BY PATRICIA C. MCKISSACK. *Illustrated by Rachel Isadora.* New York: The Dial Press, 1986.

Suggested Listening Level: Grades K–3

In a story set in the rural South perhaps a century ago, little Flossie Finley is given a basket of eggs to take to Miz Viola's cabin. Her grandmother warns her to be on the lookout for the fox, a rascal who loves eggs. Flossie sets out, not sure she knows just what a fox looks like. When she meets the old slickster, however, her wits prove to be more than a match for him. Children are likely to clap and cheer at Flossie's triumph. If you've been bothered by Little Red Riding Hood's helplessness, Flossie is the heroine for you, and you may want to discuss with children the similarities and differences in the two stories. Don't let the southern dialect of this book scare you. McKissack, who remembers her grandfather telling this story, has captured the colorful phrases and cadences of African American speech so well that anyone can bring the words alive.

Flying to the Moon and Other Strange Places BY MICHAEL COLLINS. New York: Farrar, Straus & Giroux, 1976. Paperback: Farrar, Straus & Giroux.

Suggested Listening Level: Grades 5–8

In this autobiographical account of space exploration, Astronaut Collins reveals a thoughtful perspective to young listeners. The first several chapters involve his early life—he built model planes at nine—as well as a short and fascinating account of the history of rocketry. By chapter four the listener is involved in more technical aspects of training as Collins and his fellow astronauts struggle to absorb the complicated and bewildering array of skills necessary to a space pioneer. It is the Apollo 11 flight of the *Columbia* and the lunar landing, however, that capture so much of the listener's attention. You may decide to skip some of the more technical aspects of this book, particularly details of navigation.

The last chapter, for instance, is speculation about the direction of space exploration, which has changed considerably in the years since this was published. But for technically minded listeners of fifth through eighth grades, this is a glimpse of a sensitive, thoughtful man that should be shared.

Fog Magic BY JULIA SAUER. *Illustrated by Lynd Ward.* New York: The Viking Press, 1943. Paperback: Puffin.

Suggested Listening Level: Grades 3–6

Greta had always loved the fog. Her mother worried about this fascination, but her father understood her need to explore inside the gray blanket that often covered their part of the Nova Scotia shoreline, especially Blue Cove. In the sunshine, when the water of the inlet sparkled, Blue Cove was deserted with only the shells of cellar holes left. But in the fog, when the Tollerton horn called its warning, a village appeared as it had been in the past. Greta met the Morrill family and found a best friend in Retha. She came to know the stories behind people and places taken for granted in the world outside the fog: the drowned sailors, the egg cup and silver spoon—and Princess the cat. All the life of the Cove was shared with her until her twelfth birthday, when, as her father said, "all things change and are put away to fold around you in years ahead."

This is a quiet, introspective story that is short enough to be read in three or four sessions and will entrance fourth- through sixth-grade listeners. Some adults may find the ending a bit too pat, but we've had good luck with this for fourth-graders, especially. Try it with Mollie Hunter's *A Stranger Came Ashore.*

Freddy the Politician BY WALTER R. BROOKS. *Illustrated by Kurt Wiese.* Paperback: Alfred A. Knopf. Originally published as *Wiggins for President* in 1939.

Suggested Listening Level: Grades 2–6.

Parents and grandparents who fondly remember Walter Brooks's series of books about the talking animals of the Bean Farm will be happy to hear that the publisher has recently reissued four of these volumes, so that today's children can follow the adventures and chuckle at the antics of Freddy the Pig and his friends. In *Freddy the Politician,* the animals resolve to show that they can assume responsibility, so that Farmer Bean will be able to take Mrs. Bean and the boys on a long-desired trip to Europe, leaving the animals to run the farm. They decide that the way to demonstrate their reliability is to start a bank and to found the First Animal Republic, complete with a president to oversee the farm work. Unfortunately, crafty woodpeckers arrive from Washington and, through trickery, take over both the bank and the election. The woodpeckers persuade birds from the surrounding countryside to nest on the Bean Farm until after the election, make rash campaign promises (a revolving door for the henhouse, catproof apartments for the rats), and give windy campaign speeches. (The book is a good introduction to the realities of politics, among other things.) When they lose in spite of all their dirty tricks, the rascals seize power and set up a military dictatorship that aims to rule all the animals in the state. With clever detective work on Freddy's part, common sense, and cooperation, the Bean animals outwit the interlopers and restore the peaceful community of friends. Friendship is what these books are about, Michael Cart points out in his brief introduction, and you and your children will add some very special book friends to your lives when you read Brooks's volumes.

At 253 pages and nineteen chapters, *Freddy the Politician* is longer than most of today's books for elementary-school-age children. The story meanders a bit, conveying from an earlier era the sense that the storyteller has all the time in the world. So this isn't the book to choose for the kind of group that begins to squirm if there isn't action and suspense in every paragraph. But we can testify that its lucid style and low-key humor make a two-day car trip pass much more pleasantly for children and adults, or provide about two weeks of ideal bedtime reading.

From Anna BY JEAN LITTLE. *Illustrated by Joan Sandin.* New York: Harper & Row, Publishers, 1972. Paperback: Harper.

Suggested Listening Level: Grades 3–5

It isn't easy being the youngest in a family, especially when you feel awkward and ugly and much less clever than everyone else. Only Papa seemed to appreciate Anna, but even Papa had other things on his mind as the family prepared to leave Hitler's Germany and Papa's teaching post for a grocery store in Canada. There are many exciting experiences for the Solden family in their new home, but for Anna (and the listener) it is the discovery of her own worth that brings the story to life. As part of a routine physical examination, the doctor finds that Anna needs glasses and a special school. With Miss Williams and the other children in the class, Anna begins to "blossom and grow, just like a Christmas flower."

Anna's story is a warm, loving one told with humor and yet a good deal of action. There is a considerable amount of dialogue, but the story is very straightforward. A sequel to this story of the Soldens, *Listen for the Singing,* and several other books by the author are rewarding for reading aloud, such as *Mine for Keeps* or *Far from Home.* The chapters in *From Anna* are short and episodic, so that five or six sessions should finish the story. A word of warning: Anna is a child not easily forgotten. The audience will *demand* to hear more. And her story will bring tears to the audience and reader alike—keep the Kleenex handy.

From the Mixed-Up Files of Mrs. Basil E. Frankweiler WRITTEN AND ILLUSTRATED BY ELAINE KONIGSBURG. New York: Atheneum Publishers, 1967. Paperback: Dell, Macmillan.

Suggested Listening Level: Grades 4–6

When Claudia Kincaid gets fed up with the monotony of her suburban straight-A life, she decides to run away. Because she's a fastidious and organized child, she plans carefully and selects as her destination the Metropolitan Museum in New York. As companion she chooses her younger brother Jamie (he's rich enough to bankroll the expedition). Claudia and Jamie's successful adventure has all the appeal of Robinson Crusoe, and the elegant surroundings of the museum are a great improvement over any desert island. The children sleep in a sixteenth-century canopy bed, bathe in (and replenish their funds from) the museum fountain. Furthermore, their brains are challenged as they attempt to prove that a small statue on display is the work of the great Michelangelo.

Konigsburg uses a somewhat confusing frame device to tell the story: the narrator is wealthy art patron Mrs. Frankweiler, who is relating the children's adventures to her lawyer. The identity of the narrator becomes clear only gradually, however. For that reason the book is best read to experienced listeners. This Newbery Medal–winning novel will please Manhattan-lovers and museum-lovers as well as those who value originality in fiction.

Galimoto BY KAREN WILLIAMS. *Illustrated by Catherine Stock.* New York: Lothrop, Lee & Shepard Books, 1989.

Suggested Listening Level: Grades K–3

When in an African village, a small boy decides to make a *galimoto* (a clever push-toy vehicle), his older brother laughs. "A boy with only seven years cannot make such a toy," he says. But Kondi patiently scours his Malawi village for the wire he will need, finding, trading, and begging, until he has enough. After an afternoon of labor, his new pickup leads the way in the children's moonlit parade. Scenes of contemporary village life make a fascinating backdrop for this simple tale, which quietly celebrates the satisfactions of competence, persistence, and hard work.

Ghosts I Have Been BY RICHARD PECK. New York: The Viking Press, 1977. Paperback: Dell.

Suggested Listening Level: Grades 4–7

Blossom Culp is something of an outcast in Bluff City, living as she does in a shack on the wrong side on the streetcar tracks. She asks for no special favors, however, since she prefers living by her wits to passing her life like proper girls, "up on a porch, gazing into an embroidery hoop." When Blossom suddenly develops a gift for Second Sight, she becomes a celebrity, first in Bluff City, and then as far away as London. She uses her powers first to calm a despairing and very noisy ghost, but before she is finished, her gift has put her through the harrowing experiences of going down with the *Titanic* and of witnessing in advance the carnage of modern warfare. (The book's events are set in 1913–14.)

Blossom's first-person account of the social life of Bluff City, the sights of London, and of various ghosts, real and fake, is outspoken and full of both humor and suspense. From the first scene in which a Halloween prank at Old Man Leverette's outhouse backfires, to the climax in which a tableau at Madame Tussaud's Waxworks comes to life, the action never flags. Total reading time for the book's nineteen chapters is five hours.

The Good Master WRITTEN AND ILLUSTRATED BY KATE SEREDY. New York: The Viking Press, 1935. Paperback: Penguin.

Suggested Listening Level: Grades 3–5

Jancsi is excited about the visit of city-cousin Kate, but no one is quite ready for the "bag of screaming monkeys" that is the *real* Kate. Riding horses, climbing walls and hiding in the rafters, even planting flowers, become adventures for the whole family as seen through the city-bred eyes of Kate.

Life and customs of the Hungarian countryside abound. Holidays are special times for the rural community, and the details are lovingly and faithfully included. There are four stories woven into the narrative that could be read separately, especially "The Little Rooster and the Diamond Button," which is included in many storytelling anthologies, or these stories could be included as presented. Strong-willed, energetic Kate loved the tales—and the tellers. Third- to fifth-grade audiences will be delighted to meet her.

Grandaddy's Place WRITTEN BY HELLEN V. GRIFFETH. *Illustrated by James Stevenson.* New York: Greenwillow Books, 1987.

Suggested Listening Level: Grades K–3

When Momma decides it's time Janetta knew her grandaddy, she takes her young daughter on a long train trip south. Janetta likes that, but she *doesn't* like Grandaddy's place at all. It's old and broken down and the cat and chickens and wasps all look mean. Griffeth's short, pithy chapters and Stevenson's evocative watercolors show how a feisty little girl and her grandfather gradually get to be very special friends. This is a book to be treasured for its humor and warmth. Its sequel, *Georgia Music,* is sadder but just as engaging.

The Great Brain BY JOHN D. FITZGERALD. *Illustrated by Mercer Mayer.* New York: The Dial Press, 1967. Paperback: Dell.

Suggested Listening Level: Grades 2–5

Otherwise known as Thomas Dennis Fitzgerald (T.D.), the Great Brain cannot resist moneymaking propositions, daring exploits, any challenge, even a swindle or two. His brother, J.D., relates these adventures of the Great Brain, his family, and his friends in turn-of-the-century Mormon Utah.

As a first-person account based on the childhood experience of the author, these humorous episodes can be read as individual stories or as part of a longer narrative. While many of the Great Brain's schemes are outrageous, his more thoughtful, sensitive nature emerges often enough to provide a depth of character that raises this and other titles in the series a step above merely "funny stories." Primary through middle grades will be intrigued by the Great Brain's solutions to problems. Warning: There may be an unacknowledged G.B. in the audience.

Hans Andersen: His Classic Fairy Tales TRANSLATED BY ERIK HAUGAARD. *Illustrated by Michael Foreman.* New York: Doubleday & Co., 1978.

Suggested Listening Level: Grades 3–8

Hans Christian Andersen's tales have been loved by American children ever since their first translation into English. The best translation available today is by Erik Haugaard, a Dane by birth who has lived in English-speaking countries most of his life and has written fine children's books of his own in English. This volume is a sensitive selection of seventeen of the best tales. It includes the one indispensable tale, "The Ugly Duckling," that every child deserves to hear in its complete and deeply touching form. (Everyone knows the story but often in a watered-down abridgment or a simplified cartoon version.) "The Wild Swans" and "The Tinderbox" are examples of traditional Danish fairy tales retold by Andersen. In "The Swineherd," "The Nightingale," and "The Dung Beetle," we find Andersen poking fun at the foibles of society. Perhaps the most original gift of Andersen, his ability to endow inanimate objects with life and emotions, is displayed in "The Darning Needle" and "The Steadfast Tin Soldier."

Two cautions: Most of Andersen's stories are not intended for or suited to little children. Both the romantic suffering of some tales and the tongue-in-cheek satire of others can be best appreciated by children of eight and up. "The Red Shoes," "The Snow Queen," and "The Little Match Girl" are extremely poignant at times—some would say excessively so—and have been known to haunt sensitive listeners. We recommend reading these yourself before deciding whether to share them with an audience of children.

Harriet Tubman, Conductor on the Underground Railroad BY ANN PETRY. New York: Thomas Y. Crowell, 1955. Paperback: Archway.

Suggested Listening Level: Grades 4–8

Ann Petry has written a first-rate biography about Harriet Tubman, who courageously made her way from slavery to freedom and then chose to make dangerous trips back to Tidewater Maryland to bring North more than three hundred other men, women, and children. Petry's eloquent prose creates a vivid picture of a slaveholding society, of the operation of the Underground Railroad, and of this remarkable woman. The first chapters set the scene; then the events of Harriet Tubman's life, narrated without exaggeration, build suspense and power. The last few pages are inevitably anticlimactic, for they describe the last, somewhat ordinary years of Tubman's life, but this merely sets off the amazing accomplishments of her earlier years.

Each chapter ends with an italicized passage of historical information, helping the listener to relate developments in Harriet's life to the events leading up to the Civil War, and introducing figures that were to play a part in national events or in Harriet's later life. As you read, try to indicate to your listeners the shift from the biographical narrative to this informative material. A few words or perhaps just a slight shift in tone will accomplish this. The book consists of twenty-two chapters of about eleven pages each, and total reading time is estimated at about five hours.

Hatchet BY GARY PAULSEN. New York: Bradbury Press, 1987.

Suggested Listening Level: Grades 6–8

Brian Robeson, emotionally bruised by his parents' recent divorce, is the only passenger in a small plane as he heads north to spend the summer with his dad in the Canadian wilderness. By the end of chapter one, the pilot has had a fatal heart attack. The chapter ends: "He was alone. In the roaring plane with no pilot he was alone. Alone." Needless to say, you'll have no trouble holding your listeners' attention with this novel. Bryan eventually manages to bring the plane down on a lake and to survive in the wild with only his wits and a hatchet for fifty-four days. Spine-crawling adventures alternate with quiet but compelling descriptions of the boy's attempts to devise an effective fish spear, to start a fire, and to build a raft. As Bryan becomes browner and leaner, he changes the way he thinks and feels. He will never be the same, he thinks, and neither will those who hear Brian's story brought to life by a caring reader.

The book has nineteen chapters, but Paulsen writes with great economy. Seven or eight half-hour installments would complete this unusual survival story.

The Haunting BY MARGARET MAHY. New York: Atheneum Publishers, 1982. Paperback: Scholastic.

Suggested Listening Level: Grades 4–8

Eight-year-old Barney's mother died when he was born. Now that he has Claire, his stepmother, to give him a hug when he comes home and help him with his homework, he just wants things to be ordinary. But suddenly he feels himself haunted by a ghost—a ghost who wants to take him away from Claire and his father, and from his two sisters, dark, brooding Troy and irrepressible Tabitha. Gradually, it becomes clear that Barney's "ghost" is alive, and as his story unravels, Barney learns about a family legacy of magical powers that has the potential for great joy or harm.

This story builds suspensefully to a satisfying surprise ending. *The Haunting* combines the best of two genres: mysteries (with a touch of the supernatural) and family stories. Written by a highly respected New Zealand novelist, the novel is skillfully constructed and shows a keen sensitivity to a thoughtful child's everyday worries and perceptions. The story's setting is such that it could be taking place anywhere, and the book contains no words or customs that would confuse American listeners. Total reading time for the book's twelve chapters runs about three and a half hours.

Henry Reed, Inc. BY KEITH ROBERTSON. *Illustrated by Robert McCloskey.* New York: The Viking Press, 1958. Paperback: Dell.

Suggested Listening Level: Grades 5–7

Faced with a summer in Princeton, New Jersey, and an assignment to make notes on "how things are at home" for his teacher at the American School in Naples, Italy, Henry Harris Reed decides to test the possibilities of the free-enterprise system. Working with the aid of neighbor Midge Glass, Henry comes to revise his opinion of females as well as test the endurance of his aunt and uncle, the neighbors, and "the System" itself. His efforts are earnest, logical, usually successful, and always involve at least one bit of outrageous slapstick comedy.

Henry is a serious straight man, a foil for Midge's more imaginative approach to problems. Henry occasionally delivers a rather long-winded digression that some readers may be tempted to condense or skip, but usually he gets an A-plus from listeners. When you finish the book, children may want to go on to read the sequels independently.

The Hobbit or There and Back Again (revised edition) BY J. R. R. TOLKIEN. New York: Houghton Mifflin Co., 1937, 1984.

Suggested Listening Level: Grades 4–8

In a hole in the ground there lived a hobbit. Not a nasty, dirty, wet hole, filled with ends of worms and an oozy smell, nor yet a dry, bare, sandy hole with nothing in it to sit down on or to eat: it was a hobbit-hole, and that means comfort.

Bilbo Baggins is the contented inhabitant of this hobbit-hole. Though Bilbo is devoted to his dinner and domestic comforts, as a hobbit should be, when Gandalf the wizard comes by one morning, Bilbo soon finds himself willy-nilly part of a remarkable adventure. He journeys through great perils with thirteen dwarves to try to recover a vast treasure from the dragon Smaug, and in the process proves that with determination and a stout heart, a rather ordinary being can rise to a heroic occasion.

Tolkien was a professor of Anglo-Saxon at Oxford University and drew on his wide knowledge of British folklore to create a believable world of dwarves, dragons, elves, and orcs. Names that enchant and deftly characterize, an undercurrent of humor, frequent sound effects, and rolling cadences add to the pleasure of reading this fantasy aloud. Each of the nineteen chapters is packed full of action, making this a book that provides reading for several weeks.

The House of Wings BY BETSY BYARS. *Illustrated by Daniel Schwartz.* New York: The Viking Press, 1972. Paperback: Penguin.

Suggested Listening Level: Grades 3–7

Ten-year-old Sammy's parents, on their way from Alabama to Detroit in search of work, have left him with the grandfather he's never known while they go on to find a job and get settled. The boy, enraged at being abandoned, hates this strange old man who lives in a run-down house with a parrot, an owl, and a flock of geese who wander in and out, and the story opens with Sammy's desperate flight through strange countryside with his grandfather in pursuit.

In the midst of the chase, Sammy and his grandfather come upon a wounded crane, and gradually Sammy forgets his hurt and rage in the anxiety they share about the crane's fate. Byars is noted for her portraits of old people and for her ability to delicately depict the bond that many children feel with wild creatures—both gifts contribute to this touching, suspenseful book. The story has its funny moments, too, as Sammy learns how to coexist with the various feathered creatures his grandfather has taken in.

Because the action takes only twenty-four hours, and because it builds to a moving moment of understanding, *The House of Wings* has the gripping intensity of a classic short story. Sammy's life and his grandfather's have been enriched by their first day together. So have ours.

The first of the fourteen chapters is fifteen pages long; most are seven or eight pages and can be read in about eight minutes each. *The Eighteenth Emergency, The Midnight Fox, After the Goat*

Man, The Cartoonist, and *The Night Swimmers* are other books by Betsy Byars that are successful read-alouds.

The House with a Clock in Its Walls BY JOHN BELLAIRS. *Illustrated by Edward Gorey.* New York: The Dial Press, 1973. Paperback: Dell.

Suggested Listening Level: Grades 5–8

The year is 1948. Lewis Barnavelt, a recent orphan, is traveling to his new home and an uncle he's never met. That seems a fairly standard opening for a children's book, but from this point on a zany originality defeats all conventional expectations. Lewis's new home turns out to be a huge, wonderful, and scary Victorian mansion with a mysterious ticking in its walls. Uncle Jonathan welcomes Lewis warmly, but he and his neighbor and cook, Mrs. Zimmerman, engage in all sorts of strange and secretive behavior —and unconventional language. "Weird Beard," "Frumpy," "Brush Mush," and "Hag Face" are only a few of the epithets they affectionately hurl at each other.

Lewis discovers that this pair are a wizard and a witch, and though they practice only benign magic, they are pitted against the evil magic of the house's previous owner. When Lewis himself dabbles in magic to impress a friend, he sets off a chain of events leading to a calamity only he can prevent by finding and destroying the clock in the walls!

The eccentric characters, the paraphernalia of the occult, and the aura of mystery make this a good choice for preadolescents with a taste for the ghoulish. Nostalgic middle-aged readers, on the other hand, will enjoy such memorabilia as Super Suds radio commercials. Reading time is about four hours.

How to Eat Fried Worms BY THOMAS ROCKWELL. *Illustrated by Emily McCully.* New York: Franklin Watts, 1973. Paperback: Dell.

Suggested Listening Level: Grades 3–6

Billy had eaten a lot of things that most kids can't stand: fried liver, salmon loaf, mushrooms, tongue, and pig's feet. But could he really eat one worm a day for fifteen days? Alan and Joe bet that he couldn't. "Heck," said Billy, "I can gag *anything* down for fifty dollars!" Since Alan had to pay the fifty dollars out of accumulated savings, he and Joe try a number of schemes to sidetrack the determined Billy.

There are several debates here about just what's fair in a worm-eating contest. Are night crawlers really worms? (Yes.) Can the worms be chopped or minced? (No.) How *can* they be prepared? (Boiled, stewed, fried, or fricasseed—but all in one piece.) Are worms from a manure pile eligible? (No.) The details are just deliciously yucky enough to intrigue almost any group of young listeners. Total reading time is about an hour and a half, and we recommend breaks after the first, third, fourth, eighth, eleventh, and thirteenth worms for ten- to fifteen-minute sessions. It should be noted that a new librarian began her reading-aloud career with this book and gained a dubious kind of notoriety when one motivated sixth-grade listener brought worms to the school cafeteria and pretended to eat them. One of his friends threw up all over the lunch table, but even the vice-principal had to admit the story was funny.

The Hundred Penny Box BY SHARON BELL MATHIS. *Illustrated by Leo and Diane Dillon.* New York: The Viking Press, 1975.

Suggested Listening Level: Grades 3–6

Michael loves to count the pennies in his great-great-Aunt Dew's hundred penny box—one for every year of her life—while she shares with him her rich memories. But Michael's mother makes them both unhappy when she interrupts their game to make Aunt Dew take a nap. Worse, she wants to burn the hundred penny box because it's shabby and in the way. Only Michael understands how precious the box is to Aunt Dew, and he vows to save it.

This superb story doesn't gloss over the problems of old age:

Aunt Dew's forgetfulness and her tactless ways; her monotonous singing of "Precious Lord, take my hand . . ."; the strains on the family that taking in an aged, infirm relative creates. Yet Aunt Dew's hundred-penny memories evoke a full life, and the empathy between the child and the old woman is drawn with rare skill. Leo and Diane Dillon's sepia-toned illustrations enhance the story's mood.

The contemplative mood of this quiet story can best be communicated in one reading session, which would require thirty to forty minutes.

If You Made a Million BY DAVID M. SCHWARTZ. *Illustrated by Steven Kellogg.* New York: Lothrop, Lee & Shepard Books, 1989.

Suggested Listening Level: Grades 1–5

Old-timers who grumble that "children today don't know the value of money" will love this book. But kids will love it even more, thanks to the whimsical humor of both author and illustrator. Schwartz tells youngsters how high a stack of pennies worth ten dollars would be, how many balloons or stickers a dollar would buy, and explains all about checks, interest, and loans in child-oriented terms. Meanwhile, Marvelosissimo the Magician and his child helpers caper through the pages, embroidering the text with hilarious ministories. Schwartz and Kellogg deserve to have a million readers!

Immigrant Kids BY RUSSELL FREEDMAN. New York: E.P. Dutton, 1980.

Suggested Listening Level: Grades 4–6

"Tell us what it was like when you grew up" is a familiar refrain in most families. School units on immigration and early-twentieth-century United States history also demand such background. Freedman's text is clear and flowing and just detailed enough to intrigue listeners, tempting them into the text that covers topics such as "Coming Over" and describes children and their families at home, school, play, and work. But the real pull here is the combination of text and photographs, many by the noted Jacob Riis and Lewis Hine. The wise teacher will read a chapter or a few pages and pass the book around. For parents, grandparents, aunts, and uncles, this is a book to keep close to family photo albums, or to take to family reunions. *This* is what it was like when grandparents—or perhaps great-grandparents—were kids.

In the Year of the Boar and Jackie Robinson BY BETTE BAO LORD. *Illustrated by Marc Simont.* New York: Harper & Row, Publishers, 1984. Paperback: Harper.

Suggested Listening Level: Grades 3–5

Sixth Cousin is part of a large and busy Chinese household when her engineer father sends money from America for his wife and daughter to join him. Sixth Cousin promptly takes the only American name she knows, and as Shirley Temple Wong sets out for the strange new world of Brooklyn, New York. She gamely tries to adjust, but school is a strange and painful place for Shirley until she is befriended by Mabel, "the tallest and the strongest and the scariest girl" in fifth grade. By the end of the year, Shirley has joined her classmates in passionate rooting for the Brooklyn Dodgers, especially for Jackie Robinson, who, like Shirley, is a rookie that year in a sometimes hostile environment. When Jackie Robinson comes to their school, Shirley is chosen to present to him the key to P.S. 8, and the Year of the Boar turns out to be indeed "a year of double happiness."

This book, based on the author's memories of her own first months in America, is full of humorous and heartwarming incidents that will entertain young audiences. Though listeners may find the Chinese culture described in the book's first chapter strange and a bit confusing, that will serve to waken their sympathy for Shirley's plight as she arrives to confront with courage a world so different from her own.

The book consists of twelve chapters, one for each month of this special year, and is generously illustrated by Marc Simont. Reading time ranges from ten to twenty minutes a chapter.

The Incredible Journey BY SHEILA BURNFORD. Boston: Little, Brown & Co., 1961. Paperback: Bantam.

Suggested Listening Level: Grades 3–8

Three animals—a Siamese cat, an old English bull terrier, and a young golden retriever—lonesome for their old home and human family, set off on a journey of several hundred miles through the wilds of northwest Ontario. Their adventures will keep listeners on the edge of their chairs, but the suspense and danger alternate with touches of humor and warmth. The story is very convincing, true not only to dog and cat nature but to the characteristic behaviors of each breed. In addition, the distinctive and appealing personalities of each animal are quickly established, so that we share the author's obvious affection for them.

The Incredible Journey is an excellent choice for reading aloud to older reluctant readers. They will find the narrative very easy to follow and suspenseful, yet nothing in it suggests "a little kid's book." (As a matter of fact, it was published on the regular adult list and appeared for many weeks on the best-seller list when it came out.) Children as young as seven or eight will enjoy it too, so it would be a good family choice, especially when traveling.

There are eleven chapters. The first one painstakingly describes the region and the scene of comfort and security that the animals will leave behind them. Try to extend the first reading session to include chapter two (this would require about thirty-five minutes total reading time), thus getting the animals on their way before a break in the reading. If this is not possible, ask your listeners to reserve judgment on the story until after the second session.

The Iron Giant: A Story in Five Nights BY TED HUGHES. *Drawings by Robert Nadler.* New York: Harper & Row, Publishers, 1968.

Suggested Listening Level: Grades 2–5

An Iron Giant, taller than a house, comes out of the sea and feasts on the tractors, cars, and barbed-wire fences of the nearby farms. A little boy named Hogarth lures him into a deep pit and the farmers bury him. But the Iron Giant digs his way out. Again the boy has an idea. Why not supply the Giant with scrap metal to feed on? It works and the Iron Giant lives contentedly in a junk-yard. Before the story ends, the Iron Giant has saved the world from a terrible fate by challenging and defeating a frightful monster from outer space.

This strikingly original story is the work of a distinguished English poet, known for his vision of primitive power in the natural world. From a simple, repetitive sentence-structure that would seem tedious in the hands of most writers, Hughes manages to conjure an epic dignity. The simplicity of syntax makes the book accessible to poor readers, especially if they've listened to it first. Here is a way to provide the young superhero fanatics you know with solid food for their imaginations. As the subtitle suggests, this story is best suited to five installments, one a day (or night) if possible.

Island of the Blue Dolphins BY SCOTT O'DELL. New York: Houghton Mifflin Co., 1960. Paperback: Dell.

Suggested Listening Level: Grades 4–6

This survival story, based on a historical event, has been enormously popular with children. The book chronicles the poignant life of Karana, an Indian girl born on an island off the California coast. When Russian and Aleut hunters come and kill many of the tribe, the Indians have no choice but to leave for the mainland. At the time of leaving, however, Karana discovers that her little brother is not on board the ship. She jumps overboard and is left behind with him.

The boy dies soon after this and Karana is alone in a harsh environment. She battles wild dogs, survives a tidal wave and earthquake, and attempts an unsuccessful journey in a dugout canoe to reach the mainland. The growth of her skills and her judgment, her painful wrestling with the taboos of her tribe (taboos that must be broken if she is to survive), and her eventual rescue after eighteen years make engrossing reading.

Narrated in a lucid, understated style, the book is an unflawed masterpiece. It is widely known to be a good book for reading aloud, though, so teachers should inquire in advance if children have already heard it. The twenty-nine chapters are very short—four or five pages in most cases.

Jeremy Visick BY DAVID WISEMAN. Boston: Houghton Mifflin Co., 1981.

Suggested Listening Level: Grades 5–8

Matthew Clemons was as normal as any twelve-year-old boy could be. He liked rugby, got into fights, avoided Sunday visits to Aunt Mabel, and hated history. Then a new master at the school sent the class to investigate the history "all around them." He suggested that they find out what they could about a family named Martin from the tombstone in the local churchyard, but Matthew finds himself strangely drawn to another gravestone, one for the Visick family. This one tells of the death of "Reuben, aged 40 . . . and his sons, Charles Visick, aged 20, and John Visick, aged 17, who were all killed at Wheal Maid on July 21st, 1852, and are all buried here." Below the inscription, almost faded beyond reading, there remained:

> *"And Jeremy Visick, his son*
> *aged 12 years, whose body still lies*
> *in Wheal Maid"*

So begins Matthew's compulsive involvement with Jeremy.

Throughout the spring and early summer, Matthew's knowledge of Jeremy and his family grows. Several nighttime journeys to the graveyard and to the old shed behind his family's cottage reveal ghostly visions of the Visicks as they prepare for their long days in the tin mine known as "Wheal Maid." Matthew becomes more and more intrigued with the family until finally he descends into the mine and begins the final journey with Jeremy through the depths of long-abandoned tunnels.

Cornwall and its nineteenth-century tin-mining industry may be far away from 1980s high technology, but Matthew and Jeremy span the 150 years with little difficulty. For families who still tell stories about great-grandfather or for social studies classes looking at local history, oral tradition, or nineteenth-century industrialization, the story will be a compelling one. Scenes in the early morning haze as the Visicks leave for the mine, Mrs. Visick bending over to kiss her twelve-year-old Jeremy good-bye, the stifling blackness of the tunnel will stay with your listeners long after you've gone on to other books—just as they say the persistent hammering of Cousin Jacks (Cornish miners) echoes at the bottom of a mine anywhere in the world.

The book can be completed in four sessions, but plan for a longer one at the end (chapters fifteen through twenty-three). These last chapters alternate between Matthew and Jeremy's attempts to find a way out of Wheal Maid and the Clemons family's attempt to rescue Matthew. The momentum builds so strongly that neither you nor your audience will want to stop anywhere along the way.

Journey Outside BY MARY Q. STEELE. *Illustrated by Rocco Negri.* New York: Peter Smith, 1984. Paperback: Penguin.

Suggested Listening Level: Grades 5–8

Journey Outside is an entirely original and beautifully executed book. It is the story of Dilar, a young member of the Raft People, who travel a dark underground river to the Better Place, fishing to supply their needs. No one can tell Dilar where they are going or where they have come from. All he can find out is that his grandfather's grandfather had fond memories of "day" and "green"—whatever they may be.

Dilar comes to suspect that his people are merely traveling in an endless circle and, on an impulse, steps from his raft to a ledge, letting the rafts go on without him. To escape the vicious rats that close in on him, Dilar claws his way up the rock walls, accidentally finding his way to the world above ground. His gripping adventures in several very different societies have the suspense of a good yarn and the provocativeness of keen philosophical discussion, for Dilar is searching to answer the eternal question: How should a person live? Children from ten or eleven on are remarkably responsive to such questions; *Journey Outside* will stimulate much thought and discussion.

At the book's end, Dilar is searching for a way back to the underground river so that he can show his people "the light of day and the loveliness of green growing things." Mrs. Steele's eloquent descriptions of this world's marvels—the beauty of grass and trees, of birdsong and snowstorm—will help reader and listeners to experience them anew.

Julie of the Wolves BY JEAN CRAIGHEAD GEORGE. *Illustrated by John Schoenherr*. New York: Harper & Row, Publishers, 1972. Paperback: Harper.

Suggested Listening Level: Grades 6–8

Julie of the Wolves is a remarkable story of survival and of emotional and spiritual growth. Thirteen-year-old Miyax (Julie is her Americanized name) has been left parentless by her father's presumed death. Agreeing to an arranged marriage, she discovers that her husband is retarded, and she runs away when he tries to "mate" her. Before long she is lost on the vast North Slope of Alaska. Starving, she tries to recall the old lore that her father once shared with her, and manages to communicate her needs to a wolf pack. They bring her food, and with her primitive tools and knowledge of the old ways, she constructs a good life even as the Arctic winter closes in. The wolves become her family and the dream of reaching her pen pal in San Francisco, with which she started out, recedes. But the old ways are being eroded by encroaching technology; Amaroq, leader of the pack, is shot by hunters from an airplane. Julie discovers that her father is alive but has apparently given up the ancient values of his people. She must rethink her choices: it is clear that "the hour of the wolf and the Eskimo is over."

Jean George's depiction of the fragile Arctic ecology is more persuasive than any lecture, yet smoothly integrated with the plot. Children will be interested to know that the wolf behavior depicted is based on research that Mrs. George studied and observed. She obviously respects young people's ability to face the difficult issues of our time and to handle complex and challenging fiction.

The book has three parts. It is important for listeners to realize that the second part is a flashback to the circumstances of Miyax's life before she runs away. (By the way, there is nothing explicit in the scene of Daniel's attempting to fulfill the role of husband, and it should not be embarrassing to read or hear. The scene cannot be skipped, for it explains why Julie leaves home.)

My Side of the Mountain is another popular novel by Jean George; she has written distinguished nonfiction for children as well.

Jumanji WRITTEN AND ILLUSTRATED BY CHRIS VAN ALLSBURG. Boston: Houghton Mifflin Co., 1981.

Suggested Listening Level: Grades 2–6

Warned to keep the house neat while their parents are at the opera, two imaginative youngsters begin a board game they've found in the park. In the instructions is a warning that once begun, the game will not end until a player reaches the golden city of Jumanji. As the pieces move, the two find themselves confronted by a lion, monkeys, a monsoon, sleeping sickness, rampaging rhinos, a python, a volcano, and . . . *Jumanji.*

This and other Van Allsburg picture books captivate listeners and viewers alike. Here the Caldecott award–winning black-and-white pencil drawings juxtapose the mysterious jungle with the most common household objects, a python curled around the mantel clock, for instance. Sharply delineated text and illustrations fascinate all audiences but are particularily successful with fourth and fifth grades. *The Garden of Abdul Gasazi* and Van Allsburg's second Caldecott book, *The Polar Express,* are also successful picture book read-alouds for older listeners. Try *The Mysteries of Harris Burdick* for creative writing classes up through senior high. As for *Jumanji,* we know fifth-graders who want to know where to buy the game.

Jump! The Adventures of Brer Rabbit BY JOEL CHANDLER HARRIS. ADAPTED BY VAN DYKE PARKS AND MALCOLM JONES. *Illustrated by Barry Moser.* San Diego and New York: Harcourt Brace Jovanovich, 1986.

Suggested Listening Level: Grades 1–5

The timeless animal stories brought to the Western hemisphere by African slaves, told and retold through the generations, were available in our childhood only with the difficult-to-read dialect and the compromising frame of Joel Chandler Harris's Uncle Remus. Parks and Jones have done everyone a service by choosing the best of the tales for this collection and its sequels, and retelling them without these drawbacks and with great skill and liveliness. The happy result is that today's children can revel in these wise and witty tales of "pluck and cleverness triumphing over brute strength." Barry Moser's stunning watercolor illustrations greatly enrich the volume, providing a feast for young and not-so-young eyes.

Just So Stories BY RUDYARD KIPLING. 1902. Many editions.

Suggested Listening Level: Grades 3–7

Before the High and Far-Off Times, O my Best Beloved, came the Time of the Very Beginnings; and that was in the days when the Eldest Magician was getting Things ready. First he got the Earth ready; then he got the Sea ready; and then he told all the Animals that they could come out and play.

Kipling's prose, larded with unusual and invented words, flows with a rhythm and a rollicking sense of language that set these stories as examples worth promoting in these days of diminishing articulateness. Each tale may be read independently and each is an explanation of the origin of something: how the camel got his hump, the rhinoceros his skin, the elephant his trunk. Two of them deal with the origin of the alphabet and of letter-writing, but the alphabet story is less appropriate for reading aloud because it relies on line drawings for clarification of the text.

These stories can be understood by children as young as five yet will be appreciated by older listeners, including adults. It should be noted, however, that Kipling was a Victorian gentleman and suffered from delusions of both male supremacy and white superiority. These assumptions are evident in many of the tales.

The Kite Song BY MARGERY EVERNDEN. *Decorations by Cindy Wheeler.* New York: Lothrop, Lee & Shepard Books, 1984.

Suggested Listening Level: Grades 4–6

This story of Jamie, a silent, fearful child who cannot learn to read, begins painfully with the discovery of his impoverished mother's death. Jamie's grown stepbrother Ron willingly takes him in, but life isn't easy in this working-class family living on the brink of desperation. Ron Hovanec has lost his job and can barely support his wife and two babies on irregular window-washing jobs. He has taken in another stray, too—Cousin Clem, a Vietnam vet and poet who paused in his wanderings to visit and stays on because he sees that he can help Jamie.

A very special school of caring teachers and other children with impairments helps Jamie out of his misery. A poem of Clem's, plus the buoyant demands of a mute child, Jamie's first friend, lead him to the discovery that he can read after all. Though Clem must move on and life will continue to be difficult, Jamie has shed his silence and his undeserved guilt. The red kite Clem flies is a moving symbol of the appealing protagonist's potential.

Evernden sometimes gives us Jamie's thoughts in italics, without stating "he thought." You will occasionally have to insert those words so that the listener knows that other characters can't hear certain sentences. The eighteen short chapters average ten pages and require approximately twelve minutes of reading time each.

The Knee-High Man and Other Tales BY JULIUS LESTER. *Illustrated by Ralph Pinto.* New York: The Dial Press, 1972. Paperback: Dial.

Suggested Listening Level: Grades K–5

In the first of these trickster tales, Mr. Bear remarks that he doesn't know what trouble is. Mr. Rabbit, of course, obligingly sets right out to teach him. The book consists of six short tales based on American black folklore. "Some are funny and some are sad," the author points out, but all are good stories.

The reading time is about five minutes for each tale, and they are suitable for any age group. Those who find the dialect of Joel Chandler Harris's Uncle Remus stories troublesome will be grateful to Mr. Lester for making more accessible these tales about Mr. Rabbit, one of folklore's liveliest characters.

Koko's Kitten BY DR. FRANCINE PATTERSON. *Photographs by Dr. Ronald H. Cohn.* New York: Scholastic, 1985.

Suggested Listening Level: Grades 2–6

In 1972, a graduate student named Francine Patterson gained permission to attempt to teach a baby gorilla sign language. She has been working with Koko ever since. This fascinating book chronicles in words and photographs one aspect of Koko's life that is bound to interest children: her longing for a cat and the relationship between Koko and the kitten that was given to her. When Koko, who has a five-hundred-word vocabulary in sign language, was asked what she wanted for her birthday, she signed "cat." Patterson was not surprised—Koko loved hearing her read "Puss in Boots" and "The Three Little Kittens." When Koko finally got her kitten, she carried it around like a baby gorilla, played games with it, and was very happy—even when the kitten went too far. ("Cat bite. Obnoxious," Koko once signed.) The cat's eventual death caused Koko much grief, but the book ends on a happier note, as the last photo shows another kitten snuggling in Koko's lap.

The book does a good job of presenting for children a sense of the interesting work that has been going on in human-primate communication, while also telling well a simple and touching story. The book requires twenty minutes to read aloud and is best presented without a break. Be sure to begin with the preface.

The Lemming Condition BY ALAN ARKIN. *Illustrated by Joan Sandin.* New York: Harper & Row, Publishers, 1976.

Suggested Listening Level: Grades 4–8

All around Bubber his fellow lemmings are bustling about in excitement preparing to go west. Bubber expects to go too, until his friend Crow reminds him of the ocean that lies at the foot of the cliffs to the west and asks if lemmings can swim. Once Bubber begins to question the wisdom of the mass suicide that is the lemming condition, he becomes an outsider. Instead of the acceptance and feeling of solidarity shared by all the other lemmings, Bubber is full of anxiety and despair. When the lemmings begin running, Bubber is swept along. Only at the last moment does he find the strength to resist.

Alan Arkin, distinguished actor and director, is a talented writer as well. His ability to develop character and plot with no words wasted gives this little book considerable impact. Children will like the comical interchanges between Bubber and the other sharply drawn characters, but will be receptive as well to the underlying parable. The book's six chapters can be read aloud in approximately one hour.

The Light Princess BY GEORGE MACDONALD. *Illustrated by Maurice Sendak.* New York: Farrar, Straus & Giroux, 1977. Paperback: Farrar, Straus & Giroux.

Suggested Listening Level: Grades 4–8

Imagine losing your gravity—being not only light-bodied but light-minded! A princess who floats out of the hands of nurse-maids, tutors, and parents is bad enough, but one who laughs immoderately when the enemy threatens her father's city is intolerable. The king and queen know she has been enchanted by the king's sister, the Princess Makemnoit, and they discover that only in the water of the nearby lake does the princess have any real freedom. Philosophers Hum-Drum and Kopy-Keck finally decide that if external water is efficacious, then "water from a deeper source might work a perfect cure; in short, that if the poor afflicted princess could by any means be made to cry, she might recover her lost gravity."

Enchantments, a giggling princess, a fine, fair prince, pompous philosophers—these elements of traditional lore have been whipped into an elegant froth of a tale for sophisticated listeners. MacDonald's touches of farce offer an experienced reader opportunity to rant and rave as the Princess Makemnoit (sour, spiteful creature that she is); to wave a finger portentously as a metaphysical philosopher; or to giggle with the heroine, the de*light*ful princess.

Sendak's drawings are dolefully droll and should be shared with an audience after each reading. The book can be read two or three chapters at a time and completed in less than two hours.

Linnea in Monet's Garden BY CHRISTINA BJORK. *Illustrated by Lena Anderson.* New York: Farrar, Straus & Giroux, 1987.

Suggested Listening Level: Grades 2–8

This original, entirely charming book consists of a fictitious child's travel journal, illustrated by a combination of watercolor sketches and photographs. Linnea, in whose voice the story is told, is a Swedish child with a passion for "everything that grows." Through an elderly neighbor and retired gardener, Mr. Bloom, she learns of painter Claude Monet's magnificent gardens, which have been restored and opened to the public. The two of them use their savings to travel to France, where they seek out Monet canvases in museums and then visit Monet's home and gardens. This sounds tame perhaps, but Linea's excitement is catching as she learns about impressionism and the poignant details of Monet's life. She also stands on the famous Japanese bridge overlooking Monet's treasured waterlilies and even meets a descendant of the painter.

Sketches of Linnea and Mr. Bloom are mingled with actual photographs of the artist and his family, and of his paintings and gardens. This is a book for lingering over and scrutinizing, so it would not be effective as a group read-aloud. It is tailor-made, however, for a grandparent who loves gardens or paintings to share with a grandchild.

The Lion, the Witch and the Wardrobe BY C. S. LEWIS. *Illustrated by Pauline Baynes.* New York: Macmillan Publishing Co., 1968. Paperback: Macmillan.

Suggested Listening Level: Grades 3–8

Four children have been evacuated during the London blitz to the huge old country house of an elderly professor. During a rainy-day indoor game of hide-and-seek, the youngest, Lucy, shuts herself in a large wardrobe among the fur coats. Discovering that the wardrobe has no back wall, she makes her way deeper into it and finds herself in Narnia, an unhappy land where, thanks to the evil White Witch, it is "always winter and never Christmas." With much difficulty, Lucy persuades her older siblings of the existence of Narnia and of the part they are destined to play in the restoration of the true ruler of Narnia, Aslan the Lion.

The realistic interaction among the four children is as skillfully drawn as the fantastic Talking Animals, fauns, and giants who people Narnia. Together they make this and its sequels one of the best-loved fantasies in all of children's literature.

Lewis intended *The Chronicles of Narnia* as Christian allegory, but children of all faiths respond to the compelling events and images on their own terms. The seventeen chapters each require about ten minutes reading time.

Little House in the Big Woods BY LAURA INGALLS WILDER. *Illustrated by Garth Williams.* New York: Harper & Row, Publishers, 1953. Paperback: Harper.

Suggested Listening Level: Grades K–3

Many a family now grown up looks back on the reading aloud of the "Little House" books as a treasured memory of family life. The eight books in the series* are a skillfully fictionalized account of Mrs. Wilder's childhood in a pioneering family that moved from one place to another, struggling to survive in a lovely yet often inhospitable wilderness. Each scene and event is shown through the eyes of Laura, a wonderfully lively and sensitive heroine. Mrs. Wilder was in her sixties when she began writing books, and it is remarkable how convincingly she was able to capture the perceptions of a young child. In *Little House in the Big Woods,* the first book, Laura is four and five years old; later books record her growing up, ending with marriage at eighteen to Almanzo Wilder. (*Farmer Boy* is not about the Ingalls family, but describes Almanzo's childhood on a prosperous farm in upstate New York.)

To the adult, the books are a fascinating chronicle of nineteenth-century child-rearing, a critique of the doctrine of Manifest Destiny (especially *Little House on the Prairie*), and a tribute to the courage and endurance of the western pioneers. To the child, they are exciting adventure stories and sensitive renderings of childhood experiences. Children are fascinated by how different Laura's life is from their own: Laura encounters a bear in the cow pen, Indians on the warpath, and a plague of locusts. Furthermore, she is ecstatic when Santa brings her a tin cup of her own and a whole penny! Yet today's children find Laura just like them-

* A ninth volume, *The First Four Years,* has been marketed with the series, but it was published from a manuscript found after Mrs. Wilder's death. She did not intend it as part of the series, probably because it chronicled an unremitting series of disasters in the early years of the Wilder marriage, and it does not read well aloud.

selves in many ways—they have experienced her feelings of mixed delight and terror when her daddy plays at being a "mad dog," and her fierce jealousy of sister Mary's blond hair.

The books are now established classics of children's literature and are part of the literary heritage of every American. Though they depict a somewhat idealized family, they are much less sentimental and more original than the television series that has been loosely—very loosely—based on them. *Little House in the Big Woods* consists of thirteen short chapters. The sequels become gradually longer and more complex in style, as they in effect grow up with Laura.

M.C. Higgins, the Great BY VIRGINIA HAMILTON. New York: Macmillan Publishing Co., 1974.

Suggested Listening Level: Grades 7–8

M.C. Higgins sits on top of his pole, high above the treetops where he can see all over the mountain—Sarah's Mountain, named for his great-grandmother who came here long ago fleeing slavery. He sees the thick woods and the lake and, above his family's home, the ugly spoil-heap of the strip mine.

M.C. is a black boy fast growing to manhood and all that it entails. For one thing, he can't stop thinking about the city girl who is camping by the lake. For another, he finds himself in combat with the father he loves, not only in their fierce wrestling, but in other ways. Jones Higgins forbids his son to associate with Ben Killburn or any of his "witchy" family. But M.C. cannot give up his friend. Even more serious is their disagreement over the spoil heap. M.C. believes it will slide down and kill them all; he tries to persuade his father that they must leave. But Jones's mind is closed. Sarah's Mountain is their place.

M.C. then works out his own plan. He'll bring home the dude who has been traveling over the mountains recording singers' voices. When he hears M.C.'s mother sing, he'll make a star out of her and they'll have enough money to move. Nothing works out quite as M.C. wants, but he comes to understand that the family's heritage binds them to the mountain. And Jones, overcoming old superstitions, accepts Ben.

Those who want the meaning of every act and image in a book to be crystal-clear may find Virginia Hamilton's work difficult. Symbols and images that cannot be readily explicated are central to her vision of life. The meaning of the work emerges gradually. Encourage your listeners to approach the book as they would poetry and they will find it a powerful experience.

The book's fourteen chapters are long, averaging about thirty minutes each when read aloud.

The People Could Fly: American Black Folktales offers a rich collection of twenty-four stories representing the main body of black folklore. They are divided into four sections: animal stories; "the real, extravagant, and fanciful"; tales of the supernatural; and slave tales of freedom, which includes the evocative, haunting title story. Black-and-white drawings by Leo and Diane Dillon enhance the stories, making this a truly beautiful book. Most important of all, however, is the vitality of the language and tales themselves. As Hamilton says in the Introduction:

> Remember that these folktales were once a creative way for an oppressed people to express their fears and hopes to one another. They lend themselves well to being read out loud, as they were told out loud so long ago. They can be enjoyed by young and old alike.

The Macmillan Book of Greek Gods and Heroes BY ALICE LOW. *Illustrated by Arvis Stewart.* New York: Macmillan Publishing Co., 1985.

Suggested Listening Level: Grades 4–8

In this volume, Alice Low has retold the major Greek myths and hero tales concisely, clearly, and with impressive narrative drive. Her story of the Trojan war distills a few episodes of Homer's epic without slighting their pathos and excitement; the figures of

Daedalus, Persephone, Prometheus, and many others will fire the imagination of young readers—provided you allow them to become absorbed in these tales as adventure, not as material for quizzes. Those who appreciate beauty will want to linger over this collection, for the publisher has taken pains to make it as handsome a volume as possible. Generous white space, attractive typefaces, and frequent full-color illustrations, suggestive of Aegean art, attract the eye. When our copy was discovered by a book-loving nine-year-old, he became totally absorbed by it, in spite of the noisy play that swirled around him. Over thirty stories of varying length are included here. Whether read in sequence over several days or weeks, or dipped into occasionally, the narratives are an excellent introduction to the culture, the beliefs, and the legendary history of a great civilization.

Many Moons BY JAMES THURBER. *Illustrated by Marc Simont.* New York: Harcourt Brace & World, 1943, 1970, 1990. Paperback: Harcourt Brace.

Suggested Listening Level: Grades K–4

"Anything your heart desires" is what the King promises his daughter, the Princess Lenore. "I want the moon," she says. So the King asks, in turn, the Lord High Chamberlain, the Royal Wizard, and the Royal Mathematician, but although they produce prodigious lists ranging from ambergris to wolfbane, none can get the moon. It is the Court Jester who suggests that the Princess Lenore be consulted about the size and distance of the moon, and it is the Court Jester and Princess Lenore—and the moon—who solve the problem of one moon too many.

Many of Thurber's writings make good reading aloud, from the hilarity of allegedly autobiographical essays like "The Night the Bed Fell" and "University Days" in *My Life and Hard Times* to the mock fairy tale of *The Thirteen Clocks,* with its tongue-tangling witticisms. *Many Moons,* however, is so good for a wide audience range, for a one-session book, and for its very matter-of-fact, no-nonsense princess that it just had to be included. The story stands on its own, although the illustrations give it the appearance of a picture book. The beginning reader will want to practice this a bit, as the lists produced by the Royal Consultants need to flow "trippingly" off the tongue. It is not difficult, however, and can be enjoyed by primary grades through fourth or fifth in one twenty-minute session.

Martin Luther King, Jr. (An Impact Biography) BY JACQUELINE HARRIS. Danbury, Conn.: Franklin Watts, 1983.

Suggested Listening Level: Grades 4–6

By starting with the bus boycott in December 1955 and then flashing back to the jubilation of the King family at the birth of the baby Martin, listeners who were born long after the death of this remarkable man will have a context for the dramatic events of his life. Each chapter highlights a specific event or series of events: the Montgomery bus boycott; early influences of family and teachers; the formation of the Southern Christian Leadership Conference and growing political concern; Birmingham; the march on Washington; King's death in Memphis. Dr. King's involvement in civil rights activities in the South is the focal point of these seven chapters, but his worry and concern over unemployment and injustice in all parts of the country are also presented. His growing dismay at the fragmentation of black leadership and his own lack of success with embittered segments of the black community are not slighted.

The drama of the events surrounding Dr. King's efforts to promote nonviolent change will catch the attention of youngsters whose ideas of heroism are confined to playing fields or television cartoons. The seven chapters can be read in six sessions, combining the last two chapters. Don't relegate this one to Black History Month or Dr. King's birthday.

Mary Poppins (revised edition) BY PAMELA L. TRAVERS. *Illustrated by Mary Shepard.* New York: Harcourt Brace Jovanovich, 1981. Paperback: Harcourt Brace Jovanovich (revised edition).

Suggested Listening Level: Grades 2–4

Most children know Mary Poppins from the well-loved film. But they should be introduced to the sharp-tongued, straitlaced Mary Poppins of Pamela Travers's book, for she possesses some special magic that no filmmaker has yet captured. Some children may resist, feeling they know "the best parts" from the movie. Do insist. The conversations between the babies and the "cheeky Starling," for instance, or the Dancing Cow's story—told in her own words—are too good to miss.

We would suggest, however, that the reader who is using the original edition omit the chapter "Bad Tuesday." There is no plot element here on which future action depends, and the stereotyped roles assigned to the characters from the four corners of the world are offensive to all. Fortunately, in the revised edition this chapter has been rewritten to eliminate the objectionable stereotyping.

The book can be read in about three hours. They will be three hours well spent, for Mary Poppins is one of those rare characters in literature who remains unforgettable . . . no matter which way the wind blows.

Misty of Chincoteague BY MARGUERITE HENRY. *Illustrated by Wesley Dennis.* Chicago: Rand McNally & Co., 1947. Paperback: Rand McNally.

Suggested Listening Level: Grades 3–5

"Legends be the only stories as is true!" explains Grandpa Beebe to Maureen and Paul. Some on Chincoteague Island would say it was only a legend that the wild horses on nearby Assateague were descendants of a stallion and his mares from a Spanish ship that went down in a gale. The two children care less about legends than the horses themselves, in particular a mare named Phantom. At the annual Pony Penning Day, they use hard-earned savings to buy Phantom and her new silver-and-gold colt, Misty. Phantom, "like a piece of thistledown borne by the wind, moving through space with wild abandon," wins the race with Black Comet. Later, Phantom is lured back to the wild freedom of Assateague by the stallion the Pied Piper, but by then Misty is old enough to live with the children and their grandparents quite happily as the center of attention.

The story of Phantom and Misty, as well as the stories of Misty's offspring *Sea Star* and *Stormy*, revolve around the traditional Pony Penning Days on the two islands off the Virginia coast. A good story for middle-grade animal-lovers, *Misty of Chincoteague* divides into about nine twenty-minute sessions.

The Moffats BY ELEANOR ESTES. *Illustrated by Louis Slobodkin.* New York: Harcourt Brace & World, 1941, 1968. Paperback: Harcourt Brace Jovanovich.

Suggested Listening Level: Grades 1–4

The Moffats was published over forty years ago, and it had a backward-looking "olden days" charm about it even then. This is small-town America in the days of horse-drawn wagons and coal-yards, but children today will discover that they have much in common with the four Moffat children. All the joys and worries of childhood are deftly captured: Joe's despair when he discovers he has lost the money Mama gave him for coal; the children's terror at the ghost that they set up themselves to scare the boastful Peter Frost; and Jane's relief at discovering that the Chief of Police isn't looking for reasons to arrest a little girl—he's even nice! The fatherless family is poor and can scarcely eke out an existence on Mama's dressmaking money until the next customer pays her, but humor and a sense of loving security predominate, which makes it a good choice for the primary grades.

Each chapter is a complete and satisfying episode—twelve in all. There are two other Moffat books, for those who have enjoyed this one: *Rufus M.* and *The Middle Moffat. Ginger Pye* is another of Estes' books that is still popular with children. In *The Hundred Dresses,* Estes strikes a more serious note; it captures the misery a group of children can inflict on a child who is different.

Mom Can't See Me BY SALLY HOBART ALEXANDER. *Photographs by George Ancona.* Macmillan Publishing Co., 1990.

Suggested Listening Level: Grades 1–4

So often books about disabled people are "good for you." This one about a blind mother is much more than that. Told in the voice of her nine-year-old daughter, Leslie, Alexander's story is down to earth, practical, and touching. It treats realistically a child's fear that disabilities might be passed on and extends our knowledge of how individuals can live with determination, a sense of humor, and courage. Alexander's lucid prose is complemented not only by the sensitive black-and-white photographs of Ancona but also by the careful design of the book.

More Stories Julian Tells BY ANN CAMERON. *Illustrated by Ann Strugnell.* New York: Alfred A. Knopf, 1986. Paperback: Knopf.

Suggested Listening Level: Grades K–2

Though one can now find a fair number of picture books and more than a few novels for older children about African Americans, short-chapter books for primary-grade children about this cultural group are in short supply. Ann Cameron's low-key, engaging stories about Julian and his family begin to fill this gap. *More Stories Julian Tells* is our favorite because it captures so well the small crises that occur in every family, like what happened when Julian called his little brother Huey a scaredy-cat. Huey's resulting fall when he tries to jump from the top bunk brings a response from the boys' father that Julian doesn't expect. This book could be read in five short sessions or one long one.

The same author has written a moving book about a small Guatemalan boy, abandoned by his parents but cared for with love by his hard-working grandmother. *The Most Beautiful Place in the World* provides valuable insights into what life is like in a poor country.

The Mouse and His Child BY RUSSELL HOBAN. *Illustrated by Lillian Hoban.* New York: Harper & Row, Publishers, 1967. Paperback: Avon.

Suggested Listening Level: Grades 4–8

On a toy-store counter a clockwork mouse turns around and around, swinging his child up and down by the arms as he circles. The mouse-child wants to stay forever in the cozy store, but "one does what one is wound to do"; their fate as toys is to be bought and go out into the world. They are soon broken and discarded, but a tramp repairs them, winds them, and sets them down in the road. "Be tramps," he says, and walks away.

The journey that follows, like most odysseys, is a search for a place in the world and for family. Listeners will be as caught up in the fate of these tin figures and the animals they meet as in the most realistic adventure story. At the same time, the encounters of the mouse and his child with ruthless rat criminals, forest mob violence, and a senseless war between bands of shrews will be thought-provoking for listeners of all ages. Don't expect the gentle and endearing mood of many toy fantasies. Much of this one is closer to Orwell's *Animal Farm* than to *Winnie-the-Pooh.* But the perils do give way to justice and contentment at the end.

Russell Hoban has written classic picture books (such as *Bedtime for Frances*) and highly acclaimed novels for adults (*Riddley Walker,* for instance). He pays children the compliment of using some challenging words and disturbing ideas in this book. We especially recommend it for gifted children and for young adolescents beginning to question the ways of the world. The book is divided into ten episodic chapters.

The Mousewife BY RUMER GODDEN. *Illustrated by Heidi Holder.* New York: The Viking Press, 1982.

Suggested Listening Level: Grades 2–7

Once a little mousewife befriended a dove caged in Miss Barbara

Wilkinson's parlor. Whenever she could snatch a moment from her nest-making and crumb-collecting, she visited the dejected bird. From him, she learned about flying free above the treetops and how the wind made different patterns in cornfields and how dew tasted in the early morning. She finally realized that the dove needed to be out in the world, so one night she released the lock and he escaped through an open window. The mousewife sadly wonders who will tell her now about the great world outside. But then she sees the stars. . . .

This quiet, gentle story catches the essence of a master writer as the mousewife shares the dreams of the dove to soar beyond a cage, to know the stars. So many of this author's works are successful when read aloud—from her doll stories like *Impunity Jane* to the novel *Episode of Sparrows*—but somehow this "different" mousewife is most memorable. The story can be read in one sitting.

Mr. Popper's Penguins BY RICHARD AND FLORENCE ATWATER. *Illustrated by Robert Lawson.* Boston: Little, Brown & Co., 1938. Paperback: Dell.

Suggested Listening Level: Grades K–3

Mr. Popper was a dreamer. A rather untidy, forgetful housepainter, he was destined to become the most famous person in Stillwater, for Mr. Popper dreamed of faraway places like the Antarctic. Because of his interest in an expedition to the South Pole, Mr. Popper and his family receive a penguin named Captain Cook. They find, however, that penguins are social creatures—and Captain Cook is lonely. So Greta arrives to keep the Captain company and eventually the Popper family expands to include twelve sociable penguins.

The ordinary, even prosaic, qualities of the Popper family and their town of Stillwater are wonderful contrasts to Mr. Popper's acceptance of the penguins and their antics. The chapters are short enough to be read in five to ten minutes if a group gets wiggly, but a twenty-minutes session will hold most listeners. This story with Robert Lawson's drawings is a surefire choice for primary grades, especially second- and third-graders, or as a first longer story for kindergarten or first grade.

Mrs. Frisby and the Rats of NIMH BY ROBERT C. O'BRIEN. *Illustrated by Zena Bernstein.* New York: Atheneum Publishers, 1971. Paperback: Atheneum.

Suggested Listening Level: Grades 4–7

Mrs. Frisby is at her wit's end. The fieldmouse widow and mother has a sick son and needs help in moving him out of the way of spring planting. As a last resort she consults the rats under the rose bush and finds there an unexpectedly sophisticated civilization. It turns out that the rats and Mr. Frisby had been part of an experimental group at the National Institute of Mental Health (NIMH), and the series of injections that they got not only enhanced their mental abilities but prolonged their life span.

"By teaching us how to read, they taught us how to get away," explains Nicodemus, leader of the rats of NIMH, to Mrs. Frisby. Now, five years after they escaped from NIMH, the group is working on the Plan, a long-range scheme for survival that won't involve stealing as a way of life.

Mrs. Frisby's own courage and initiative are supplemented by the rats' help, and her problem is resolved. The success of the rats' noble experiment is still in doubt, however, when the book ends. Thought-provoking and engrossing, the story is just plausible enough to spark stimulating discussions by fifth- and sixth-grade listeners. This surefire novel is also suitable for a wide age range of listeners because it operates on many levels, and the twenty-eight chapters combine into approximately fourteen twenty-minute sessions.

My Father's Dragon BY RUTH STILES GANNETT. *Illustrated by Ruth Chrisman Gannett.* New York: Random House, 1948.

Suggested Listening Level: Grades K–4

Does your father tell tall tales? One father told his child about his rescue of a dragon from Wild Island where lazy animals kept it prisoner. It seems that the dragon (a baby about the size of a large bear, with a long tail, yellow and blue stripes, gold wings, and bright red eyes and horn) was required to fly those lazy animals across the river that nearly split Wild Island in two. So the child's father set off to befuddle the lazy animals, rescue that baby dragon, and fly away home.

Stuff and nonsense? Of course, but it is so absurd and so full of colorful detail that younger audiences are captured just as surely as the baby dragon was. We have found that tall tales are sometimes over the heads of children under eight or nine, but images of a lion with seven different-colored hair ribbons in his mane (because his mother hates messy manes) or seventeen crocodiles tail-to-tail as a bridge across the river, or tigers chewing gum until it turns green enough to plant, are vivid enough to convince even younger listeners that this is funny. The ten chapters can be read in about an hour and a half, and the adventures of the dragon and the narrator's father continue in *The Dragons of Blueland*.

Over Sea, Under Stone BY SUSAN COOPER. *Illustrated by Margery Gill.* New York: Harcourt Brace & World, 1966. Paperback: Harcourt Brace Jovanovich.

Suggested Listening Level: Grades 4–7

The Drew children, Simon, Jane, and Barney, discover an ancient manuscript in the attic of their summer home in Cornwall, and find themselves thereby drawn into a life-and-death struggle. The narrative is both a classic mystery story in which the children race into and out of heart-stopping dangers as they try to get the treasure before the bad guys do, and, on another level, the lofty and perilous quest for the Grail itself—King Arthur's legacy to the forces of Light in their eternal battle against the Dark. The staunch figure of Great-uncle Merry, university professor and world authority on Arthurian matters, plays an important part in guiding and occasionally rescuing the children in their quest.

A few minor characters speak a Cornish dialect; we recommend trying out a few of these lines in advance to determine whether you want to attempt the accent or ignore it. Susan Cooper has written four more books that carry on the battle of the Light versus the Dark; none of these is as firmly rooted in a realistic narrative as this one, however. Written in the mode of "high fantasy," they are increasingly dominated by the marvels of ancient folklore.

It should be noted that Jane is, in this first book, a rather stereotyped female, very much in the shadow of her more heroic brothers. In the third volume of the series, *Greenwitch*, she takes the central role.

For younger listeners try *The Silver Cow*, a picture book retelling of an old Welsh tale. Gwilym Hughes, "with a heart as small and mean as his black beady eyes," loses cows, coins, and even his son because of his selfishness. Cooper's way with words and thorough knowledge of Welsh tales provides an ideal introduction to longer and more complex stories of any culture.

Owls in the Family BY FARLEY MOWAT. *Illustrated by Robert Frankenberg*. Boston: Atlantic–Little, Brown, 1961. Paperback: Bantam.

Suggested Listening Level: Grades 3–6

Billy already had a few pets when he approached his parents about keeping an owl blown out of its nest after a heavy windstorm. There were about thirty gophers snared on the Saskatchewan prairie with the help of Bruce and Murray, and rats from the medical school where Murray's father was a professor (no one was quite sure how many because they kept having babies so fast), a box of garter snakes under the back porch, and pigeons—about ten of them, but they kept bringing friends and relations for visits. And Mutt, of course, but he wasn't just a dog—he was family. So an owl didn't seem so overwhelming when one thought about it. Later, when Wol was joined by a timid, bedraggled second owl named Weeps, the menagerie was complete. But life with owls and rats and gophers and pigeons and snakes was not calm, and

Billy had a difficult time keeping animals and humans separate and happy.

This first-person account based on the author's Canadian childhood is a perfect choice for third- through sixth-grade classes restless with the lure of spring and the itch to be outside. The episodic chapters are "knee-slappers" and the action is fast-paced, taking approximately two and a half hours reading time. Slightly older children find Mowat's adventure novels, such as *Lost in the Barrens*, totally engrossing.

Ozma of Oz BY L. FRANK BAUM. *Illustrated by John R. Neill.* Chicago: The Reilly and Lee Co., 1907. (Out of print) Paperback: Ballantine.

Suggested Listening Level: Grades 2–5

Why do we suggest *Ozma of Oz* rather than Baum's first and best-known book, *The Wizard of Oz*? Because nearly all American children are well acquainted with the film version of *The Wizard of Oz* from its annual television screenings; because we, like most other critics, think that the film improves upon the book, which is therefore likely to prove a disappointment; and because we believe that Baum had not yet perfected his craft when he wrote *The Wizard of Oz*. *Ozma of Oz* seems to us a better book. In particular, it reads aloud better.

In this book children will find Dorothy reunited with her dear friends from Oz: the Scarecrow, the Tin Woodman, and the Cowardly Lion. And she has acquired amusing new friends—Billina, a talking hen of strong opinions and quick wits; Tiktok, a mechanical man who serves Dorothy devotedly; and the capable and gracious Ozma, girl ruler of Oz. From the storm at sea in chapter one that blows Dorothy and Billina overboard, to the successful rescue of the Queen of Ev and her ten children from the diabolically clever enchantments of the Nome King, the listener's interest never flags. Dorothy is as appealing as ever—open, brave, and self-assured. When a princess commands haughtily: "Tell me, . . . are you of royal blood?" our heroine replies, "Better than that, ma'am, . . . I came from Kansas."

Our only caution for readers-aloud is that Baum describes the mechanical man's words as "uttered all in the same tone, without any change of expression." Most listeners cannot make sense out of expressionless words, and besides, it is tiresome to read without inflection for long. We recommend, therefore, that you make Tiktok's speech only slightly mechanical.

The Peppermint Pig BY NINA BAWDEN. Philadelphia: J. B. Lippincott Co., 1975. Paperback: Penguin.

Suggested Listening Level: Grades 4–8

Looking for an opening that will grab kids' attention? Try this one:

> Old Granny Greengrass had her finger chopped off in the butcher's when she was buying half a leg of lamb. She had pointed to the place where she wanted her joint to be cut but then she decided she needed a bigger piece and pointed again. Unfortunately, Mr. Grummett, the butcher, was already bringing his sharp chopper down. He chopped straight through her finger and it flew like a snapped twig into a pile of sawdust in the corner of the shop. It was hard to tell who was more surprised, Granny Greengrass, or the butcher. But she didn't blame him. She said, "I could never make up my mind and stick to it, Mr. Grummett, that's always been my trouble."

Poll, nine, and Theo, ten and a half, love to hear their mother tell this old family story. Big brother George says they're partial to bloodthirsty stories because their own lives are so snug and comfortable. Before long, though, their comfortable life is behind them. Their father confesses to a theft he didn't commit, loses his job, and goes away to America to make his fortune. While he's gone, the rest of the family must leave London to live with their father's sisters in a Norfolk village. For Poll, it is a wonderful and terrible year. The best thing in it is Johnnie, a runt pig who becomes an adored pet with the run of the household. But the inevitable slaughter of Johnnie, and Poll's growing certainty that her father will never return, are a part of the year too. Poll, feisty and sensitive, makes this coming-of-age novel one that appeals to children and adults, boys and girls. The story is so universal that the few unfamiliar British words and phrases provide flavor without offering any real difficulty. The book consists of nine chapters, each about thirty minutes long.

Peter the Great WRITTEN AND ILLUSTRATED BY DIANE STANLEY. New York: Four Winds Press, 1986.

Suggested Listening Level: Grades 3–6

Tsar of all the Russias, Peter stood six feet seven inches tall, slept on the ground when necessary, and had a passion for knowing how things worked. He was spoiled, imperious, overbearing, loving, and hardworking, and changed his vast country by sheer force of his own personal drive. In this biography, Stanley is wise enough to let Peter's actions speak for themselves so that listeners can be caught up in the momentum of his vigor and spirit.

The illustrations are meticulously detailed and rich, reminding one of both the miniatures and the iconography so typical of sixteenth- and seventeenth-century Russian art. This short historical biography should fascinate youngsters who may tend to forget that there was life outside the "thirteen original colonies" and that it was also exciting and challenging and influenced the lives of people on half a continent.

The Phantom Tollbooth BY NORTON JUSTER. *Illustrated by Jules Feiffer.* New York: Random House, 1961. Paperback: Random House.

Suggested Listening Level: Grades 4–6

Milo is bored by everything until he discovers in his room a turnpike tollbooth, complete with a strange map. When he gamely sets out in his toy car, the tollbooth admits him to a strange land where the marvels and adventures quickly banish his boredom. In the cities of Dictionopolis and Digitopolis, Milo's dull school subjects take on new meaning, and he discovers that he has to think his way out of trouble. Idioms become literal as Milo meets a Spelling Bee, gets stuck in the Doldrums, visits the Land of Infinity ("a dreadfully poor place . . . they can never manage to make ends meet"), and attends a banquet where the speakers have to eat their words. Among the memorable characters he encounters are Faintly Macabre, the not-so-wicked witch, and Kakofonous A. Dischord, Doctor of Dissonance. Milo's adventures end happily as he restores peace to the land by rescuing the Princesses Rhyme and Reason from the Mountains of Ignorance.

Some children love this book's wordplay and intellectual gymnastics; others find it tedious in its absence of character development. Clearly, listeners need good vocabularies and a grounding in mathematics to appreciate much of the humor. We recommend a flexible approach when reading this aloud to a group. Try out the first two chapters and let your listeners' reactions determine whether you read on to the end or leave it for those children who are interested to finish independently.

The Piemakers BY HELEN CRESSWELL. *Illustrated by Judith Gwyn Brown.* New York: Macmillan Publishing Co., 1967, 1980.

Suggested Listening Level: Grades 3–6

Gravella Roller knew her father Arthy was the best piemaker in Danby Dale. All the Rollers were fine piemakers, whether the pie was beef or pork or pigeon, but the trouble was that Cousin Crispin of the Gorby Rollers was *also* considered a fine piemaker. So when the king declared a contest to find a pie "the biggest and the best by common consent," the honor of Danby Dale was at stake. The entire village turned out to help Arthy and his wife, Jem, prepare the biggest pie ever—enough to feed two thousand people.

There are inevitable problems with such a venture. The size of the pie dish, for instance, means it must be floated down the river to Danby, but with Arthy at the helm, one knows the Danby

Rollers will triumph. This fanciful tale of the English Downs is as light as Arthy's piecrust and reads in about two and a half hours. Third- through sixth-grade listeners are appreciative of both the action and the aroma of a pie big enough to feed two thousand friends.

You may also want to try the hilarious adventures of the eccentric Bagthorpe clan. The tone is British; the humor universal. We like *Ordinary Jack*, which introduces the lot.

Pinch BY LARRY CALLEN. *Illustrated by Marvin Friedman.* Boston: Little, Brown & Co., 1976.

Suggested Listening Level: Grades 5–7

Pinch Grimball is a twentieth-century Tom Sawyer who lives in Four Corners, a small southern town where a hunting pig contest is the year's most exciting event. This year Pinch wants to train his own hunting pig and manages with some fine luck to parlay a quarter into a frog, then into two chickens, and finally into a pig named Homer.

The characters in this humorous novel of rich local color are as believable as the murky bayou just beyond the Grimball farm: Mr. Tony Carmouche, store owner, part-time sheriff, part-time most anything; Mr. John Barrow, "tall and skinny with spidery legs . . . and clothes that hang on him like bat wings"; Charley Redlinger, the best friend anyone could ask for; and the dangerous Sweet boys. Our list contains a remarkable number of books about pigs, but we couldn't resist adding this one, which has a flavor all its own. The chapters are short and episodic; the book can be read in five or six sessions, depending on the time available.

Pippi Longstocking BY ASTRID LINDGREN. *Translated by Florence Lamborn. Illustrated by Louis S. Glanzman.* New York: The Viking Press, 1950. Paperback: Puffin.

Suggested Listening Level: Grades 2–5

Pippi Longstocking is a heroine after a child's own heart. She lives by herself, her mother being an angel in heaven and her father a captain lost at sea. Pippi is sure that her father will return one day and that her mother is "watching her little girl through a peep-hole in the sky." "Don't you worry about me. I'll always come out on top," Pippi calls up to her often, and that confidence of hers allows children to concentrate on the benefits of her solitary state. She gives her pet monkey and horse the run of the house, she has a suitcase full of gold coins that will buy anything she desires, and after totally disrupting a classroom, she's given the teacher's fervent permission to stay home from school.

Though Pippi's friends, Annika and Tommy, are prime examples of sex-role stereotyping, Pippi's thoroughgoing defiance of convention ends by calling into question all such repressive categories. No one who hears this story will ever forget carrot-topped Pippi, dancing before the roaring flames after she performs a heroic rescue. She is the image of childhood energy and its challenge to stuffy grown-up conventions. Allow fifteen minutes for each of the book's eleven chapters.

Portrait of Ivan BY PAULA FOX. *Illustrated by Saul Lambert.* Englewood Cliffs, N.J.: Bradbury Press, 1969, 1985.

Suggested Listening Level: Grades 4–6

Ivan's widowed father has commissioned an artist to paint his son's portrait. Through the growing relationship between the young artist and his subject, Ivan comes to new ways of seeing the world. Matt takes Ivan with him on a working trip to Florida where, messing about in a rowboat with a new friend, Ivan is for once free of adult supervision. By sketching an imagined scene of Ivan's mother's childhood, Matt helps Ivan fill the empty space that his father's grieving silence has created around her memory.

The story chronicles the gradual release of a boy from the safe but pent-up world of wealthy urban childhood. Yet every child who has begun to view the world differently from his or her parents, every child who has exchanged the comfortable, home-centered world of childhood for wider horizons, will understand what has happened to Ivan.

In this subtle, quiet book the meaning gradually accumulates. Some listeners will want to reread the book to ponder the questions Fox raises about human relationships and memory, about photography, drawing, and writing as ways of keeping alive the past. As in all of her distinguished fiction, this prize-winning author respects the acuteness and sensitivity of her young readers.

The eight chapters of the novel can be read in less than two hours.

One-Eyed Cat—published in 1984—is another challenging, introspective book for young readers. Its tone is predominantly somber, and any child who has had a guilty secret will empathize with Ned, who thinks he has wounded a cat with the air rifle his father forbade him to use. Fox has never been more brilliant in her sure depiction of moral growth and the mysterious relations of parents and children. Not for all children—or adults either—but rewarding for those who enjoy books that are both quiet and deep.

The Pushcart War BY JEAN MERRILL. *Illustrated by Ronni Solbert.* Boston: Addison-Wesley Publishing Co., 1964. Paperback: Dell.

Suggested Listening Level: Grades 3–7

Tension has been building in Manhattan. Overcrowded streets are to blame. Pushcart peddlers are tired of being shoved about by bullying trucks, and truck drivers are fed up with pushcarts taking up precious parking spaces. Then the mammoth trucking corporations declare war on the peddlers in secret, hoping to make them scapegoats for the public's anger. When Morris the Florist is knocked into a barrel of pickles by a Mighty Mammoth truck and his pushcart demolished, however, the peddlers decide to fight back. Events escalate into a hilarious epic battle, thanks to the peddlers' secret weapon—shooting tacks into truck tires with peashooters.

This is a clever and subtle David and Goliath story, a tongue-in-cheek account of a mythical war that will leave your audience thinking as well as smiling. It would be hard to name another book that is both as funny and as ultimately serious as this one.

The challenge for the reader is that the book is written as a history of a real event. There is extensive dialogue, and interspersed with the narrative are news bulletins, diary entries, and transcriptions of interviews. To be most effective, some preparation and practice is recommended. The thirty-six short chapters could be combined in groups of two or three.

Queenie Peavy BY ROBERT BURCH. *Illustrated by Jerry Lazare.* New York: The Viking Press, 1966.

Suggested Listening Level: Grades 4–8

"Queenie Peavy was the only girl in Cotton Junction who could chew tobacco. She could also spit it—and with deadly aim. She could do a number of things with a considerable degree of accuracy, most of them unworthy of her attention." Hiding behind a tough veneer of pride, Queenie lives in the shadow of the federal penitentiary in Atlanta where her father is imprisoned. Through the sometimes painful events of the story, Queenie's idealized image of her father is gradually replaced by a recognition of him as he is. Queenie discovers that she can face life as *it* is, not just as she wants it to be. Yet she also learns that she can give pleasure to others with her singing and that her gentle touch with babies is appreciated. Queenie's prickly personality makes this an absorbing growing-up story that stays with one after the last chapter is read.

The microcosm of the junior high school world with students, teachers, and principals, with assemblies and wienie roasts, with gossip and cliques, is convincingly portrayed. The chapters are episodic enough to provide natural divisions, but they can be combined for seven or eight thirty-minute sessions. We recommend this for fourth grade through eighth *and* family groups.

A Racecourse for Andy BY PATRICIA WRIGHTSON. *Illustrated by Margaret Horder.* New York: Harcourt Brace Jovanovich, 1968. (Out of print)

Suggested Listening Level: Grades 4–7

Five boys have grown up playing together, so the four others are patient and protective toward Andy, as they gradually realize that he is retarded. It was as if "Andy lived behind a closed window. When he smiled his warm smile and spoke a little too loudly, it was as if he were speaking through the glass." A favorite game of the group is pretending to own and swap various public buildings and facilities around the city of Sydney; it is a game Andy can't seem to understand and from which he feels left out.

Then one day an old tramp "sells" Andy the Beecham Park Racecourse for three dollars, and Andy, in all seriousness, believes himself the new owner. Since those in authority at the racetrack let Andy come and go as he pleases and indulge him in his fantasy, he is proud and happy. The other boys, however, who are afraid Andy's delusions will end up hurting him, wrestle with difficult issues. Should they tell Andy the truth and force him to face it? Are they just jealous of his new privileges? Can anyone "own" greyhounds and races and flowers anyway? The working-out of this delicate predicament is handled with great sensitivity by Patricia Wrightson, one of Australia's most distinguished writers for children.

The few Australian terms should pose no difficulty for American children, as the context makes their meaning clear. The book consists of twelve chapters, each roughly ten to twelve minutes long.

Wrightson has recently won the prestigious Hans Christian Andersen Medal for her distinguished contribution to children's literature. Her stories about her native Australia introduce Aboriginal lore, which is the source of much of her inspiration. *The Nargun and the Stars* is wonderfully evocative of a brooding landscape and a young boy's struggle to overcome ancient forces he barely understands. It is both a suspenseful adventure and a touching account of an orphan's closeness to his two elderly guardians.

Ramona the Pest BY BEVERLY CLEARY. *Illustrated by Louis Darling.* New York: William Morrow & Co., 1968. Paperback: Dell.

Suggested Listening Level: Grades K–3

Ramona Quimby doesn't understand grown-ups. How can mothers sigh that children grow up so quickly when she's been waiting years just to get to kindergarten? The first day of school doesn't quite measure up to Ramona's high hopes, however. When her teacher asks her to "sit here for the present," Ramona is disappointed because no "present" materializes. Then she has to sit out of the game just because she pulled Susan's corkscrew curl to see if it would go "boing." And she finds it especially difficult to figure out what a dawnzer is in "Oh say can you see by the dawnzer lee light."

Beverly Cleary's appreciation both of the intense feelings small children experience and of the humor in them has made her a perennial favorite with children. Though young readers usually prefer stories about children their own age or slightly older, the great popularity of *Ramona the Pest* and its sequels shows that, like adults, children can enjoy looking back through fiction at their younger selves and feeling fondly superior.

When read one chapter at a sitting, *Ramona the Pest* is a sure success with first- through third-graders (there are eight chapters in all). Of the sequels, *Ramona and Her Father* is particularly interesting, portraying family stress from a seven-year-old's perspective, when Mr. Quimby loses his job. *The Mouse and the Motorcycle* is another favorite Cleary book, especially with no-nonsense third-graders.

Rascal: A Memoir of a Better Era BY STERLING NORTH. *Illustrated by John Schoenherr.* New York: E. P. Dutton, 1963, 1984. Paperback: Avon.

Suggested Listening Level: Grades 4–7

Rascal, a young raccoon, is without a doubt one of the most winning pets ever to appear in a book. He eats in a high chair (when he's not walking across the table to dip into the sugar bowl) and rides in his young master's bicycle basket like an animated figurehead. Rascal's human-childlike qualities and the scrapes they get him into give him the appeal of a real-life Paddington Bear.

Rascal is more than a winsome pet story, however. North deftly captures the atmosphere of small-town Wisconsin during World War I and, even more vividly, the lavish beauty of northern farms, lakes, and streams. (North, boy and man, is a passionate fisherman.) In addition, the motherless child Sterling is a winning protagonist. Left alone a great deal by his lawyer father, Sterling is a poignant figure, but an enviable one as well. If he sometimes gets lonely, he also is allowed to take over the living room for months to build a large canoe. And his freedom to ramble about at will, with Rascal as an eager and curious companion, is an eleven-year-old's dream come true.

Each of the book's nine chapters makes a satisfying read-aloud session.

The Rescuers BY MARGERY SHARP. *Illustrated by Garth Williams.* Boston: Little, Brown & Co., 1959. Paperback: Dell.

Suggested Listening Level: Grades 3–5

Did you know that mice the world over have organized a Prisoners' Aid Society? Besides providing companionship and doing tricks to cheer those in prison, mice devote themselves to securing the liberty of unfortunate captives whenever possible. When Madam Chairwoman proposes that the Society take on the mission of freeing a Norwegian poet from the dungeons of the infamous Black Castle, however, the membership is dismayed. No mouse has been able to even reach the prisoners' cells there, the jailer's cat is "twice natural size and four times as fast," and none of them speaks Norwegian. But Madam Chairwoman has a plan, one that depends on an unlikely rescue party of Bernard, a rough but gallant pantry mouse, Nils, a seagoing Norwegian mouse recruited for the task, and Miss Bianca, the pampered pet of the Ambassador's son.

There is never a dull moment in the chronicle of their heroic adventure, and Margery Sharp's delightful prose style is a rare treat for both reader and listeners. The fourteen chapters divide the book into manageable segments for reading sessions.

The Return of the Twelves BY PAULINE CLARKE. *Illustrated by Bernarda Bryson.* First American edition, New York: Coward, McCann & Geoghegan, 1962. (Out of print) Paperback: Dell.

Suggested Listening Level: Grades 4–6

Max is the first to learn the secret of the twelve antique wooden soldiers tucked away in the attic of the English farmhouse to which the Morleys have just moved. Then his sister Jane and finally his older brother Phillip watch and listen to the twelve as they come alive and relate all manner of wondrous adventures. Butter Crashey, the Patriarch, "one hundred and forty years old and full of years and wisdom," tells the three Morley children enough about the soldiers' past to make it clear that the twelve once belonged to the Brontë children. The three Morleys read Branwell Brontë's *History of the Young Men* and decide to help the twelve return to their ancestral home, Haworth Parsonage, now a Brontë museum. When an American scholar threatens to take the soldiers to be displayed in the United States, the soldiers resolve to set out intrepidly across the English countryside to return to their rightful place on the Haworth mantel shelf.

This is a delightful reading experience for families. As in Mary Norton's *The Borrowers,* the speculation about life just beyond the corner of the eye is intriguing. The action here is very straightforward and can be handled in eight to ten sessions.

Richard Kennedy: Collected Stories BY RICHARD KENNEDY. *Illustrated by Marcia Sewall.* New York: Harper & Row, Publishers, 1987.

Suggested Listening Level: Grades 1–8

Richard Kennedy has been publishing wonderful stories since the mid-seventies. At first, they attracted little notice and he supported himself working as a janitor, but gradually the number of his admirers grew. We can now rejoice at having so many of his skillful tales in one volume. It is a must for lovers of reading-aloud. Kennedy has such a mastery of different styles and such a fertile imagination that the fourteen stories and two poems vary enormously in impact and mood. Some of them, like the hilarious "The Contests at Cowlick," are suitable for young children. A few, such as "The Porcelain Man," will best be appreciated by older children. Still others ("Oliver Hyde's Dishcloth Concert") are for all ages.

Roll of Thunder, Hear My Cry BY MILDRED D. TAYLOR. *Illustrated by Jerry Pinkney.* New York: The Dial Press, 1976. Paperback: Bantam.

Suggested Listening Level: Grades 4–6

This Newbery Medal–winning book tells of the good and bad times in the lives of the Logans, a family trying to hold on to their land in Mississippi during the Great Depression. Written by a young black woman, it is based on stories told by her father about his own boyhood. Through the dramatic events of the book, the young listener learns with nine-year-old Cassie Logan about the existence of bigotry and injustice. Yet the terror of night riders and lynchings, the humiliation of insults and inferior schooling, are made bearable by the courage and warmth of the adult Logans. The suspense builds steadily to a haunting ending.

Mildred Taylor's relative inexperience as a writer at the time the book was written shows occasionally in an awkward phrase or clumsiness in narration (there is an excess of eavesdropping to maintain Cassie as the point-of-view character, for instance), but the suspense and emotional force of the story carry reader and listener over any rough spots. Fast-moving and touching, this novel has become a great favorite with children. A fairly good adaptation of the book was made for television. The novel is divided into twelve chapters, each suitable for one reading session.

Two more recent novels by Taylor, *The Gold Cadillac* and *The Friendship,* are equally powerful renditions of troubling events from her family's past. Available in one paperback volume, either story can be read aloud in less than an hour.

Roller Skates BY RUTH SAWYER. *Illustrated by Valenti Angelo.* New York: The Viking Press, 1969. Paperback: Dell.

Suggested Listening Level: Grades 4–6

A whole year of freedom! Having seen her wealthy parents off to Europe and escaped the clutches of tyrannical Aunt Emily, Lucinda arrives to spend her "orphan year" with Miss Peters and Miss Nettie, as she says, "blissfully unhampered." Her roller skates take her all over New York City with all the exuberance of ten-year-old innocence as she makes delightful new friends: Mr. Gilligan and his hansom cab, Tony Coppino and the bambinos, and Trinket, a tiny child to cherish and share secrets with.

The story is based on the author's reminiscences of her own tenth year and catches for the reader/listener the poignancy of growing up. Although the setting of turn-of-the-century New York adds much to Lucinda's experiences (her excursions to Mr. Louis Sherry's for candy, for instance), it is Lucinda's face-to-face encounter with the death of Mrs. Grose and the even more searing loss of Trinket that raise her experiences above the common-place.

The book begins with a rather coy introduction that we find more effective to omit or summarize, beginning the actual reading with chapter one. Episodic chapters provide easy divisions for eight or nine sessions.

Rootabaga Stories BY CARL SANDBURG. 1922. Many editions.

Suggested Listening Level: Grades 4–8

In the Rootabaga Country the pigs wear bibs, and the railroad tracks change from straight to zigzag, and the mothers and fathers fix them. The biggest city in the big, big Rootabaga Country is the Village of Liver-and-Onions, and the Village of Cream Puffs is "a light little village on the upland corn prairie many miles past the sunset in the west." Here in the Rootabaga Country, mothers and fathers and uncles and aunts tell stories about the Huckabuck Family, the Potato Face Blind Man, Jason Squiff the cistern cleaner, and the White Horse Girl and the Blue Wind Boy.

Sandburg's feel for the land and for the people of the Midwest is evident in these nonsense stories. Most of the tales are rather short, taking no more than five or ten minutes to read, but the poet's ear for rhythm and alliteration make practice essential. While these stories may not appeal to every reader, listeners who are introduced to them will never hear a train whistle on a lonely Kansas prairie without remembering the two skyscrapers who had a child—and lost it.

Saint George and the Dragon RETOLD BY MARGARET HODGES. *Illustrated by Trina Schart Hyman.* Boston: Little, Brown & Co., 1984.

Suggested Listening Level: Grades 3–6

The Red Cross Knight rode across the plains "in the days when monsters and giants and fairy folk lived in England." He knew nothing of his background, not even his name, but he was dedicated to the Queen of the Fairies and had vowed to vanquish "a dragon grim and horrible," even if it cost him his life. So begins this tale of honor and death-defying action forming a legend so enduring, it still stirs the imagination.

Based on Sir Edmund Spenser's *Faerie Queene,* a sixteenth-century allegorical poem, this retelling captures in prose the trustworthy, intrepid knight who nearly dies in his battle with the dragon. Hyman's Caldecott award–winning illustrations present splendid images of the dignity and otherworldliness of the knight and his fair Una. For listeners whose heroes carry not a shield but inarticulate bravado, the fearsome battle may offer a glimpse of true courage.

Sarah, Plain and Tall BY PATRICIA MACLACHLAN. New York: Harper & Row, Publishers, 1985. Paperback: Harper.

Suggested Listening Level: Grades 2–8

Anna and Caleb want to know if Sarah Elizabeth Wheaton can sing. She has answered their father's advertisement for a new wife and mother. When Sarah arrives at the prairie home of the Witting family, she has brought a few things to remind her of the Maine coast and the sea she loves so much: Seal, her cat; a moon snail "that was curled and smelled of salt" for Caleb; and for Anna, "the smoothest, whitest stone that she had ever seen." A trial month is all that they have for Sarah to decide if missing the sea has been too great a price to pay for a farm in the middle of the prairie, and a family, and singing.

Your listeners will not soon forget the intrepid Sarah and her new family. The longing of the children to hear their father singing, to know a mother's care; the loneliness of the father; and Sarah, cut off from family and friends and the sound and smell of the sea, but growing to love her new family—all these emotions are as carefully presented as the colors of the prairie sky. *Sarah . . .* should be read aloud to children and to college classes, at family reunions, and with families newly formed, or shared with anyone who will listen. It can be read aloud in about forty minutes or in two sessions, breaking after chapter four.

Save Queen of Sheba BY LOUISE MOERI. New York: E. P. Dutton, 1981. Paperback: Avon.

Suggested Listening Level: Grades 4–8

Save Queen of Sheba is a survival story that will have you and your child listeners on the edge of your seats. The story opens as a twelve-year-old boy groggily returns to consciousness. He has been half scalped and left for dead by a Sioux war party that attacked a wagon train traveling to the Oregon Territory. King David (that's his unusual name) explores the horror of massacre and destruction around him and finds no one left alive but himself and his little sister, Queen of Sheba. He discovers evidence, though, that his parents may have escaped to Fort Laramie. Can the injured boy get himself and his frail and stubborn small sister across the vast barren spaces to safety? In his ordeal, King David proves worthy of the father whose stern notions of courage and honor guide him. And all indirectly, listeners learn a great deal about the motives and conditions, high ideals and grim realities of the celebrated western migration. A riveting story for those who can take the initial grisly descriptions of violent death.

The seventeen chapters would work well in seven twenty-minute sessions of two chapters each and one longer session of the final three chapters.

The Secret Garden BY FRANCES HODGSON BURNETT. *Illustrated by Tasha Tudor.* 1909. New York: J. B. Lippincott Co., 1962, 1985. Paperback: Dell.

Suggested Listening Level: Grades 4–7

Mary Lennox is a very unattractive child—thin, pale, and sour-looking. To make things worse, when we meet her at the opening of the story, she is "as tyrannical and selfish a little pig as ever lived." The transformation of this unlikely heroine into a lively, loving, and attractive child is the subject of *The Secret Garden*. When a cholera epidemic leaves Mary suddenly orphaned, she is sent from India to a huge old manor house in Yorkshire, the home of her uncle. A mysterious, brooding figure, he is rarely at home and shows no interest in the child.

In this pathetic state, Mary might be expected to become more disagreeable than ever. That she does not is due to her discovery of Colin, an invalid cousin shut away in the recesses of the mansion, of robust and cheerful Dickon with his gift of nurturing plant and animal life, and of the growing things that transform the bleak Yorkshire winter into luxuriant spring. Together the three children bring back to life the walled garden that Mr. Craven has shut up since his wife's death ten years earlier, and the garden in turn brings Colin to health and Mr. Craven out of his grief.

The story is both a hymn of tribute to the healing power of the natural world and a psychologically acute study. Its "happily ever after" resolution is as satisfying as the best fairy tale.

The Yorkshire dialect that is spoken by some of the characters looks a bit intimidating on the page, but it's easier to manage than it looks once you get under way. The book has twenty-seven chapters averaging fifteen minutes apiece. Although this makes it longer than the typical children's book today, most children become caught up in the story and enjoy every minute of it.

Shadow of a Bull BY MAIA WOJCIECHOWSKA. *Illustrated by Alvin Smith.* New York: Atheneum Publishers, 1964. Paperback: Atheneum.

Suggested Listening Level: Grades 4–6

In the small Spanish town of Arcangel, the people all long for the day when Manolo, the son of a great bullfighter, is himself old enough to fight bulls. They are sure he will be as great as his father, who ten years ago was killed in the bullring—and then the town will be famous and full of life again. But Manolo has no desire to fight bulls, nothing like the fierce desire that makes his friend Juan willing to take any risks to face the magnificent, terrible animals. Manolo is full of fear. He sees no way to escape his fate, however, for six men who have been good to Manolo and his mother, followers of his father's career, have taught him all they know about bullfighting; he cannot disappoint them.

Tension builds relentlessly in the book as the time for Manolo to face his first bull approaches, and the climactic scene is orchestrated skillfully. The world of bullfighting and its meaning to Spaniards is so vividly realized that the novel far transcends the subject of physical courage; it is a novel about discovering one's identity and claiming it.

The book consists of fifteen short chapters and a helpful glossary defining bullfighting terms and indicating their pronunciation.

Shakespeare Stories BY LEON GARFIELD. *Illustrated by Michael Foreman.* New York: Schocken Books, 1985.

Suggested Listening Level: Grades 4–8+

This volume contains powerful prose retellings of twelve of Shakespeare's plays. Of all children's writers today, Leon Garfield seems the best suited to the ambitious task of providing simplified versions for children of our language's greatest plays. He writes with great energy, and revels in a bold use of figurative language that marks him as one indebted to the Bard. Some might ask, why retell the stories at all, but Shakespeare often chose subjects that interest children, and there are fortunate young people who have the opportunity to see one of the plays performed on stage. For those children, the experience will be greatly enhanced by listening first to one of Garfield's adaptations. Garfield chose to work with all the great tragedies, two history plays, plus *The Merchant of Venice, Twelfth Night, Midsummer Night's Dream, The Taming of the Shrew,* and *The Tempest.* This volume supersedes the old *Tales from Shakespeare* by Charles and Mary Lamb, in our opinion.

These retellings make the plots clear, yet don't slight character, on which so much depends in a Shakespearean play. If Garfield sometimes *tells* us what we need to know about a character, where the drama would *show* it, his interpretations seem always sensitive and defensible. The reteller comes into his own, however, in brief descriptive passages, invented to fill out sparse stage directions. A typical case is the opening of *The Tempest.* Prospero and Miranda are watching the ship, which is foundering in the tempest Prospero's magic has raised. "As it heaved and tossed, its masts scribbled frantic messages against the blotchy sky, and its rigging all fell down like a madman's hair. Tiny figures, black as fleas, and with patched white faces, clung where they could; and shrieks and screams, small as the squealing of mice, drifted to the watchers on the shore." A bit overwritten, you say? Perhaps, but guaranteed to reach out and pull in the young listener.

If you've never thought of trying Shakespeare out on children, this book may change your mind. The Suggested Listening Level may be extended downward, in fact, for those who can't wait to share a passion for Shakespeare with the children in their care. We know one day camp counselor who was also working backstage evenings on a production of *Twelfth Night.* One day at camp she ran out of ideas for story time and so launched into a telling of that play (minus one subplot). The four-year-olds in her group were held spellbound. She was just yielding to their pleas for another such story when a child from another group approached and shyly asked, "May five-year-olds listen too?"

Short Takes EDITED BY ELIZABETH SEGEL. *Illustrated by Joseph A. Smith.* New York: Lothrop, Lee & Shepard Books, 1986.

Suggested Listening Level: Grades 4–7

If you're looking for one-session stories that will interest middle-grade listeners, try one of these. The nine selections by first-rate authors are appealing on many levels. "On Shark's Tooth Beach" by E. L. Konigsburg is the story of a young boy living in Florida with his American father and Vietnamese mother. Ned often meets other beachcombers, but one is more irritating than the others. He introduces himself as "President Bob, boy . . . I'm president of a college, upstate Michigan. But I'm retired now. . . ." President Bob challenges Ned to see who can find the most fossilized shark's teeth. When Ned discovers not only four teeth but part of a jaw, he feels that he has won the undeclared war. Looking at the older man, however, Ned realizes that he would lose more than a shark's jaw with four teeth attached if he gave in to President Bob's dare. His self-respect is more important than a fossil any day.

Some of the stories are shorter, others longer, but all have that sense of wholeness that makes good short stories such a pleasure to read—and to hear. In Philippa Pearce's "The Great Blackberry Pick," Val begins to understand that not all families are as rigid and bleak as her own. "The Snakeskin Bag" by Constance Greene is both funny and thought-provoking, identifying some of the difficulties of being new to a group. You'll find this an ideal collection to use when you need one or two stories to read just before or just after reading a longer novel.

The Shrinking of Treehorn BY FLORENCE PARRY HEIDE. *Illustrated by Edward Gorey.* New York: Holiday House, 1971.

Suggested Listening Level: Grades 4–7

Nobody's listening. Children all suspect this, but Treehorn knows it better than most as he shrinks in size day by day, until he is small enough to stand under the bed and play a game "to grow on." Nobody listens to him. His mother and father urge him to behave. His teacher suggests that shrinking is inappropriate behavior in her classroom. Bus drivers, even good friends, pay no attention to the *real* Treehorn.

This short, sophisticated story will strike a chord in anyone who has ever been ignored. It is deceptive in its simplicity and should be shared with older groups, fourth or fifth grades through junior high. For families, it may be a source of much discussion. Edward Gorey's illustrations add to the wry humor of Treehorn's problem, but the story line moves successfully on its own.

Sideways Stories from Wayside School BY LOUIS SACHAR. *Illustrated by Dennis Hockerman.* Chicago: Follett Publishing Co., 1978. Paperback: Avon.

Suggested Listening Level: Grades 2–4

The builders of Wayside School made a mistake and built it thirty stories high and one room wide, instead of the reverse. The result gives the children lots of playground space but creates many funny situations. This zany book will captivate children right from the first chapter, in which a mean teacher turns misbehaving children into apples. They eventually turn the tables on her with hilarious results. Students in ordinary schools will love hearing all thirty short chapters about the wild and wacky goings-on in this "sideways school." They won't let you stop a session after just one chapter, though, so begin at your own risk.

Slake's Limbo BY FELICE HOLMAN. New York: Charles Scribner's Sons, 1974. Paperback: Dell.

Suggested Listening Level: Grades 6–8

. . . It is simplest and most practical to believe that Slake was born an orphan at the age of thirteen, small, near-sighted, dreaming, bruised, an outlander in the city of his birth (and in the world), a lad of shifting, fitful faith with a token in his pocket. In other ways he was not so different from the rest of the young raised with house keys around their necks, rearing themselves in litter-strewn streets.

So Aremis Slake, repeatedly harassed by a gang in his neighborhood, takes refuge in New York's subway and there survives for one hundred twenty-one days. Willis Joe Whinney, a motorman on the subway, also seeks refuge from his world in dreams about sheep ranching in Australia. Willis Joe and Slake have only one chance encounter, but each is changed, and as the book draws to a close, the reader/listener catches sight of the bright blue sky that pulls Slake back into the world above the subway.

Slake's story is a dramatic, moving one that can catch the reader on many levels. Daily routines established by Slake simply to exist are intriguing, but more than that, the isolation of an individual in a crowded, rushed society is starkly revealed. This is not a happy book, but it is compelling. The relatively short narrative can be broken after chapters three, seven, eleven, and thirteen into approximately twenty- to thirty-minute sessions.

Snow Company BY MARC HARSHMAN. *Illustrated by Leslie W. Bowman.* New York: E. P. Dutton (Cobblehill Books), 1990.

Suggested Listening Level: Grades K–3

The snow is building up as Teddy and younger brother Ronnie return from school. Shortly after, the first visitor arrives. Jim, whose truck is stranded near the mailbox, is followed by Mrs. Hart, a retired schoolteacher, and pretty Mrs. Mason and her baby. Stories, chili and cornbread, and a sense of neighbor helping neighbor warm the company stranded by the storm. Your listeners will be warmed too. Bowman's frosty landscape conveys perfectly the mood of nostalgia that the story evokes.

Sounder BY WILLIAM ARMSTRONG. *Illustrated by James Barkley.* New York: Harper and Row Publishers, 1969. Paperback. Harper.

Suggested Listening Level: Grades 6–8

Sounder contains some of the most painful scenes in children's fiction, yet, as in classic tragedy, the beauty of the language and the stature of the characters transform the story into an uplifting experience. A boy stands helplessly by as sheriff's men brutally arrest his father and shoot the family's magnificent coonhound, Sounder. The father, a sharecropper, has in desperation stolen a ham to feed his hungry family. Though grievously wounded in the head, the dog survives, restless and mute, waiting six long years for the return of his master from a chain gang. All that while, the boy searches for his father, whenever the field work allows. The family is finally reunited, but both the father and the dog soon die of their injuries. A note of hope lingers, however: the education that the boy has been able to acquire promises a way out of the inhuman oppression the family has known.

Just as medieval morality plays portrayed the life of Everyman to dramatize universal events and emotions, so the loyalty and long suffering of the dog Sounder serve to dramatize the dignity and long suffering of this poor black family. Some critics have felt that Armstrong's decision not to give the characters names demeans them, but children recognize the love and trust and endurance of this family that just might be Everyfamily. Little more than two hours reading time is required, but don't rush this one. Allow time for discussion, for thought, for tears.

Soup BY ROBERT NEWTON PECK. *Illustrated by Charles C. Gehm.* New York: Alfred A. Knopf, 1974. Paperback: Dell.

Suggested Listening Level: Grades 3–5

Boyhood pleasures in the rural Vermont of the 1920s are celebrated in this engaging small volume: a good piece of rope, small green apples and sassafras whips to send them flying, acorn pipes and cornsilk tobacco. The boys in question are the narrator and his best friend, Soup, who is "a regular genius" at getting the boys in trouble. One hilarious episode in the "bad boy" vein follows another until the last chapter adds a new and touching dimension to the boys' friendship.

Peck's language is as high-spirited as the boys' antics—richly figurative in a robust, down-to-earth idiom. The author, who drew on memories of his own childhood for *Soup* and its sequel, zeroes in perfectly on third-grade psychology, even to the bathroom humor with which the boys frequently regale each other. Young listeners will love it, but adults who prefer to avoid the vulgar terms for bodily functions may find themselves uncomfortable with this book. Grandparents not averse to letting their hair down, however, will particularly enjoy sharing with children Peck's nostalgic vignettes of days gone by.

The ten very brief chapters can be read aloud in about one hour.

Space Demons BY GILLIAN RUBENSTEIN. New York: The Dial Press, 1987. Archway Paperback, 1989.

Suggested Listening Level: Grades 6–8

Drawn into a computer game that his father brings back from Japan, Andrew is caught up in the urge to bring others into the game with him by the compelling message "Respond to Hate." Eventually three other members of his junior-high class are captured by the game. The four find that they are able to get in and out of the world of the game only by hatred and anger, emotions that follow them into the real world of school and family. They face the menace of the demons who attack with ever growing force and even follow each of them back into reality.

The story is action packed and full of dramatic events as the demons seem to close in, dangerously blending reality and fantasy. All of the young people must face the emotions that feed the game and then begin to control themselves and eventually the demons. While the moral is obvious, the story is as compelling as the game, and junior-high audiences are sure to want to talk about implications in their own lives. The twenty-two chapters are short and can be read in five or six sessions.

Stevie WRITTEN AND ILLUSTRATED BY JOHN STEPTOE. New York: Harper & Row, Publishers, 1969.

Suggested Listening Level: Grades K–2

John Steptoe was still a teenager when he created this remarkable book. Luminous illustrations, created with vivid pastels on dark backgrounds, accompany the musings of a young black boy, Robert. He remembers Stevie, the little tot his mother used to care for, as a pest, and complains about all the trouble he caused. Now that Stevie no longer comes, however, Robert begins to realize that he misses the little guy. Older siblings and youngsters whose mothers care for other children will understand Robert's mixed feelings. This picture book for primary-grade children can be read whenever you have a few minutes to spare.

Children of all ages are drawn into Steptoe's handsome version of an African Cinderella tale, *Mufaro's Beautiful Daughters.* In this story, both sisters are beautiful. This makes clear that it is Nyasha's kind ways, not her looks, that lead the handsome prince to choose her for his wife over her mean-spirited sister Manyara. Steptoe used his own family as models for the characters, and the love and pride with which they are rendered are unmistakable.

A Stranger at Green Knowe BY LUCY BOSTON. *Illustrated by Peter Boston.* New York: Harcourt Brace & World, 1961. Paperback: Harcourt Brace Jovanovich.

Suggested Listening Level: Grades 4–8

Ping, a Chinese orphan refugee, visits the monkey house of the London zoo. The miserable creatures depress him until he catches sight of the magnificent gorilla, Hanno, like him taken from the beautiful forest to live in a world of concrete. Hanno's power and noble rage move Ping deeply and he, quite simply, falls in love. Later, Ping is invited by elderly Mrs. Oldknowe to visit her centuries-old home, complete with moat. While Ping is there, Hanno escapes and makes his way north, taking refuge in the bamboo thickets within the moat at Green Knowe. There Ping tries to protect him from capture. Though this is not possible —there is no place for Hanno in our world—Ping does provide the great beast with companionship and freedom for a few precious days.

Many elements combine to make this a superb novel. The description in the opening pages of a gorilla family's life in the equatorial jungle and its destruction in the terror of pursuit and capture will remain with the reader always. The relationship between the old lady and the gentle child is developed with remarkable subtlety. In addition, Mrs. Boston's courage in raising profound questions without supplying easy answers contributes to the deeply moving story.

Lucy Boston, who lives in the nine-hundred-year-old house that she writes about, has set other novels at Green Knowe in which Ping, Mrs. Oldknowe, and other characters figure. Each volume is quite different; all reflect the skill and intelligence of a remarkable writer.

A Stranger at Green Knowe is divided into three unequal parts. Parts one and two can each be read in one long session (about forty minutes apiece) or two shorter sessions. The long final part contains frequent breaks that provide logical stopping places. Total time to read the book aloud is estimated at just under three hours.

A Stranger Came Ashore BY MOLLIE HUNTER. New York: Harper & Row, Publishers, 1975. Paperback: Harper.

Suggested Listening Level: Grades 4–6

In the Shetland Islands there are many stories about the selkies, the seals who take human shape and live on the land for a time. It is said that the selkies aren't really animals but a kind of folk doomed to live in the sea. Fallen angels they are, and they're ruled by a great bull seal who lives in a jeweled palace and lures golden-haired young lasses to his kingdom. Anyway, this is the tale told to Robbie Henderson by his Old Da when Robbie shares with his grandfather his uneasiness about the shipwrecked sailor, Finn Learson. And Robbie's sister Elspeth has golden hair and seems bedazzled by the dark-eyed stranger. The tangled threads don't sort themselves out, however, until the final night of the Christmas festival, when Robbie and Elspeth and Finn Learson each fight for what they want.

This is definitely a "page-turner." The action and suspense build page by page, and fourth- through sixth-graders will hardly allow stopping for a sip of water. The setting is as authentic as master Scottish storyteller Mollie Hunter can make it; even land-locked listeners will be able to hear sea breakers pounding on the rocky shore.

Striped Ice Cream BY JOAN LEXAU. *Illustrated by John Wilson.* Philadelphia: J. B. Lippincott Co., 1968. (Out of print) Paperback: Scholastic.

Suggested Listening Level: Grades 2–5

In *Striped Ice Cream,* Joan Lexau has captured the hurts that come with being the youngest in a family of several children. Seven-year-old Becky "spent a lot of time thinking that no matter how old she got, she would never catch up to the others"—her four older siblings. Soon it will be Becky's birthday, and because all of the children need new shoes, Becky fears there will be no presents and none of her favorite "striped ice cream" on her birthday. Her sisters and brother manage to make her a special birthday gift, but their efforts to keep it a secret make Becky feel more left out than ever. Yet it all comes around to a happy ending.

Mrs. Lexau handles sensitively the subject of a "father-absent" black family struggling to obtain the necessities of life while keeping its pride intact. The loving warmth of the close-knit family remind one of *The Moffats* and *All-of-a-Kind Family.* Reading time is approximately two hours.

Sugaring Time BY KATHRYN LASKY. *Photographs by Christopher G. Knight.* New York: Macmillan Publishing Co., 1983.

Suggested Listening Level: Grades K–4

Kathryn Lasky's poetic prose celebrates a time of year "when winter seems tired and spring is only a hoped-for thing"—sugaring time. Her words and her husband's black-and-white photographs describe vividly the maple sugar harvest on a family farm in Vermont. The Lacey family taps trees in the old way, using buckets, not plastic tubing, and a team of Belgian horses to gather the sap. A young reader can identify with the three Lacey children, who ride on the sled or cross-country ski ahead of it, and who savor the rewards of a pancake feast and a sugar-on-snow party. Lasky doesn't just detail the facts about this picturesque activity; they're there, but subordinate to the delicious anticipation that builds as everyone waits for the right weather, for the trails to be broken out, for the sap to flow, and then for the boiling. If you live in maple country, hearing this book would be ideal to prepare children for a demonstration of maple syruping; for those far from the sugarbush, there could be no better introduction than this book that, like sap-boiling time, "celebrates mud and greenness, sweetness and renewed life."

The book has seven chapters of varying length, but is best read in one sitting. Lasky's other titles are equally distinguished; *Puppeteer* is particularly interesting.

Summer of the Monkeys BY WILSON RAWLS. New York: Doubleday & Co., 1976. Paperback: Dell.

Suggested Listening Level: Grades 4–8

Jay Berry Lee at fourteen lived a wild and free boy's life on a farm in Ozark country of Oklahoma at the turn of the century. "I had a dandy pocketknife, and a darn good dog; that was about all a boy could hope for in those days," he says. But that's before he discovers thirty trained monkeys and a chimpanzee in the wooded river bottoms. They have escaped the wreck of a circus train, and when Jay Berry learns that the circus is offering a big cash reward for their capture, he dreams of earning it and buying himself a pony and a .22.

With his Grandpa's advice, Jay Berry lays his plans for catching the monkeys, but those monkeys outsmart him at every go-around, with hilarious results. The action is fast and funny in this can't-miss story. A poignant note, verging on melodrama, is added by Jay Berry's gentle twin sister, who needs an expensive operation to straighten a twisted leg. Few writers can touch the emotions as surely as this master storyteller, who wrote of a bygone era with firsthand knowledge and affection. No wonder *Summer of the Monkeys* has won several awards voted by children themselves. The book's nineteen chapters will stretch out over seven or eight hours of read-aloud enjoyment.

Superduper Teddy BY JOHANNA HURWITZ. *Illustrated by Lillian Hoban.* New York: William Morrow & Co., 1980, 1990.

Suggested Listening Level: Grades K–2.

Many children will identify with Teddy, a shy five-year-old who wears his Superman cape whenever possible because it makes him feel "bigger and stronger and smarter" than his older sister Nora. The six short chapters relate Teddy's everyday triumphs with a sure grasp of the child's viewpoint, and Lillian Hoban's sketches of Teddy and his family are just right. This author's lively stories make ideal first chapter books, and you can read more about Teddy, Nora, and their friend Russell in other titles by Hurwitz.

The Sword and the Circle: King Arthur and the Knights of the Round Table BY ROSEMARY SUTCLIFF. New York: E. P. Dutton, 1981.

Suggested Listening Level: Grades 5–8+

An accomplished historical novelist, Sutcliff weaves together Arthurian legend from many sources to create a seamless narrative. *The Sword and the Circle* begins with the boy Merlin and carries the story through the founding of the Round Table and the adventures of that fellowship up to the arrival of Perceval. In an elevated yet well-paced style that avoids the pseudo-archaic, Sutcliff captures the romantic deeds and loves of Gawain, Lancelot, Tristan, Guenever, Arthur, and many other knights and ladies. Young listeners will be transfixed as you read the Green Knight's challenge: "Let any man here stand forth as champion against me, and he may take from my hand this axe . . . and with it strike me one blow . . . in the place of my choosing." The condition, however, is that the man must yield the Green Knight the right to strike a return blow in the same place, if he is able, a year and a day later. Gawain accepts the challenge and is horrified when the Green Knight bares his neck. His horror grows when the headless knight picks up the head Gawain has severed, turns it to Gawain, and says as he rides away: "See that you keep your oath." How Gawain manages to keep his oath *and* his head is a story that will hold even a difficult audience.

Sutcliff doesn't flinch at reporting the adulteries that make up part of the story, but she discreetly implies, rather than depicts, the occasional scene of passion. Throughout, she makes clear from the actions of the characters the nobler elements of that influential code we call chivalry. Stories like these can compete successfully with the shallow figures of the latest film massacre *if* an adult introduces them with enthusiasm to hero-seeking children.

Most of the thirteen chapters can be read in half an hour, but two or three require nearly an hour. These could be read in two parts, however, if necessary. Two sequels complete Sutcliff's version of Arthurian legend, *The Light Beyond the Forest* and *The Road to Camlann*.

The Talking Stone: An Anthology of Native American Tales and Legends EDITED BY DOROTHY DE WIT. *Illustrated by Donald Crews.* New York: Greenwillow Books, 1979.

Suggested Listening Level: Grades 3–8

The Talking Stone, a collection of Native American tales, is wonderful in every sense of that word. The editor has selected from the thousands of stories that have been collected, twenty-seven that have great appeal to young listeners. The tales represent all the major tribal groups of the North American continent, from the Northeast Woodlands to the California Plateau, from the Plains to the Canadian Pacific tribes. A succinct introduction to each section acquaints the listener with the distinctive characteristics of the particular group's culture and stories. Decorations by an award-winning illustrator and a handsome layout enhance the book's attractiveness.

But it's the tales themselves that make this book a standout.

Several offer memorable explanations for natural phenomena, such as how songbirds gained their bright feathers, how Rabbit stole fire and gave it to all the people, and how another trickster, Skinkoots, stole the springtime. Some narrate the exploits of heroes, often child heroes, such as Small Star. This Pawnee boy, too poor to own a horse, lovingly molds and cares for a mud pony, which comes to life and helps him become a great chief. De Wit's retelling of the Algonquin Cinderella tale, "Little Burnt Face," provides an especially moving version of that universally appealing story. In these tales, language flows gracefully and events are shaped into satisfying narratives, delighting reader and listeners.

The title story explains how Orphan Boy listens to the Spirit of the Rock and learns from it all the stories of the Seneca people. It concludes: "On and on he spoke, one tale after another, just as he had heard them from the talking stone. And the people listened, with their ears and their hearts, and did not sleep." Your young audience, too, will remain wide-awake and attentive, listening to these stories with their ears and with their hearts.

Tatterhood and Other Tales EDITED BY ETHEL JOHNSTON PHELPS. *Illustrated by Pamela Baldwin Ford.* Old Westbury, N.Y.: The Feminist Press, 1978. Paperback: Feminist Press.

Suggested Listening Level: Grades K–8

Because the influential collections of fairy tales for children were edited by Victorian gentlemen like Andrew Lang and Joseph Jacobs, the tales best known to us feature beautiful passive young women waiting for handsome brave young men to rescue them from difficulties. The only strong women in these tales tend to be old, ugly, and evil. Such stories reinforced the Victorian ideal of masculinity and femininity as polar opposites. In recent years, students of folklore have discovered many tales that depict women and men in more varied roles, and the best of these tales are as appealing as the old favorites. Several collections of folktales have appeared by now that feature appealing, active women —young and old, pretty and plain. *Tatterhood and Other Tales* is one of the best. Included in it are the comical Japanese tall tale of "Three Strong Women" who train a great wrestler; "Unanana and the Elephant," an African tale of a clever woman who rescues her children from an elephant's belly; and "Kate Crackernuts," a Scottish tale that depicts the devotion between two stepsisters as one endures great dangers to free the other from an evil spell. The collection is wider ranging than most: tales from Egypt, Ecuador, China, and a California Native American tribe are included as well as European tales.

Nothing can or should take the place of such tales as "Cinderella" and "Snow White," stories of deep power and beauty. These twenty-five tales provide, however, an ideal supplement to the traditional fairy tale collections.

Thank You, Jackie Robinson BY BARBARA COHEN. *Illustrated by Richard Cuffari.* New York: Lothrop, Lee & Shepard Books, 1974.

Suggested Listening Level: Grades 3–6

Sam Greene leads a solitary life in a family of two big sisters and a busy widowed mother who runs an inn. Then a new cook arrives, an elderly black man who shares Sam's passion for the Brooklyn Dodgers. The two become friends as they listen to broadcasts of the Dodger games and root for their favorite player, rookie Jackie Robinson. Davy and his daughter take Sam to his first Dodger game, and then Sam and Davy travel to other ballparks where the Dodgers are playing. When Davy has a heart attack, Sam overcomes his shyness to approach Jackie Robinson before a game and have a ball autographed for his friend. Sam gradually comes to realize what Jackie Robinson's success means to a sixty-year-old black man. And it is Jackie Robinson's grace and his courage against the odds of injustice and of time itself that alone comfort Sam after Davy's death.

The play-by-play action that figures occasionally in the book may intimidate readers and listeners who are not baseball fans, but don't be put off, for *Thank You, Jackie Robinson,* like all the best sports fiction, is much more than a sports story. It can be read in five or six twenty-minute sessions.

This talented writer has many other books that we find successful for reading aloud. Two picture books are particularly worthy of mention. *Mollie's Pilgrim,* adapted for an Academy Award–winning film, is the story of a young Jewish immigrant whose mother fashions a doll for the Thanksgiving model Pilgrim village that shows Mollie and her classmates that "it takes all kinds of Pilgrims to make a Thanksgiving." *Gooseberries to Oranges* chronicles from a child's perspective the momentous journey from an Eastern European village to a teeming American city.

A Toad for Tuesday BY RUSSELL ERICKSON. *Illustrated by Lawrence Di Fiori.* New York: Lothrop, Lee & Shepard Books, 1974. Paperback: Dell.

Suggested Listening Level: Grades K–3

Everyone knows toads don't go out in winter—not even to deliver the finest of beetle brittle to dear old Aunt Toolia. But Warton did go out on a sunny winter's day and began an adventure that nearly cost him his life, though it won him an unlikely new friend.

In the world of anthropomorphized creatures, two toads, Warton and Morton, an owl named George, and an army of mice on skis led by an intrepid adventurer named Sy are not only believable but deftly define human foibles and follies. This sprightly tale can be read in two sessions: a break naturally occurs after the first cup of clover blossom tea shared by George and Warton. It is suitable for the primary grades, although for kindergarten listeners you may wish to read it in three sessions.

Tom's Midnight Garden BY PHILIPPA PEARCE. Philadelphia: J. B. Lippincott Co., 1959, 1984. Paperback: Dell.

Suggested Listening Level: Grades 5–8

What does it mean when a clock strikes thirteen? Tom, who has been exiled during his brother's illness to the dreary little flat of

Aunt Gwen and Uncle Tom, finds the thirteenth hour allows him to walk into a garden that doesn't exist—at least not in this time. The garden is part of the lawn that surrounded the building sixty years before, when it was a mansion. Whenever the clock invites him, Tom enters the midnight garden and plays with the mysterious little girl he meets there. As his expeditions continue he discovers that although *he* doesn't change, the young girl, Hatty, does. She is growing older. As the time for Tom to return to his family approaches, Hatty is a young woman about to be married and the bond between the two seems to be weakening. Tom wants desperately to see her once more, to prove that the garden is more than a dream. When his need evokes a glimpse of the real Hatty, Tom at last understands the mystery of the garden.

Pearce not only develops this as an adventure story, but offers an intriguing speculation on the nature of time. She transforms the inescapable fact of growing old from an abstraction beyond children's grasp to a moving reality. British critic John Rowe Townsend has termed *Tom's Midnight Garden* the best English children's book since World War II. It is not a first book to read aloud, for listeners will need some patience with the beginning, but it goes very well in eight or nine sessions for middle grades. It is also deeply satisfying family fare.

Philippa Pearce's *Lion at School & Other Stories* is that rare item, a collection of short stories for primary-grade children. Most are realistic narratives marked by Pearce's usual sensitivity to the passions and fantasies of real children.

Treasure Island BY ROBERT LOUIS STEVENSON. 1883. Many editions.

Suggested Listening Level: Grades 5–8

This classic tale hasn't lost a bit of its appeal in one hundred years. The tarry pigtails and bloody dirks of the motley pirate crew, the unique mixture of irresistible charm and malevolence that is Long John Silver, and the enviable, plucky Jim Hawkins are as vivid today as when Stevenson created them for the amusement of his adolescent stepson during a rainy stay in Scotland. Jim's adventure is a child's fantasy come true. At the story's start, Jim leads a humdrum life as an innkeeper's son, but the arrival and subsequent death of an irascible old pirate brings ample excitement and danger, for Jim comes into possession of a treasure map left by the old buccaneer. On the voyage to find the treasure, mutiny and murder repeatedly threaten, but Jim, through luck, wit, and daring, saves the day time and again.

Some girls think they won't like *Treasure Island,* perhaps because it's so often labeled "a boy's book." Yet if they can be persuaded to keep an open mind, they'll soon be scrambling into the mizzen shrouds with Jim, and puzzling over the enigma of Long John Silver.

Don't worry about understanding all the nautical language. It supplies flavor and authenticity, but knowing every term isn't necessary for an understanding of the plot. The book consists of thirty-four chapters arranged in six parts. If your listeners' attention spans hold out, three chapters at a session works well.

Tuck Everlasting BY NATALIE BABBITT. New York: Farrar, Straus & Giroux, 1975. Paperback: Farrar, Straus & Giroux.

Suggested Listening Level: Grades 3–8

Hot, dusty days of August, days that "hang at the top of summer," enclose the events that bring the Tuck family and ten-year-old Winnie Foster together. When Winnie decides to run away from her nagging family, she stumbles across Jesse Tuck and his secret bubbling pool of water that has given the Tuck family immortality. They never grow older, never become sick, and, of course, never die. In short, they never change. But life *is* change, and as Tuck himself says, "You can't call it living what we got. We just *are,* we just be." Their ominous secret is sought after by an outsider who wants to exploit the water. In a violent confrontation with the Tucks, the man is killed. Winnie realizes the necessity of keeping the secret and protecting the Tucks, but she must also decide whether or not to join them by drinking the water herself.

The wooded setting and the hot, humid weather pervade this

speculative, thought-provoking fantasy. The action is fast enough for even beginning listeners, and the story can be read in three or four twenty-minute sessions. Yet Winnie's forced choice between immortality and growing old is intriguing enough to capture the interest of a family or a group with a wide age range. This paperback would be a perfect addition to a backpack on a camping trip.

Turn Homeward, Hannalee BY PATRICIA BEATTY. New York: William Morrow & Co., 1984.

Suggested Listening Level: Grades 4–8

"Turn homeward, Hannalee" is the parting plea Hannalee Reed hears from her mother when Yankee soldiers seize her and her younger brother from their Georgia village to take them north for the duration of the war. Hannalee and Jem, like all the Reeds, are workers in a textile mill. With the War Between the States in progress, the mill is making cloth and rope for Confederate troops, so Sherman's soldiers come, burn down the mill, and take away the young women and children who constitute the wartime work force. Hannalee resolves to get back to her mother, who has been widowed by war and is expecting a baby. The book is a gripping account of a plucky girl's successful attempts to survive all the threats that war poses to innocent noncombatants. So that the siblings can stay together, Hannalee disguises Jem as a girl, but they are ultimately separated. Escaping from the Indiana home where she works as a household drudge, a virtual prisoner, Hannalee sets out to find Jem. The hardships and dangers of this journey and of crossing army lines to return home make this a riveting story, and while Beatty gives full weight to the suffering imposed by the war, the book does have an essentially happy ending.

Beatty points out in an interesting author's note that the first part of this novel is factual, the second half, fictional. In 1864, 1,800 mill workers were indeed relocated to the north from two Georgia towns by the Union army. Once they reached Tennessee and Kentucky, these figures simply disappeared from history.

Beatty, a talented historical novelist, has used her skills to imagine what might have been the fate of some of these young people. Reader and listener alike will be gripped by the unrelenting suspense of the book's ten chapters. Each can be read in twenty to thirty minutes, except chapter two, which runs to almost forty minutes.

Watership Down BY RICHARD ADAMS. New York: Macmillan Publishing Co., 1974. Paperback: Avon.

Suggested Listening Level: Grades 5–8

In a peaceful rabbit warren, a young rabbit has a premonition of terrible danger (which turns out to be the gassing of the rabbits and destruction of the warren to make way for a housing development). The chief rabbit ignores young Fiver's advice to evacuate, so Fiver and his brother Hazel lead a small group of rabbits on a journey to find a new home. Their odyssey is full of perils—their natural enemies, their own fears and habits, hostile rabbits. Comforted and heartened by the legends of their shrewd ancestor rabbit, however, they survive to found a new and more humane (if one may use that word) warren.

The rabbits Adams depicts are true to rabbit behavior and yet each is fully individualized, and the listener quickly becomes deeply involved in the fate of the stalwart band. Adams even invents a rabbit language, for which he provides a glossary, but one soon finds rabbit words incorporated into one's own vocabulary.

The book is easy to criticize. The title (which refers to the location of the new warren) does not attract the reader. Adams indulges too much in ruminating digressions (they can be skipped so as not to lose the attention of the audience). Moreover, his is an old English clubman's view of the world. Creatures the rabbits view as inferior "talk funny"—in this case, broken English with a Mediterranean accent and occasional vulgar phrases. And females seem to be an afterthought with Adams, as they are with his rabbits, who never think of including females in their community until they are ready to breed. Yet when all is said and done, *Watership Down* is an absorbing read and a remarkable achievement.

The epigraphs that begin each chapter, taken from such towering figures as Aeschylus, Shakespeare, and Jane Austen, may be over the heads of some children but are worth reading aloud (when possible; some are not translated into English). They add to the solemn atmosphere of the saga. This is a long book: fifty chapters and a brief epilogue.

The Wednesday Surprise BY EVE BUNTING. *Illustrated by Donald Carrick.* New York: Clarion Books, 1989.

Suggested Listening Level: Grades K–2

Every Wednesday evening Anna's grandmother comes to stay with her while the rest of the family goes out. The two spend their time together reading books and preparing a surprise for Anna's father's birthday. Listeners will be moved as Dad is to discover what it is: Grandma has learned to read, thanks to Anna's good teaching. Carrick's soft pastel paintings mirror the warmth of the text. An added bonus of sharing this picture book might well be to reduce the shame children often feel about older family members who missed out on learning to read.

Another fine picture book by Eva Bunting, *The Wall,* sensitively treats the sadness a small boy feels when he and his father visit the Vietnam Memorial in Washington, where they look for his grandfather's name on the granite wall. Ronald Himler's soft watercolors exactly complement this touching story of family love and loss.

Weird Henry Berg BY SARAH SARGENT. New York: Crown Publishers, 1980. Paperback: Dell.

Suggested Listening Level: Grades 5–8

If Henry had to name one thing that made him feel special—not weird, but special—it was the newly hatched lizard he named

Vincent. On the other hand, Millie Levenson did consider herself somewhat weird, voting for "radicals" and sprinkling garlic salt on her baked potatoes at the senior citizen dinners. What brings these unlikely conspirators together is the creature Millie found wandering the streets threatening her dog late one night. Eight feet tall, bright green with eyes that gleamed gold in the street-light glow, Aelf was in search of a "young one" hatched from an egg one hundred years old.

"A young one?" questioned Millie. "What kind of a young one?"

"A dragon, of course."

Henry and Millie become involved in protecting Henry's liz-ard/dragon, and through a series of misadventures, the two realize that the only way to save Vincent is to return him to the Welsh hills and the other dragons.

An absolute matter-of-fact tone strengthens the involvement of listeners in this story. Henry is bright but doing poorly in school, fearing to become involved with anyone since his father's death from drugs. He's also alienated from his mother, but these problems only serve to point up the "real" difficulties of living with a dragon. Even the most diffident fifth-, sixth-, or seventh-grade individualist should be captivated by this most unusual pet. The eleven chapters can probably be read in five or six sessions of about twenty-five minutes each. This will work with skeptics as well as believers because all middle school kids understand feeling weird.

Westmark BY LLOYD ALEXANDER. New York: E. P. Dutton, 1981. Paperback: Dell.

Suggested Listening Level: Grades 5–8

Like many of Lloyd Alexander's best books, *Westmark* is about political power and personal morality. In this case, these issues are embodied in a dashing plot enacted by a motley crew of characters: a grief-stricken king manipulated by an evil prime minister; a lovable charlatan; a female street waif of mysterious origins and strange powers; young revolutionaries; and an appealing adolescent hero—Theo, a printer's devil or apprentice. One hair-raising episode follows another in the pell-mell plot until the author neatly gathers up all the threads in a surprising yet satisfying resolution.

The twenty-nine chapters of *Westmark* are very short (five to seven pages in most cases), so they can be combined to suit the time available for a reading session. The book's division into four parts should be observed by making a part-ending coincide with the end of a reading session whenever possible. Total reading-aloud time is approximately eight hours. Fantasy buffs may also want to try Alexander's famous Prydain series—a five-book cycle based loosely on Welsh legend.

Whale Watch: An Audubon Reader BY ADA AND FRANK GRAHAM. *Illustrated by D. D. Tyler.* New York: Delacorte Press, 1978. Paperback: Dell.

Suggested Listening Level: Grades 3–8

For children who want passionately to know all about real creatures, the Grahams have written a remarkable book. Packed into just 112 pages is accurate information about the biology, ecology, history, and politics of whales and whaling. Each chapter takes us into the subject from a different angle. The first gives us the viewpoint of a young student observer of whale behavior from a rocky island off the Maine coast. Next we learn about an old-time whale hunt and the beginning of mechanized slaughter of the whale from the log kept by a scientist in 1912. An account of the birth of whales and one of the boycott aimed at saving these amazing mammals from extinction constitute other chapters that are especially interesting. Though the book doesn't have the overall narrative thrust of a novel, each chapter is given a satisfying shape and is written in a lively style. It makes a good "chapter-a-day" book.

Whale Watch is particularly valuable as a case study in twentieth-century technology. It is clear that without technological advances, the survival of whales would not be in jeopardy. (In 1931

new technology enabled men to kill 25,000 blue whales in Antarc-
tica alone, the authors tell us, whereas that species was so de-
pleted by 1964–65 that only 20 were killed in that year.) Sonar
locates the whales, diesel engines speed after them, harpoon
bombs kill them efficiently. Yet technology has also enabled us to
study the whales and begin to appreciate how remarkable they
are. The book ends on a hopeful note, depicting the new interest
and sympathy humans are belatedly developing for these fellow
mammals. The Grahams' book is an absorbing and civilizing introduction to whales and whale watchers.

The Wheel on the School BY MEINDERT DEJONG. *Illustrated by
Maurice Sendak.* New York: Harper & Brothers, 1954. Paperback:
Harper.

Suggested Listening Level: Grades 2–4

Everyone knows that storks bring good luck to the houses they
nest on, but until Lina writes a composition about storks, none of
the six children in the Dutch village school wonder why no storks
nest in Shora. When they begin to wonder, things begin to happen. Before long the entire village is caught up in the search for a
wagon wheel, which, placed on top of a peaked Shora roof, can
serve as a platform for a stork's nest. The strength and wits of
everyone are needed to find, repair, and mount the wheel, then
to rescue two storm-tossed storks from drowning.

Although the story takes place far away—in a treeless village
rimmed with dikes—and long ago—when women and even little
girls wore heavy, billowing skirts that hindered their activity—
Meindert DeJong penetrates straight to universal feelings of
childhood that transcend all surface differences.

Of DeJong's many other books, *Shadrach* is particularly appealing in its sensitive depiction of a little child's intense longing for a
pet. *The House of Sixty Fathers* is a grim but powerful account of a
Chinese boy who is separated from his family at the time of the
Japanese invasion.

The fifteen chapters of *The Wheel on the School* make it quite long for the audience to whom it will most appeal: seven- to nine-year-olds. Children who are good listeners, however, will be captivated by it.

Where the Buffaloes Begin BY OLAF BAKER. *Illustrated by Stephen Gammell.* New York: Frederick Warne & Co., 1981. Paperback: Penguin.

Suggested Listening Level: Grades 3–6

"Over the blazing campfires, when the wind moans eerily through the thickets of juniper and fir, they still speak of the great lake to the south where the buffaloes begin." Little Wolf had heard of the story from Nawa, wiser than all, older than any, and he set off to find the lake and the buffalo. He heard the noise that never ceases from far beneath the lake and saw the buffalo and was one with them. Trapped in a stampede, Little Wolf's courage led the buffalo herd back to his people in time to save the camp from raiders.

Lean lyrical prose will make your listeners gasp with Little Wolf as the buffaloes rise from the mists of the lake. The prose thunders and subsides as the story mounts in intensity. This is a grand story to read for any occasion, but it was especially effective for one family in a van at dusk riding across the prairie. Even after a long day of driving, tired bones and spirits were revived as Little Wolf cried out his greeting to his massive, shaggy-haired brothers. It works in less dramatic settings—classrooms or living rooms—but be sure to share with your audience the evocative atmosphere created by the dramatic black-and-white illustrations. This picture book for older groups can be read in about twenty-five minutes.

Where the Forest Meets the Sea BY JEANNIE BAKER. New York: Greenwillow Books, 1987.

Suggested Listening Level: Grades K–5

A young boy and his father take a small boat through a reef to get to an ancient rainforest. The boy explores the forest, projecting himself back one hundred million years. The artist uses "collage construction" of clay, paint, and natural materials to depict the diverse textures and colors of the magnificent landscape. She also ingeniously creates ghostly suggestions of creatures and people from earlier times. The boy is sad when they must leave. Though his father promises they will come again, the boy wonders whether the forest will still be there when they do. Baker's final spread shows the suggestion of hotels and condominiums superimposed on the scene. This is one of the most powerful and creative picture books in recent years.

Where the Lilies Bloom BY VERA AND BILL CLEAVER. Philadelphia: J. B. Lippincott Co., 1969.

Suggested Listening Level: Grades 4–8

Set in the Great Smoky Mountains of North Carolina, this is the story of Mary Call Luther, a feisty, no-nonsense fourteen-year-old. Hungry for education, she finds her ambitions are thwarted by her responsibilities. She worries about her older sister, "cloudy-headed" Devola, "so free and innocent, so womanly in form but with a child's heart and a child's mind," about Ima Dean and Romey, "so carefree . . . with never a thought in their little heads as to how they're going to get decently raised," and about her sharecropper father, "coughing his life away." The story is told in Mary Call's forthright, eloquent voice, and seldom has a first-person narration achieved such moving intimacy. "And I get scared and I think but how am I going to do this? Who will show me how and who will help me?" she asks.

The struggles of the children to keep their father's death a secret from the authorities and to survive the winter make compelling reading. Part of the solution is found in the ancient art of wildcrafting, gathering and selling medicinal roots and herbs from the mountains. Another part is Mary Call's learning to accept help from others. The Cleavers have written many other books, some of them very good ones, but none equal this story of the "wondrous glory" and "awful anxiety" of independence. Each of the fifteen chapters would make a good read-aloud session, but your listeners probably won't let you stop with just one.

The White Archer: An Eskimo Legend WRITTEN AND ILLUS-TRATED BY JAMES HOUSTON. New York: Harcourt Brace & World, 1967. (Out of print) Paperback: Harcourt Brace Jovanovich.

Suggested Listening Level: Grades 5–8

The Eskimo boy Kungo escapes when Indian warriors massacre his parents and take his sister into captivity. The family's only offense had been extending the customary hospitality to travelers, not knowing them to be raiders of an Indian camp.

With the bloody scene stamped on his memory, the boy prepares himself for revenge. He travels to a distant island where an old man and woman take him in. The old man undertakes to make Kungo into a great archer. It is a slow process and Kungo is often impatient, but after four years he has become a great archer and a man. Kungo then sets out to exercise his vengeance. He learns, however, when he reaches the Indian camp that his sister has been adopted by the tribe and is married to a young warrior. The tale's benign resolution holds no surprises, but the endless cycle that violence spawns needs to be discovered anew by each person; it is a theme worth repeating. Middle-school readers will be stirred by the book's issues of loyalty and justice. Houston includes much detail about Eskimo ways, however, so the book requires an audience of willing and thoughtful listeners.

James Houston is a Canadian artist who for years lived with Eskimos, helping in the development of Inuit art. He has done us a comparable service in retelling for the rest of the world this and other Eskimo legends.

The White Archer has no chapter divisions, so the reader should plan ahead for breaks in the reading sessions. The entire book can be read in about two hours.

The White Mountains BY JOHN CHRISTOPHER. New York: Macmillan Publishing Co., 1967. Paperback: Macmillan.

Suggested Listening Level: Grades 4–6

Will Parker's friend Jack was the only one who asked questions or wondered about why things were the way they were. But he didn't ask any more questions after the Capping Ceremony, a ceremony that changed young people into followers of the system imposed by the Tripods. *No one* questioned the rules and regulations of life in the small villages and towns dotting the English countryside, not even the mindless vagrants who wandered about after their capping had somehow failed. One day, however, Will is approached by a vagrant who is not at all what he appears to be, a wanderer who persuades Will that there is hope for a better, freer life if he can just reach the White Mountains.

Set in an indefinite future time, this taut adventure story will capture readers just as surely as the machine-like Tripods dominate the humans they cap. Listeners will be intrigued with the artifacts from an earlier civilization, such as watches and railroad tracks that are discovered by Will and his two companions as they journey to the stronghold in the mountains. The ten chapters, each about twenty to twenty-five minutes, are episodic enough to form good breaks, but we recommend that you plan some longer sessions in anticipation of audience demand. Will's story is continued in *The Pool of Fire* and *City of Gold and Lead*.

The Wind in the Willows BY KENNETH GRAHAME, 1908. *Illustrated by Ernest H. Shepard.* New York: Charles Scribner's Sons, 1933. Paperback: Many editions.

Suggested Listening Level: Grades 2–8

From the moment Mole flings down his spring-cleaning tools, follows the imperious call of spring, and catches his first glimpse of the river, *The Wind in the Willows* casts a powerful spell. Few writers can match Grahame's skill at evoking the beauty of the natural world, the love of one's own home-place, and the charm of small wild creatures. The story consists of two plot-threads, each with its distinctive mood. There are the mellow and lyrical chapters devoted primarily to the friendship and activities of Mole and Ratty. The chapters that star the rich and swaggering yet good-natured Toad, on the other hand, are humorous, even lapsing into slapstick at times. The threads frequently overlap and then come together in the last part of the book, the epic battle of Toad Hall.

The story originated as episodes in a bedtime story that was continued by letter when Grahame's son Alistair was away on holiday; it is tailor-made for reading aloud. Yet action is minimal in some chapters, and not everyone has a taste for Grahame's highly wrought prose. We therefore don't recommend it for all groups of children (though they might enjoy one of the livelier chapters, such as "The Open Road"). It well deserves its reputation as a classic, however, and will please some children—and adults—like no other book in the world.

Winnie-the-Pooh BY A. A. MILNE. *Illustrated by Ernest H. Shepard.* New York: E. P. Dutton, 1926. Paperback: Dell.

Suggested Listening Level: Grades K–3

These whimsical tales of young Christopher Robin and his friends Pooh and Piglet, Eeyore, Rabbit, Owl, Kanga, and Roo, have entered the lore of childhood all over the English-speaking world. Much in the stories is provided for the adult reader's amusement. As a result, a patronizing tone creeps in occasionally that may make some readers uncomfortable. Yet there is plenty here to delight the child listener: the appealing fantasy of toys come to life; Christopher Robin's superior adult-like role as brave and wise protector to all the others; the sharply drawn personalities of the toy animals.

Film versions and abridged editions of these stories abound. Be sure that your children's acquaintance with Pooh doesn't end with them. The great distinction of the stories is Milne's skillfully crafted language, both in the prose and in the verses that are scattered through the chapters, and for that, you must seek out the original.

The ten chapters provide ten reading sessions, each concluding with a comforting resolution that makes the stories good bedtime fare.

The Witch of Blackbird Pond BY ELIZABETH SPEARE. Boston: Houghton Mifflin Co., 1958. Paperback: Dell.

Suggested Listening Level: Grades 5–8

Imagine stepping from a life of cultured ease on a Caribbean plantation into the grim piety and primitive conditions of colonial Connecticut in 1687. This is the trying experience of Kit Tyler, who is forced to leave sunny Barbados when her grandfather dies in debt. Kit goes to her only other relatives, her aunt's family in a cold and unfriendly New England. The family takes her in but are shocked by her secular ways and frivolous clothes. Kit must cope with unaccustomed drudgery, a cousin's jealousy, and a disapproving community. A wealthy suitor offers her a quick way to respectability, but she resists that temptation. Her only comfort and understanding come from another outcast, an old Quaker woman, rumored to be a witch, who lives alone on the flats near Blackbird Pond. In the gripping climax of the story, Kit saves old Hannah from an ignorant mob, but she is then tried for witchcraft herself.

Because most American women in years gone by led uneventful domestic lives subordinated to men, the great majority of American historical novels for children have featured male protagonists. In *The Witch of Blackbird Pond*, Elizabeth Speare has created an active, adventurous heroine without violating the carefully developed seventeenth-century setting. The twenty-one chapters could be read one at a time or in groups of two.

A recent book by Speare, *The Sign of the Beaver,* also explores the conflicts that occur when two very different cultures meet. Young Matt is on his own in the Maine woods as his colonist father attempts to bring back the rest of the family. He is befriended by an old Indian who wants Matt to teach his grandson "the white man's words and markings." Attean is an unwilling pupil and Matt a reluctant teacher, but the two learn that each has much to gain from the other. Matt's knowledge and appreciation of Indian ways grow immeasurably and enable him to survive for more than seven months until his family returns. The twenty-six chapters are very short and can be read in six sessions with a longer one in the beginning to introduce the two boys to your audience.

The Wizard of Earthsea BY URSULA LE GUIN. *Illustrated by Ruth Robbins.* New York: Houghton Mifflin, Parnassus Press, 1968. Paperback: Bantam.

Suggested Listening Level: Grades 6–8

In the wide-flung island world of Earthsea, a boy discovers that he has the power to call a falcon from the sky or to work the weather to protect his village from pillaging raiders. These are Duny's first steps toward becoming a mage, one of the greatest of all mages. The path to greatness takes him through great pain and peril, however, even to "the lightless coasts of death's kingdom." At the School for Wizards, Ged (as Duny is now called) is taught that magic is not for entertainment or for power but "must follow knowledge and serve need." When challenged to a contest of powers by a despised rival, however, Ged rashly ignores this lesson and, in doing so, looses an awful evil on the world. From then on, this horror pursues him until he turns in desperation to face it. The courage he musters and the lesson he learns in that moment make him worthy at last of his great gifts.

In this gripping and profound fantasy, Le Guin has created an elaborate world, conjured up by lovely and suggestive place-names. In a classroom reading some students may be intimidated by all the names, in fact, so it is a good idea to reassure them that they can sit back and enjoy the story—there will be no tests on the geography of Earthsea. *The Wizard of Earthsea* is the first of a trilogy, but it is totally self-contained and stands on its own. We recommend ten reading sessions, one for each longish chapter.

The Wolves of Willoughby Chase BY JOAN AIKEN. *Illustrated by Pat Marriott.* New York: Doubleday & Co., 1962. Paperback: Dell.

Suggested Listening Level: Grades 4–6

The author claims this novel is set in a history that never was, within reach but turned upside down with the Stuarts on the throne of England instead of Queen Victoria. One doesn't have to be a history buff to follow this melodrama, however, for the plethora of detail and strong sense of characterization catch both reader and listener from the very first wolf-howl.

Arriving at Willoughby Chase in a swirling snowstorm, the ominous Miss Slighcarp ("a tall, thin lady clad from neck to toe in a traveling dress of swathed gray twill") is only the first of several threats to Bonnie, dark and impetuous, and her cousin, the fair, sweet, and loyal Sylvia. Miss Slighcarp is joined by Josiah Grimshaw, and when Bonnie's father is called away on an extended trip, the two villains banish our heroines to a dreadful charity school where misdeeds are punished by isolation in the coal cellar. Clever Bonnie is aided by a vagabond named Simon, however, and the three children escape from the charity school to find safety with poor Aunt Jane, who needs their help as much as they need hers. Before the final curtain falls, parents return, the villains are punished, and wolf-howls fade into soft, warm dreams.

Rich, vivid detail and exciting "cliff-hanging" episodes make this and its sequels experiences middle-grade listeners should not miss. The ten chapters of this novel require about twenty-five to thirty minutes reading time each.

The Wonderful Flight to the Mushroom Planet BY ELEANOR CAMERON. *Illustrated by Robert Henneberger.* Boston: Atlantic–Little, Brown, 1954.

Suggested Listening Level: Grades 2–5

" 'Great jumping kadiddle fish!' shouted Chuck. 'You must invent all *sorts* of miraculous things, Mr. Bass.' " Chuck and David have brought their homemade spaceship to Mr. Tyco M. Bass's house at

5 Thallo Street. They are answering a green-inked newspaper notice looking for a boy and a spaceship and promising adventure and "a chance to do a good deed." Although an inventor of marvelous contraptions, Mr. Bass needs their help to save his ancestral planet, Basidium, where there has been a loss of a special food that keeps the inhabitants healthy.

A remarkable blend of fantasy and speculative science, Cameron's saga of the Mushroom Planet has survived more than thirty years. The story is lively, and even audiences born after moonwalks will be fascinated by the view of the earth from the homemade spaceship. The first two parts are each about an hour and a half of reading time, with chapters grouping comfortably into twenty-minute sessions. The third part is much shorter and may be read in one long, thirty-minute session.

There are five other titles in the Mushroom Planet series.

A Wrinkle in Time BY MADELEINE L'ENGLE. New York: Farrar, Straus & Giroux, 1962. Paperback: Dell.

Suggested Listening Level: Grades 4–6

Meg Murry's scientist father has been gone for nearly a year without any word, and Meg heartily resents the nosy prying of neighbors. Just when her troubles begin to overwhelm her, Charles Wallace, her unusually talented five-year-old brother, discovers three new neighbors whose abilities are far beyond any that even Charles Wallace can imagine. For one thing, they understand and can complete a tesseract, travel in the fifth dimension. These beings, acting as guardian angels, guide the two Murry children on a quest through time and space to save Mr. Murry and the planet Earth from the terrible IT.

Children find this combination adventure and family story compelling and thought-provoking. The evil of IT is easily identified as the enemy and Meg's efforts to save her imprisoned father allow young listeners to win the battle against tremendous odds. There are no gray areas here: right is right.

The book reads in about three hours, but the first chapter is a leisurely introduction to the action; you may wish to do some summarizing. The dialogue of the three spirits also may present some difficulty. Mrs. Who has a habit of spouting quotations in various languages, from Greek to Portuguese to Italian. She immediately states the author and gives a translation, though, so you can skip the Greek or Portuguese or Italian if your language skills don't stretch that far. Mrs. Which draws out all her words and offers wonderful opportunities for those with a dramatic flair.

The Young Landlords BY WALTER DEAN MYERS. New York: The Viking Press, 1979. Paperback: Avon.

Suggested Listening Level: Grades 6–8

When a group of fifteen-year-old inner-city kids decide to form an Action Group to improve the neighborhood, they don't know what they're getting themselves into. After they criticize the landlord of a run-down apartment building, Paul, the book's narrator, finds that the building has been transferred to his name. The group accepts the challenge of running the building, and the complications that follow provide an equal measure of humor and insight into urban problems. Suspense is added when Paul and his buddies try to help a friend whom they believe has been unjustly accused of theft. The action gets complicated, but the book holds the interest of young adolescents, including those with learning disabilities. In the course of the book, Paul becomes closer to his overbearing but basically loving father, and everyone learns that there are solutions, but not simple ones. Myers reproduces convincingly the conversation of an appealing group of black teenagers. If your listeners like this book, you might suggest they go on to read *Cool Clyde, Fast Sam, and Stuff* by the same author.

Allow a total of four and one-half hours to read aloud the book's twenty chapters.

Zlateh the Goat and Other Stories BY ISAAC BASHEVIS SINGER. TRANSLATED FROM THE YIDDISH BY THE AUTHOR AND ELIZABETH SHUB. *Illustrated by Maurice Sendak.* New York: Harper & Row, Publishers, 1966. Paperback: Harper.

Suggested Listening Level: Grades 1–8

For the stories in this, Singer's first volume of stories for children, the Nobel prize–winning author draws on the rich lore of his Eastern European Jewish childhood.

One of the most appealing of the stories is "The First Shlemiel." When Mrs. Shlemiel has to go out and leaves her husband to mind the rooster and the baby, she tells him that the jam she is saving for Hanukkah is poison, so he won't eat it up. Alas, Shlemiel falls asleep, the rooster escapes, and the baby falls out of the cradle, bumping his head. Shlemiel trembles at the thought of his wife's coming anger and decides there's no point in living such a life. But how to end it? Aha—that pot of poison . . .

Two other pieces are silly stories of Chelm, the village of fools, and there are spooky stories that feature the devil himself. The title story is a realistic tale of a boy and his beloved goat, who save each other's lives during a terrible blizzard. It and several of the other stories are set at Hanukkah time and might be shared as part of holiday festivities. In the years since this book was published, Singer has written many more good stories for children, including *Day of Pleasure,* an autobiographical account of growing up in Warsaw.

The volume *Stories for Children* collects thirty-six of Singer's remarkable children's stories. Though it lacks the first-rate illustrations of the versions in which most of Singer's stories first appeared, this volume plus the one described above provide the means to introduce children to the humor, humanity, and mysticism of this gifted storyteller. (Only one story appears in both of these books.)

VIII/Narrowing It Down:

CROSS-LISTINGS OF THE RECOMMENDED BOOKS FOR SCHOOL-AGE CHILDREN BY SUBJECT, LENGTH, AND TYPE

When you need to choose one book, knowing 175 good ones is hardly better than knowing none. To help you choose the best book for particular children at a particular time, we have drawn up a cross-listing of the recommended titles according to the categories that, in our experience, people most often specify when searching for children's books. The suggested listening level following each annotation will help also in locating the right book, of course. Books for little children don't lend themselves to this sort of listing, so only books from our List for School-Age Children are included here.

Since some of the best books on our list don't fit neatly into any category, we hope you will use these cross-listings only as a rough guide for specific needs or interests and will also browse through the main annotated list in Chapter VII for books that look appealing.

SUREFIRE—easy-to-follow stories of universal appeal; good for inexperienced listeners and/or readers

Babe, the Gallant Pig
The Best Christmas Pageant Ever
By the Great Horn Spoon!
Charlotte's Web
The Cricket in Times Square
Do Bananas Chew Gum?
Fantastic Mr. Fox

The Fighting Ground
Flossie and the Fox
The Great Brain
Hatchet
How to Eat Fried Worms
If You Made a Million

Mr. Popper's Penguins
Mrs. Frisby and the Rats of NIMH
Owls in the Family
Ozma of Oz
Pippi Longstocking
Ramona the Pest
Sarah, Plain and Tall
Save Queen of Sheba
Sideways Stories from Wayside School
Space Demons
Summer of the Monkeys
Superduper Teddy
A Toad for Tuesday
The Wonderful Flight to the Mushroom Planet

WIDE AGE RANGE—recommended for reading to children widely
spaced in age; good for family reading

Abel's Island
About Wise Men and Simpletons
The Adventures of Tom Sawyer
The Animal Family
Annie and the Old One
Babe, the Gallant Pig
Beat the Story-Drum, Pum-Pum
The Best Christmas Pageant Ever
The Brave Little Toaster
Buffalo Woman
By the Great Horn Spoon!
Charlotte's Web
Cheaper by the Dozen
The Dollhouse Caper
Fantastic Mr. Fox
Favorite Folktales from Around the World
Freddy the Politician
The Great Brain
The Hobbit

The House of Wings
How to Eat Fried Worms
The Incredible Journey
Jumanji
Jump!
Just So Stories
The Knee-High Man and Other Tales
The Lemming Condition
Linnea in Monet's Garden
The Lion, the Witch and the Wardrobe
Many Moons
The Mousewife
Owls in the Family
The Piemakers
Ramona the Pest
The Rescuers
Richard Kennedy: Collected Stories
Rootabaga Stories
Sarah, Plain and Tall
Summer of the Monkeys
The Talking Stone
Tatterhood and Other Tales
Tuck Everlasting
Where the Buffaloes Begin
Where the Forest Meets the Sea
The Wind in the Willows
Zlateh the Goat and Other Stories

ONE-SESSION READS—stories short enough to be completed in one sitting; some of these volumes contain one story, and others are collections of one-session stories

About Wise Men and Simpletons
American Tall Tales
And Then What Happened, Paul Revere?
Annie and the Old One
Auks, Rocks and the Odd Dinosaur

Beat the Story-Drum, Pum-Pum
Blackberries in the Dark
Brothers
Buffalo Woman
The Doubleday Illustrated Children's Bible
Favorite Folktales from Around the World
Flossie and the Fox
Galimoto
Grandaddy's Place
Hans Andersen: His Classic Fairy Tales
The Hundred Penny Box
Jumanji
Jump!
Just So Stories
The Knee-High Man and Other Tales
Linnea in Monet's Garden
Many Moons
Mom Can't See Me
The Mousewife
Peter the Great
Rootabaga Stories
Saint George and the Dragon
Shakespeare Stories
Short Takes
The Shrinking of Treehorn
Snow Company
Stevie
Sugaring Time
The Talking Stone
Tatterhood and Other Tales
The Wednesday Surprise
Where the Buffaloes Begin
Where the Forest Meets the Sea
Zlateh the Goat and Other Stories

SHORTER STORIES—books that can be read in two hours or less but are longer than one-session reads

Abel's Island
All Times, All Peoples
The Animal Family
Badger on the Barge and Other Stories
The Best Christmas Pageant Ever
A Blue-Eyed Daisy
The Brave Little Toaster
Burnish Me Bright
Chimney Sweeps, Yesterday and Today
The Courage of Sarah Noble
The Dollhouse Caper
Fantastic Mr. Fox
The Fighting Ground
Fog Magic
The Iron Giant: A Story in Five Nights
The Lemming Condition
The Light Princess
Martin Luther King, Jr.
More Stories Julian Tells
Owls in the Family
Portrait of Ivan
Sarah, Plain and Tall
Soup
Superduper Teddy
Striped Ice Cream
A Toad for Tuesday
The White Archer

LONGER READS—stories that spin out over many reading sessions

The Adventures of Tom Sawyer
. . . and Now Miguel
Dicey's Song
Freddy the Politician
The Hobbit
M.C. Higgins, the Great
The Secret Garden

Summer of the Monkeys
Treasure Island
Watership Down
The Wind in the Willows
The Wizard of Earthsea

Books with SEQUELS—stories that are continued for more than one volume

The Adventures of Tom Sawyer
The Alfred Summer
Alice's Adventures in Wonderland
All-of-a-Kind Family
Anastasia Again!
A Bear Called Paddington
The Borrowers
The Bully of Barkham Street
Burnish Me Bright
Cheaper by the Dozen
The Cricket in Times Square
Dicey's Song
Five Children and It
Freddy the Politician
From Anna
Ghosts I Have Been
The Good Master
Grandaddy's Place
The Great Brain
Henry Reed, Inc.
The House with a Clock in Its Walls
Jump!
The Lion, the Witch and the Wardrobe
Little House in the Big Woods
Mary Poppins
Misty of Chincoteague
The Moffats
More Stories Julian Tells

My Father's Dragon
Over Sea, Under Stone
Ozma of Oz
Ramona the Pest
The Rescuers
Roll of Thunder, Hear My Cry
Roller Skates
The Shrinking of Treehorn
Sideways Stories from Wayside School
Soup
A Stranger at Green Knowe
Superduper Teddy
A Toad for Tuesday
Where the Lilies Bloom
The White Mountains
Winnie-the-Pooh
The Wizard of Earthsea
The Wolves of Willoughby Chase
The Wonderful Flight to the Mushroom Planet
A Wrinkle in Time

ADVENTURE—stories of action and suspense

The Adventures of Tom Sawyer
April Morning
The Brave Little Toaster
By the Great Horn Spoon!
Escape from Warsaw
Fantastic Mr. Fox
The Fighting Ground
Ghosts I Have Been
Hatchet
The Hobbit
The Incredible Journey
Jeremy Visick
Journey Outside
Julie of the Wolves

The Mouse and His Child
Mrs. Frisby and the Rats of NIMH
Over Sea, Under Stone
Ozma of Oz
The Rescuers
Saint George and the Dragon
Save Queen of Sheba
Shakespeare Stories
Space Demons
Summer of the Monkeys
The Sword and the Circle
The Talking Stone
A Toad for Tuesday
Treasure Island
Watership Down
Westmark
The Wheel on the School
The White Mountains
The Wizard of Earthsea
The Wolves of Willoughby Chase
The Wonderful Flight to the Mushroom Planet

ANIMALS—real and fanciful birds and beasts

Abel's Island
The Animal Family
Babe, the Gallant Pig
A Bear Called Paddington
Beat the Story-Drum, Pum-Pum
Ben and Me
Buffalo Woman
Charlotte's Web
The Cricket in Times Square
Fantastic Mr. Fox
The Fledgling
Flossie and the Fox
Freddy the Politician

The House of Wings
The Incredible Journey
Julie and the Wolves
Jump!
Just So Stories
Koko's Kitten
The Lemming Condition
The Lion, the Witch and the Wardrobe
Misty of Chincoteague
The Mouse and His Child
The Mousewife
Mr. Popper's Penguins
Mrs. Frisby and the Rats of NIMH
My Father's Dragon
Owls in the Family
The Peppermint Pig
Pinch
Rascal
Sounder
A Stranger at Green Knowe
Summer of the Monkeys
The Talking Stone
A Toad for Tuesday
Watership Down
Whale Watch
The Wheel on the School
Where the Buffaloes Begin
The Wind in the Willows

All kinds of FAMILIES

The Alfred Summer
All-of-a-Kind Family
Anatasia Again!
. . . and Now Miguel
The Animal Family
Annie and the Old One

Badger on the Barge
The Best Christmas Pageant Ever
Blackberries in the Dark
A Blue-Eyed Daisy
The Borrowers
Brothers
Buffalo Woman
The Bully of Barkham Street
Calico Bush
Cheaper by the Dozen
Childtimes
The Courage of Sarah Noble
Dicey's Song
The Dollhouse Caper
Dragonwings
The Ears of Louis
The Endless Steppe
The Eternal Spring of Mr. Ito
Escape from Warsaw
A Fair Wind for Troy
Five Children and It
The Good Master
Grandaddy's Place
The Great Brain
The Haunting
The Hundred Penny Box
In the Year of the Boar and Jackie Robinson
Jeremy Visick
Jump!
Kite Song
Little House in the Big Woods
M.C. Higgins, the Great
Mrs. Frisby and the Rats of NIMH
The Moffats
Mom Can't See Me
More Stories Julian Tells
The Most Beautiful Place in the World

The Mouse and His Child
The Peppermint Pig
Pinch
Portrait of Ivan
Ramona the Pest
Rascal
Roll of Thunder, Hear My Cry
Sarah, Plain and Tall
Save Queen of Sheba
Short Takes
The Shrinking of Treehorn
Snow Company
Sounder
Stevie
Striped Ice Cream
Summer of the Monkeys
Superduper Teddy
The Wednesday Surprise
Where the Lilies Bloom
A Wrinkle in Time
The Young Landlords

FOLKLORE—folk and fairy tales, myth and legend

About Wise Men and Simpletons
American Tall Tales
Beat the Story-Drum, Pum-Pum
Brothers
Buffalo Woman
A Fair Wind for Troy
Favorite Folktales from Around the World
Jump!
The Knee-High Man and Other Tales
The Macmillan Book of Greek Gods and Heroes
Saint George and the Dragon
The Sword and the Circle
The Talking Stone

Tatterhood and Other Tales
Where the Buffaloes Begin
The White Archer
Zlateh the Goat and Other Stories

HISTORICAL PERSPECTIVES—books that illumine the past

Across Five Aprils
The Adventures of Tom Sawyer
All-of-a-Kind Family
All Times, All Peoples
. . . and Now Miguel
And Then What Happened, Paul Revere?
April Morning
Ben and Me
By the Great Horn Spoon!
Calico Bush
Chimney Sweeps, Yesterday and Today
Commodore Perry and the Land of the Shogun
The Courage of Sarah Noble
The Doubleday Illustrated Children's Bible
Dragonwings
The Endless Steppe
Escape from Warsaw
The Eternal Spring of Mr. Ito
A Fair Wind for Troy
The Fighting Ground
Ghosts I Have Been
The Good Master
Harriet Tubman, Conductor on the Underground Railroad
Jeremy Visick
Linnea in Monet's Garden
Little House in the Big Woods
Martin Luther King, Jr.
Peter the Great
Roll of Thunder, Hear My Cry
Sarah, Plain and Tall

Save Queen of Sheba
Shakespeare Stories
Sounder
The Talking Stone
Whale Watch
The Witch of Blackbird Pond

HUMOR—witty books, funny books

Abel's Island
Alice's Adventures in Wonderland
American Tall Tales
Anastasia Again!
Babe, the Gallant Pig
A Bear Called Paddington
Beat the Story-Drum, Pum-Pum
Ben and Me
The Best Christmas Pageant Ever
The Brave Little Toaster
By the Great Horn Spoon!
Cheaper by the Dozen
Do Bananas Chew Gum?
The Ears of Louis
Fantastic Mr. Fox
Favorite Folktales from Around the World
Five Children and It
Flossie and the Fox
Freddy the Politician
Ghosts I Have Been
Grandaddy's Place
The Great Brain
Henry Reed, Inc.
How to Eat Fried Worms
Jump!
The Light Princess
Many Moons
The Moffats

Mr. Popper's Penguins
My Father's Dragon
Owls in the Family
The Phantom Tollbooth
The Piemakers
Pinch
Pippi Longstocking
The Pushcart War
Ramona the Pest
The Shrinking of Treehorn
Sideways Stories from Wayside School
Soup
Summer of the Monkeys
Weird Henry Berg
Winnie-the-Pooh
The Young Landlords

MYSTERIES—books that keep you guessing

The Dollhouse Caper
The Egypt Game
Fog Magic
Freddy the Politician
From the Mixed-up Files of Mrs. Basil E. Frankweiler
Ghosts I Have Been
The Haunting
The House with a Clock in Its Walls
Jeremy Visick
Journey Outside
The Return of the Twelves
A Stranger Came Ashore
Tom's Midnight Garden
Westmark

NONFICTION—accounts of the real world

All Times, All Peoples
And Then What Happened, Paul Revere?

Auks, Rocks and the Odd Dinosaur
Child of the Silent Night
Childtimes
Chimney Sweeps, Yesterday and Today
Commodore Perry and the Land of the Shogun
The Endless Steppe
Flying to the Moon
Harriet Tubman, Conductor on the Underground Railroad
If You Made a Million
Immigrant Kids
Koko's Kitten
Martin Luther King, Jr.
Mom Can't See Me
Peter the Great
Rascal
Sugaring Time
Whale Watch

OTHER WORLDS—imaginary realms of one sort or another

Alice's Adventures in Wonderland
The Animal Family
The Borrowers
Favorite Folktales from Around the World
Fog Magic
The Hobbit
Journey Outside
Jumanji
The Macmillan Book of Greek Gods and Heroes
The Mouse and His Child
My Father's Dragon
The Phantom Tollbooth
Shakespeare Stories
Space Demons
The Sword and the Circle
The Talking Stone
Tom's Midnight Garden

The White Mountains
The Wizard of Earthsea
A Wrinkle in Time

STRANGE CREATURES—tales of ghosts, giants, goblins and such

Alice's Adventures in Wonderland
American Tall Tales
The Animal Family
Auks, Rocks and the Odd Dinosaur
Favorite Folktales from Around the World
Ghosts I Have Been
The Haunting
The Hobbit
The House with a Clock in Its Walls
The Iron Giant
The Lion, the Witch and the Wardrobe
The Macmillan Book of Greek Gods and Heroes
My Father's Dragon
Ozma of Oz
The Phantom Tollbooth
Saint George and the Dragon
A Stranger Came Ashore
The Sword and the Circle
The Talking Stone
Weird Henry Berg
The White Mountains
The Wizard of Earthsea
The Wonderful Flight to the Mushroom Planet
A Wrinkle in Time

SURVIVAL STORIES—Crusoe's descendants

Abel's Island
The Brave Little Toaster
Escape from Warsaw
The Endless Steppe
Fantastic Mr. Fox

Hatchet
The Incredible Journey
Island of the Blue Dolphins
Journey Outside
Julie of the Wolves
Mrs. Frisby and the Rats of NIMH
Save Queen of Sheba
Slake's Limbo
A Toad for Tuesday
Treasure Island
Watership Down

IX/Book-Places:

FOR TRAVELERS AND STAY-AT-HOMES, A CROSS-LISTING OF BOOKS BY SETTINGS

This chapter lists books in which a specific setting plays a prominent part and arranges them by location, so that readers interested in a particular city, region, or country can locate books that depict that area. Just as a young child's familiarity with the classic picture book *Make Way for Ducklings* adds to the delight of a swanboat ride in Boston's Public Gardens, so a reading of . . . *and Now Miguel* will add a rich dimension to a family's stay in New Mexico. And books can deepen the understanding and appreciation of our everyday surroundings as well. New York City dwellers learn from *Roller Skates* what their city was like to a ten-year-old in the 1890s—and discover in *The Pushcart War* what it may be like in years to come if the traffic gets any worse! (The *y* after a title in this list indicates that the book is on the BOOKLIST FOR YOUNGER READERS.)

NORTH AMERICA

The Talking Stone: every section of North America
Miss Rumphius: New England coast *(y)*
The Fox Went Out on a Chilly Night: New England *(y)*
Calico Bush: coast of Maine
The Ox-Cart Man: New Hampshire *(y)*
Whale Watch: Maine
Sugaring Time: Vermont
And Then What Happened, Paul Revere? Boston, Massachusetts
Make Way for Ducklings: Boston, Massachusetts *(y)*

April Morning: Lexington, Massachusetts
The Fledgling: Concord, Massachusetts
Thy Friend, Obadiah: Nantucket Island *(y)*
The Witch of Blackbird Pond: Connecticut
The Courage of Sarah Noble: Connecticut
Freddy the Politician: upstate New York
All-of-a-Kind Family: New York City
The Cricket in Times Square: New York City
From the Mixed-Up Files of Mrs. Basil E. Frankweiler: New York City
In the Year of the Boar and Jackie Robinson: Brooklyn, New York
The Pushcart War: New York City
Roller Skates: New York City
Slake's Limbo: New York City
The Fighting Ground: New Jersey
Ben and Me: Philadelphia
Harriet Tubman, Conductor on the Underground Railroad: tidewater Maryland
Dicey's Song: Maryland shore
Misty of Chincoteague: Virginia shore

A Blue-Eyed Daisy: Appalachia
Come a Tide: Appalachia *(y)*
When the Relatives Came: Appalachia *(y)*
Childtimes: North Carolina; Washington, D.C.
Where the Lilies Bloom: Great Smoky Mountains, North
  Carolina
Grandaddy's Place: Georgia
Queenie Peavy: Georgia
Flossie and the Fox: southern United States
Jump!: southern United States
Sounder: southern United States
Portrait of Ivan: Florida
Roll of Thunder, Hear My Cry: Mississippi
Pinch: Louisiana
Rootabaga Stories: midwestern United States
Across Five Aprils: southern Illinois
The Adventures of Tom Sawyer: Hannibal, Missouri
Little House in the Back Woods: Wisconsin (sequels: Kansas,
  Minnesota, South Dakota)
Rascal: Wisconsin
Weird Henry Berg: Wisconsin
Buffalo Woman: Great Plains
Where the Buffaloes Begin: Great Plains
Sarah, Plain and Tall: Kansas
Summer of the Monkeys: Oklahoma
The Great Brain: Utah
. . . and Now Miguel: northern New Mexico
Annie and the Old One: southwest United States
Save Queen of Sheba: Wyoming
The Egypt Game: California
Island of the Blue Dolphins: California coastal islands
By the Great Horn Spoon! San Francisco, California
Dragonwings: San Francisco, California
The Eternal Spring of Mr. Ito: Vancouver, British Columbia
Julie of the Wolves: Alaska
Hatchet: Canadian wilderness
The White Archer: Canadian Arctic

Owls in the Family: Saskatchewan
The Incredible Journey: northwest Ontario
Fog Magic: Nova Scotia
The Chalk Doll: Jamaica *(y)*

GREAT BRITAIN

A Bear Called Paddington: London
Mary Poppins: London
Watership Down: Hampshire
Jeremy Visick: Cornwall
Over Sea, Under Stone: Cornwall
A Stranger at Green Knowe: the Midlands (also the Belgian
    Congo)
Tom's Midnight Garden: East Anglia
The Peppermint Pig: Norfolk
The Return of the Twelves: Yorkshire
The Secret Garden: Yorkshire
Saint George and the Dragon: England
*The Sword and the Circle: King Arthur and the Knights of
    the Round Table:* England, Wales, Ireland
Babe, the Gallant Pig: England
Little Tim and the Brave Sea Captain: England *(y)*
A Stranger Came Ashore: Shetland Islands

CONTINENTAL EUROPE

The Wheel on the School: Holland
Madeline: Paris *(y)*
Burnish Me Bright: France
Linnea in Monet's Garden: France
Stone Soup: France *(y)*
The Story of Babar: France *(y)*
Shadow of a Bull: Spain
The Story of Ferdinand: Spain *(y)*
Strega Nona: Italy *(y)*
The Good Master: Hungary
Zlateh the Goat and Other Stories: Poland

Escape from Warsaw: Warsaw, Poland, and Germany
Children of the Fox: Greece
A Fair Wind for Troy: Greece
The Macmillan Book of Greek Gods and Heroes: Greece
Peter the Great: Russia
Aunt America: Ukraine, Soviet Union
The Endless Steppe: Siberia (also Vilna, Poland)

MIDDLE EAST

Brothers: Jerusalem

ASIA

The Story About Ping: China *(y)*
Commodore Perry in the Land of the Shogun: Japan
The Funny Little Women: Japan *(y)*

AFRICA

Beat the Story-Drum, Pum-Pum: Africa
A Story, a Story: Africa *(y)*
Anansi: Ghana *(y)*
Galimoto: Malawi
Jambo Means Hello: East Africa *(y)*
Bringing the Rain to Kapiti Plain: Kenya *(y)*

AUSTRALIA

A Racecourse for Andy: Sydney
Where the Forest Meets the Sea: Daintree Rainforest

Appendix A: Poetry

Any program of reading aloud should include poetry, for poetry more than any other form of literature is written to be heard. A carefully selected poem, presented with enthusiasm, may very well become part of a family's or a class's common experience, to be quoted with relish again and again. "And the highwayman came riding, riding, riding . . ." chanted one group of children as they left the library. They had been intrigued by comic book superheroes, Spider-Man™ being the current favorite, and Alfred Noyes's poem turned out to be a perfect choice. A first-grade class demanded Ogden Nash's "The Tale of Custard the Dragon" over and over again and could quote whole segments.

There are so many wonderful volumes of poetry for children available—anthologies, illustrated versions of one poem, and collections of a single poet's work—that to list and annotate them all would require a volume by itself. Therefore, we have listed twelve titles to represent hundreds. Brief comments indicate why we recommend them as a starting point, but we urge you to look at others that please you and your audience.

A Child's Garden of Verses BY ROBERT LOUIS STEVENSON. Multiple editions.

Today's children find, just as their grandparents did, that Stevenson knows all about what it's like to be a child—from the injustice of "Bed in Summer" to the sheer delight of "The Swing." His poems are available in many editions, including an inexpensive paperback selection of those poems that most appeal to younger children, illustrated by the outstanding artist Erik Blegvad (Random House, 1978).

The Golden Treasury of Poetry EDITED BY LOUIS UNTERMEYER. *Illustrated by Joan Walsh Anglund.* Western Publishing Co., Golden Press, 1959.

Well-known anthologist Louis Untermeyer has compiled a collection of range and depth—from Mother Goose to William Butler Yeats; from Father William to the Pied Piper to Annabel Lee. The volume contains little recent poetry, however, so it needs to be used in conjunction with one of the other collections. This fat book would be a perfect gift for a grandmother or a new teacher.

I Am the Darker Brother: An Anthology of Modern Poems by Black Americans EDITED BY ARNOLD ADOFF. Macmillan Publishing Co., 1970.

"I too sing America," wrote Langston Hughes. This collection contains poems by Hughes, Gwendolyn Brooks, and many other distinguished poets.

Joyful Noise: Poems for Two Voices BY PAUL FLEISCHMAN. New York: Harper & Row, Publishers, 1988.

Paul Fleischman won the Newbery Medal from the American Library Association for this delightful collection of poems spoken about and in the voices of different insects. Varied moods are deftly caught, from the sadness of a requiem for those insects dead in the first frost, to the humorous duet of a book-lice couple whose taste in edible literature differs.

Knock at a Star: A Child's Introduction to Poetry BY X. J. KENNEDY AND DOROTHY M. KENNEDY. Little, Brown & Co., 1982. Paperback: Little, Brown.

The Kennedys have put together for children aged eight to twelve an unbeatable combination of wonderful poems and intelligent comments, explaining all about poetry in terms young readers can understand. The last section, "Do It Yourself," contains good ideas and advice for children's own poetry-writing. The "Afterword for Adults" is the most sensible brief discussion of children and poetry that we've seen.

O Frabjous Day: Poetry for Holidays and Special Occasions ED-ITED BY MYRA COHN LIVINGSTON. Macmillan Publishing Co., 1977.

A fine poet and critic, Livingston here assembles a collection of holiday poems that is both distinguished and delightful. With this book on hand, you'll want to make poetry reading a part of every celebration.

One at a Time BY DAVID MCCORD. *Illustrated by Harry B. Kane.* Little, Brown & Co., 1977.

David McCord has the ear of a master poet, the vision of a child, and the sense of a wizard. This is a selection of his best.

Piping Down the Valleys Wild EDITED BY NANCY LARRICK. *Illustrated by Ellen Raskin.* Delacorte Press, 1975. Paperback: Dell.

Larrick has compiled a good basic anthology for the elementary-school-age child that combines high literary standards with a sensitivity to children's own poetry preferences.

The Poetry Troupe: An Anthology of Poems to Read Aloud COM-PILED AND DECORATED BY ISABEL WILNER. Charles Scribner's Sons, 1977, 1986.

This excellent collection is partly based on children's selections of poems they like to read aloud.

Read-Aloud Rhymes for the Very Young SELECTED BY JACK PRELUTSKY. *Illustrated by Marc Brown.* Alfred A. Knopf, 1986.

This collection is for the little ones—from babyhood to kindergarten. The rhymes that chronicle the child's world are set off by appealing illustrations and decorations on each page, making this a volume children will ask for often and remember fondly.

Reflections on a Gift of Watermelon Pickle and Other Modern Verse COMPILED BY STEPHEN DUNNING, EDWARD LUEDERS, AND HUGH SMITH. Lothrop, Lee & Shepard Books, 1967.

This is an unusually attractive anthology of contemporary poetry for older listeners.

Sing a Song of Popcorn: Every Child's Book of Poems. SELECTED BY BEATRICE SCHENK DE REGNIERS, EVA MOORE, MARY MICHAELS WHITE, AND JAN CARR. *Illustrated by nine Caldecott Medal artists.* New York: Scholastic, 1988.
An elegant and delightful volume of children's favorite poems, the book is arranged in sections by subject—Mostly Weather, Spooky Poems, and so on. Each section is illustrated by a different distinguished illustrator, among them Marcia Brown, Trina Schart Hyman, and Maurice Sendak. This one will be saved by lucky children for *their* children.

When We Were Very Young BY A. A. MILNE. *Illustrated by Ernest H. Shepard.* E. P. Dutton. 1924. Paperback: Dutton, 1966; Dell, 1976.
Nobody should grow up without meeting James James Morrison Morrison . . . or hearing the thumps and bumps on the stairs.

Where the Sidewalk Ends WRITTEN AND ILLUSTRATED BY SHEL SILVERSTEIN. Harper & Row, Publishers, 1974.
Children delight in Silverstein's witty and irreverent verse and pictures, and so do adults, judging from the many months this book spent on the best-seller list.

GENERAL GUIDELINES FOR READING POETRY TO CHILDREN

Before you begin, read a few poems to yourself so that they are not mechanical, with a forced rhythm or rhyme. (If you can substitute "de dum, de dum, de dum" for a line, your reading is forced.) Then choose some that you enjoy to try with your listeners.
For children up through six or seven, for the most part select rhyming poems with a decided rhythm. These children like hu-

morous poems and poems that tell a story. They are less enthusiastic about descriptive poems heavily dependent on figurative language. Older children, too, like humorous and narrative poetry, rhythm, and rhyme, but they also respond to free verse, to lyric poetry, to serious subjects, and to more abstract imagery and figurative language.

Don't restrict yourself either to the classic poets of childhood or to contemporary poets who write for children. Every child deserves to know *A Child's Garden of Verses* and the work of Edward Lear, Walter de la Mare, and A. A. Milne—poems and verses that have delighted children for generations. Her or his introduction to poetry would be incomplete, however, without also knowing the excellent work of contemporary poets who have written for children, such as David McCord, Karla Kuskin, Nikki Giovanni, X. J. Kennedy, and Myra Cohn Livingston.

Don't overlook poems that were not written with children in mind as readers but are simple enough for them to appreciate. Children respond enthusiastically to the poetry of William Blake, Robert Frost, Langston Hughes, Emily Dickinson, and Theodore Roethke, among others.

Finally, don't feel you have to explain the "meaning" of a poem after reading it or that the child listener should be able to do so. Children's felt response to poetry (as to other forms of literature) is far in advance of their ability to talk about it abstractly. It helps to keep in mind, too, that if the content of a poem could be expressed in prose, there would be no need to write it as a poem.

Appendix B: A Selected Bibliography

For adults who want to explore further expert opinion on reading aloud to children and related subjects.

BOOKS

Anderson, Richard C., et al. *Becoming a Nation of Readers: The Report of the Commission on Reading*. National Institute of Education, 1985. Top experts in the field of reading survey research and make recommendations, strongly endorsing reading aloud.

Butler, Dorothy. *Babies Need Books*. Atheneum, 1980. Sound advice on sharing books with children from infancy through age five.

Chambers, Aidan. *Introducing Books to Children,* Second edition. Horn Book, 1983. A comprehensive and thoughtful exploration by a first-rate critic and caring teacher.

Clark, Margaret M. *Young Fluent Readers*. Heinemann, 1986.

Cochrane-Smith, Marilyn. *The Making of a Reader*. Ablex, 1983. Close observations of a nursery-school classroom reveal how adults assist children in acquiring the knowledge they need to understand print—without formal teaching.

Cullinan, Bernice E. *Children's Literature in the Reading Program*. International Reading Association, 1987.

Hart-Hewins, Linda, and Jan Wells. *Borrow-a-Book: Your Classroom Library Goes Home*. Scholastic, 1988.

Hearne, Betsy. *Choosing Books for Children: A Commonsense*

Guide. Revised edition. Delacorte, 1990. An intelligent and lively resource for parents.

Heath, Shirley Brice. *Ways with Words: Language, Life, and Work in Communities and Classrooms.* Cambridge, 1983. A brilliant ethnographic study of three subcultures' patterns of life and language, with interesting implications for fostering a love of reading in diverse children.

Hill, Mary W. *Home: Where Reading and Writing Begin.* Heinemann, 1989.

Jalongo, Mary Renck. *Young Children and Picture Books: Literature from Infancy to Six.* NAEYC, 1988.

Kobrin, Beverly. *Eyeopeners! How to Choose and Use Children's Books about Real People, Places, and Things.* Penguin, 1988.

Lamme, Linda. *Growing Up Reading.* Acropolis, 1985. An early childhood expert's suggestions for parents who want to encourage a love of reading in their children.

Larrick, Nancy. *A Parent's Guide to Children's Reading.* Fifth edition. Westminster, 1983. This has long been a valuable asset to concerned parents.

McLane, Joan Brooks, and Gillian Dowley McNamee. *Early Literacy.* Harvard University Press, 1990.

Schickedanz, Judith A. *More than the ABCs: The Early Stages of Reading and Writing.* NAEYC, 1986.

Schwartz, Judith I. *Encouraging Early Literacy: An Integrated Approach to Reading and Writing in K–3.* Heinemann, 1988.

Singer, Dorothy G., Jerome L. Singer, and Diana M. Zuckerman. *Teaching Television.* Dial Press, 1981. Television-watching tends to squeeze out reading time. This book will help you to limit television's negative impact on your children and to exploit its potential for stimulating growth and learning.

Strickland, Dorothy S., and Lesley Mandel Morrow, eds. *Emerging Literacy: Young Children Learn to Read and Write.* International Reading Association, 1989.

Taylor, Denny. *Family Literacy: Young Children Learning to Read and Write.* Heinemann, 1983. A detailed account of how young children in six families learned to read and write.

Taylor, Denny, and Catherine Dorsey-Gaines. *Growing Up Literate: Learning from Inner-City Families.* Heinemann, 1988.

Trelease, Jim. *The Read-Aloud Handbook,* Second revised edition. Viking–Penguin, 1989.

ARTICLES

Heath, Shirley Brice, and Charlene Thomas. "The Achievement of Preschool Literacy for Mother and Child," in *Awakening to Literacy.* Edited by Hillel Goelman, Antoinette Oberg, and Frank Smith. Heinemann, 1984, 51–74. A fascinating account of how an adolescent mother and school dropout provided her toddler with an early literate environment through reading to him.

Segel, Elizabeth. "Pushing Preschool Literacy: Equal Opportunity or Cultural Imperialism?" *Children's Literature Association Quarterly* 11 (Summer 1986), 59–62.

————. "Side-by-Side Storybook Reading for Every Child: An Impossible Dream?" *The New Advocate* 3 (Spring 1990), 131–37.

Smith, Frank. "Demonstrations, Engagement and Sensitivity: The Choice Between People and Programs." *Language Arts* 58 (September 1981), 634–42. Warns that technology is restricting the time available for teacher-originated activities like reading aloud.

Teale, William H. "Positive Environments for Learning to Read: What Studies of Early Readers Tell Us." *Language Arts* 55 (November/December 1978), 922–32.

————. "Reading to Young Children: Its Significance for Literacy Development," in *Awakening to Literacy,* cited above, 110–21. These two articles by Teale skillfully summarize the most significant research on reading to children.

Title Index

Author Index

About the Authors

MARGARET MARY KIMMEL is professor and chair of the Department of Library Science, School of Library and Information Science, University of Pittsburgh. She is past president of both the Association for Library Services to Children of the American Library Association and of the United States Board on Books for Young People.

ELIZABETH SEGEL is co-director of Beginning with Books, a prevention-oriented literacy outreach program affiliated with the Carnegie Library of Pittsburgh, and is review editor of the journal *Children's Literature in Education*. She compiled and edited *Short Takes*, a collection of short stories for children by distinguished authors.